D1447938

AFFINITY

AFFINITY

Reclaiming the Divine Flow of Creation

Amorah Quan Yin

Bear & Company
Rochester, Vermont

Bear & Company
One Park Street
Rochester, Vermont 05767
www.InnerTraditions.com

Copyright © 2001 by Amorah Quan Yin

All rights reserved. No part of this book may be reproduced or utilized in any form or by any means, electronic or mechanical, including photocopying, recording, or by any information storage and retrieval system, without permission in writing from the publisher.

Library of Congress Cataloging-in-Publication Data

Quan Yin, Amorah
  Affinity : reclaiming the divine flow of creation / Amorah Quan Yin.
    p. cm.
  ISBN 1-879181-64-9 (pbk.)
  1. Parapsychology. 2. Spiritual life. I. Title.
  BF1031 .Y455 2001
  133.9'3—dc21

                              2001003504

Printed and bound in Canada

10 9 8 7 6 5 4 3 2 1

Text design and layout by Rachel Goldenberg
This book was typeset in Legacy

Contents

Part 4

Embodying Divine Qualities

Introduction

The art of spiritual awakening and enlightenment is one of establishing connection with your own Divine Essence so that you may experience yourself and your life free of contrivance, control, contraction, inhibition, and illusion-based identity. The path to this experience is already carved for you through the Divine Flow of Affinity.

Affinity is known as a force of attraction to a particular thing or being. It can also be described as a commonality or likeness between two things. In Earth science, affinity can represent physical body structure similarities that indicate a common origin between biological groups. When manifested on a spiritual level, affinity with your Divine Essence (herein referred to as *self-affinity*) allows you to be real and experience Divine Flow: the rhythm that carries you joyously to fulfilling your life purpose and spiritual mission.

Humans today are living mostly in the identity of the ego persona, ruled by their own thoughts and emotions. If a person feels fear, he or she usually makes decisions based on that fear. If we think we are not likable or lovable, we live in low self-esteem and become underachievers. In this place of ego-personality identity, the things we are attracted to do not seem to support us, and life is a struggle. Rather than experiencing a Divine Flow that directs and carries us, we experience something of a choked drip, where every action seems thwarted by resistance, and a persistent sense of lack weighs heavily upon us. These examples of human conditions exist because most humans have never had the realization that they can choose to believe in and act on these thoughts and emotions—or they can choose to change them. These thoughts and emotions are believed by most humans to be the very defining factors of their human pseudo-reality. Yet there is a great spiritual movement happening simultaneously, in which millions of us are seeking some new source of Truth with which to define our personal realities and self-identities. This seeking of Truth must lead one home to self-affinity—to being who we really are in every way.

The dance of affinity is an ecstatic experience of spiritual awakening. As inherent likeness to our Divine Essence is restored, we naturally begin to attract and choose people and situations that are in affinity with our Higher Self. We shift from a frequency of karmic magnetism and ego identity into one of healthy, fulfilling attractions with the positive connections that inherently support our spiritual evolution. In this place of Divine Flow, what is in the highest good naturally occurs and self-affinity with our Divine Essence is naturally perpetuated and strengthened. We experience harmonious alignment with ourselves, our lives, and All That Is.

This book is intended to assist you in gradually dissolving your ego back into Divine Essence. As you walk through and beyond time, space, emotions, attitudes, thoughts, and the flow of energy in these pages, you will step into an adventure of self-discovery and healing. You will be impulsed to become more mature on many levels and to find hope on every level. It gives you the tools for living in self-affinity and Divine Flow. It is up to you to determine whether this book becomes another New Age collection of somewhat interesting thoughts or whether you wish to apply these tools in your daily interactions with yourself and others in order to realize your goals of spiritual growth. Is that not exactly how you really want it? For how could you have hope of becoming a living Master, and finding enlightenment and freedom to be who you really are, unless you do it for yourself? And yet here you will find many guides and teachers—from the depths of Earth's sacred centers to the "heights" of multiple galaxies—who will join you in these pages to lovingly guide you toward your own Truth.

As this collection of channelings, teachings, and guided meditations came together, it was a thrilling experience to find that Divine Flow and continuum existed before I had any notion of a theme. I expected this book to be simply a collection of channelings about many wonderful spiritual themes. Though there is great diversity within the beings whom I have channeled and the teachings brought forth, there is great unity in that diversity. Each unique chapter originates from the goal of leading us back into affinity with ourselves and the Divine Essence in order to live and love in Divine Flow.

Finding your way home to self-affinity and Divine Flow is like studying the individual threads of a great tapestry and repairing or replacing the broken and faded ones, while seeing the whole tapestry's creation simultaneously. All the polyester fibers of artificial ego reality will be replaced with the purest silk fibers of your Divine Essence. Each of the chapters in this book that brings the light of understanding about what it takes to be whole again provides a few threads for the tapestry. As spiritual discipline, transcendence of judgment, cellular healing, and inner child healing are woven together with all the other aspects of this tapestry of affinity, the whole of the Creation is revealed in all its beauty and glory. And you are part of that beauty and glory. When the repair and reclamation begin to happen in Divine Flow, the result is predictably wondrous. May the channelings, loving connections to higher-dimensional Light Beings, teachings, and meditations in this book prove to be a gentle and loving way home to your Divine Flow with Creation, deep self-affinity, and affinity with the Divine Source and All That Is, on all levels. May your tapestry be rewoven in Grace and Love always.

Part 1

Divine Flow of Creation

As we begin the journey of reclaiming Divine Flow, it is natural that we start at the beginning of all consciousness, the Original Creation. In Original Creation, innocence, love, beauty, adoration, awareness, and wonder were natural states of being. In Original Creation, all possibilities of existence and experience were yet to be explored. These materials are intended to set the groundwork for you to recover your own origins and connection to Divine Source: Oneness, God/Goddess, All That Is, Creator, Great Spirit, I Am.

This is the story of Creation as I personally experienced it. These chapters are some of the most important material with which I have been gifted. Through hypnosis I was led to a deep place in my own psyche, subconcious, and beyond body consciousness in order to recover my memories of the origins of my own individuated consciousness, or Divine Essence.

Pleiadian Archangel An-Ra says that when one person remembers and shares her experience of remembering, it impulses others to remember their own stories. Whether you remember your experiences lucidly, or simply gain a gentler inner understanding of the nature of your personal reality, recognition of the innocent nature of original consciousness is of primary importance. This will give you a reference point to which you may aspire as a spiritual seeker of Truth, Love, Mastery, and Divine Flow. Without original innocence as a reference point, how can you hope to permanently transform and transcend your own negative ego's thoughts and emotional reactions? And without these releases, transformation, and transcendence, how can you hope to find your Divine Flow within self-affinity, not to mention affinity with Divine Source and All That Is?

After completion of the hypnosis work, I rearranged the sessions into the sequential order in which they originally occurred. This was tricky, considering that these experiences actually happened outside of the time and space continuum! I have written these sessions in a form as close as possible to the actual transcript of the hypnosis sessions while still having them remain intelligible.

The first three chapters of this book will be familiar to those of you who have read my book *The Pleiadian Tantric Workbook: Awakening Your Divine Ba*. They were also the first three chapters of that book. These chapters seemed inherently vital, however, in the journey of awakening to the Divine Flow of your I Am, since they explain the birth of Divine Flow—as well as how Divine Flow was first interrupted. Therefore, I choose to reintroduce this material within this new context and the broader perspective of this book.

An-Ra says of this work, "It is time now to remember everything."

1

Birth of the I Am Presence

Before undergoing the following hypnosis sessions, I was instructed by An-Ra, the Pleiadian archangel who was guiding me, that it was time for me to remember fully the story of who I was before I came to the Milky Way. I also needed to remember my spirit's first experience of individuation. At that time, I presumed that An-Ra was referring to the creation of my soul. Therefore, I was quite surprised to find myself literally going back to *The Creation*.

I was taken to a binary solar ring called Ninevah, in the Andromeda galaxy. There I lucidly experienced being a very large, tenth-dimensional, Light Being. This Light Being had a male deity as partner, and together they held within their combined consciousness that entire solar ring. That solar ring is composed of six planets, five of which orbit between the two suns in a figure-eight pattern: the infinity symbol. The sixth planet orbits a single sun, just as Earth does in our solar ring. I was a Supreme Being, as was my partner. Supreme Beings are Light Beings who are responsible for protecting and overlighting a planet, solar ring, galaxy, or other designated territory. I was the Goddess Erotica. When I (she) first told me her name, I must confess that my human self squirmed and thought, "Oh my God, I'm in trouble!" However, after the hypnosis session was complete, that reaction changed. My definition of the erotic expanded to become even more than what I had always thought of as sacred sex. What I experienced was such a powerful and all-encompassing love that I was overwhelmed to the point of scarcely being

8

capable of speech. The truly erotic is like a sacred cosmic rhythm, the Divine Flow of Light Beings emerging into individuality, and then returning back into Oneness over and over again in a continual dance of ecstasy. At that level of consciousness, love is the key ingredient to all sexual experience.

During this session I was also given audience with the Elohim, the Creator Gods and Goddesses. While the Elohim eloquently formed the words that I channeled, I was expanded and deeply altered. As the transcript begins, I have already been taken into a deep hypnotic state and experienced a personal clearing in order to reach the deep levels necessary. The collective consciousness of the Elohim spoke as a single voice to and through me. The transcript follows:

> *The Elohim:* When we came together as the Elohim, we were what you think of as the archetypes of God/Goddess/All That Is, All That Ever Has Been, and All That Ever Shall Be. Before Creation there was only Oneness. Within Oneness came a divine thought as Oneness awakened to the realization "I am." It was the realization that Oneness existed. From ecstasy came a voice, "I am that I am." And from that "I am that I am" came awareness of self as One, and with awareness of self as One came desire for experience through reflection, through another. And there was no other; there was only One, and One was All That Is, and that One chose to mirror itself back to itself in order to objectify itself to itself. And that objectification became deity. And deity became portions. And the reflection saw love in the other and became One again in union. The experience of reunion was so great that Oneness again mirrored itself in order to reunite, and the birth of sacred union came through desire for the experience of reuniting the reflected self to the reflector. When this process had occurred over what you would call billions or trillions of centuries, there was a desire within Oneness to know objectification from the mirrored part and the self at the same moment of existence. The Elohim Council was born from that divine spark of inspired objectification. It was what you might call the birth of the first children.

> Oneness created a mirror image of itself, which it fell in love with, as it always did. Because it was mirrored, it was a mutual love experience of union. While in that individuated state, there was a decision to mirror again, which had not been done before that point in conscious existence. When the mirrored self and the reflector mirrored at the same exact moment in time—in your words—two more beings

were created, each mirroring the individuated self. There was a wave of amazement as Oneness in its mirrored form suddenly found three other aspects reflecting the same thing. When the original two parts of Oneness reunited, the newest reflected pair united at the same time with each other, not with the original pair. These two simultaneous unions each impulsed the other's union and created another wave of amazement. They were immediately reflected again, creating yet another. And with each creation, the mirroring created so much awe, wonder, ecstatic inspiration, discovery, and joyful pleasure that the original Oneness wondered what would happen if each of those who had been mirrored by itself had the power to mirror—since each was a part of all Creation and all of Creation is part of the same Oneness. Each of these was told to mirror outside itself. Obedient children, as we were, we became the Elohim. It began with two, then four; and when the four impulsed outside themselves, there were eight. When the eight joined with the original two—which you may call the Holy Mother and Holy Father—they experienced themselves as Oneness again. Yet, from that Oneness, great waves of love spread, and those waves created individuation again. Individuation inspired admiration and adoration for Creation, which resulted in the desire for union. It was a circular, or spiral, experience, you might say. You, Amorah, were part of that beginning in the twelfth round of creation and became an Elohim Goddess, a mirror, a reflector. Further divisions began from there.

What you call the Divine Plan is not as complete as you have thought it to be. The Divine Plan was simply that each of the twelve individuations who are the original Council of the Elohim could explore creation and the possibilities of existence. Each pair of reflector and reflected was given sovereignty and autonomy to create and to maintain its own creations. We, the Elohim, are twelve large androgynous beings, each composed of the reflector and the reflected—or female and male, in your terms—when in our individuations before reuniting. When reunited, each pair becomes one androgynous being again. In other words, the council of twelve, within itself, was and is a council of twenty-four, half male and half female, or twelve Creator Gods and twelve Creator Goddesses. Within the twelve united forms, twelve galactic centers were birthed through which the divine couples could radiate and emanate the love from their unions, and creation continued on the next level. Each pair that constituted an androgynous One created, maintained, and contained what you call a galaxy within its consciousness. When the couple was together it was like water and flow, or electricity and light. The goddess was the mirror, and the male god was that which was reflected in the mirror, and while in union as a single being of androgynous Light they were given the power to create whatever they desired to create, whatever they might imagine.

Each of the twelve Elohim couples possessed unique qualities of its own. These qualities were due to the particular frequencies held by the Holy Mother and Holy Father at the time of each conception. Just as your soul contains the energy of the union of the mother and father who physically birthed you, so does it contain the frequencies of your higher-dimensional parents who originated your soul. All of existence, even the Elohim, were created in much the same way. What we wish for you to understand is that the male/female split and the original Creation are two parts of the same thing. When female and male, the mirror and the reflected, are not in harmony, there is no peace. Understanding how Creation began with complete union between equals inspired to love one another, inspired by one another, is the way back to God/Goddess/All That Is, or Oneness—and to healing the male/female split.

The only plan, beyond the Elohim being empowered for their own creations, was that at some point in time and space and beyond it, they would all come back together in Oneness again and blend and share one another's experiences. This is what creates both the urge for enlightenment and the urge for sacred marriage, union. It is why human sexual energy is so strong. It is not just the desire to create children that creates the sexual urge; it is the urge toward Oneness.

We end our communications with you with much for you to absorb, distill, and dissolve into yourself. And we wish to say now that responsibility born of anything but love is truly irresponsible. For only through love can any act bring a positive end result. So-la-re-en-lo, with greatest love and devotion.

The Goddess Erotica spoke as the session continued. My consciousness was so completely blended with the consciousness of this "bigger self" that I could scarcely speak. My words were very slow and stilted. It was quite difficult to maintain enough contact with my body to allow my mouth to utter the words. When you read phrases about Creation, and singing existence, it is the Goddess Erotica speaking: she of whom I am only the third-dimensional self. She is my eleventh-dimensional self, which contains all aspects of myself from the tenth dimension and down.

> **Goddess Erotica:** Sleep perchance to dream, dream perchance to re-member, remember perchance to know, know perchance to be, be perchance to be. Simply be perchance to be. I am always here. You don't have to be in an altered state to know me now. We will go through a few weeks of experience together during your next stage of integration and remembrance, and then you will write. For now, return to this world of time and space knowing that you are limited by nothing, other than your own choices. We are love.

In a separate hypnosis session, which I also recorded, I was able to experience my own consciousness during the Creation. The early stages of that session follow so that you will be able to sense the fullness of the experience. This was no doubt the most expansive and deepest hypnotic state I have ever known. I had experienced deep trance states before, but this was in a category all its own. The energies did not exactly translate through my physical body. It was more that I was just pure consciousness outside of time and space, experiencing Creation all over again and remembering it in such a way that I could bring the energies and memories back to my body when I returned. When I did come back to my body, it took several hours to get all of me back in. I felt so expanded that trying to fit back into my body—even though I am a large-bodied woman—seemed like attempting to put a camel through the eye of a needle. My cells spun so fast, as my body received the newly awakened me with all of the frequencies of my experiences, that it was like being inside a psychedelic light show complete with bizarre, and mostly wonderful, sensations. The complete integration took weeks. The Pleiadians worked with me faithfully and continually, guiding me each step of the way. Sometimes I was told to do a next level of cellular clearing on myself, or soul healing through the Interdimensional Chamber of Light, or other techniques given in *The Pleiadian Workbook: Awakening Your Divine Ka*. Mainly, the integration was facilitated by my own step-by-step introduction to Dolphin Tantra as taught in *The Pleiadian Tantric Workbook: Awakening Your Divine Ba*. In general, the integrations from the hypnosis work in these first chapters have been extremely gracious and joyful—ecstatically so at times. When this next part of the session began, I was still experiencing myself as Amorah and was individuated from the Goddess Erotica.

Amorah: My goddess-self from Andromeda, the Goddess Erotica, is holding my right hand, and there is an emissarial group of Andromedans, Pleiadians, and three Sirians who are all here together, like a council. They are actually members of the Higher Council, but they are presenting themselves to me in a way that they have never done before. All twelve members are here, and they want to say something. They say that they are here to present me with an opportunity to go back to the source of All That Is, and to return to this galaxy and to Earth with more of myself than I go there with at this time. To do so, they send an emissary along from the Higher Council who is from Andromeda. They are letting me know that this is a high honor, that they rarely guide or accompany individuals on such journeys; generally, other beings are appointed as guides—beings who work with the Higher Council. The reason they are here with me is because of the nature of my service on Earth, my Higher Self's request, and the fact that it was long ago agreed that when this time came an emissary from the Higher Council would accompany me. This would ensure that the vibrations were clear, since the information was intended to be shared with readers and students. The Higher Council also agreed to help me be sure that my body was ready. That is why, when I knew I needed to do a cleanse, I intuitively went to them to ask them about the cleanse even though I had never bothered them with such mundane details before.*

A member of the Higher Council: The Christ teachings are most imminent at this time, as you well know; but how imminent they are you are about to find out more clearly than you have ever known before. Therefore, we leave you now with our Andromedan member, and with your twin star—the Goddess, as you call her.

Amorah: They are telling me to call her my twin star, and she will help me understand more about our relationship to one another at this time. They also affirm my assumption that she has a strong connection to Mother Mary.

---

*The Higher Council had guided me, just a week and a half before, to begin an all-organic raw foods cleanse, which I now know was to prepare me for this session and its integration. They were preparing my body for the vibrations that were going to be incoming on this day.

The Andromedan: It is more like an aspect of Mother Mary's galactic consciousness, rather than her Ascended Master consciousness with which you are more consciously familiar. So you are in quite good company today, Amorah.

Steve, the regressionist: Is there a name for the Andromedan member of the Higher Council?

Amorah: I cannot see that member as individuated from the Council yet. It feels like a male presence at my left side. It is interesting that the males are at my left and the females are at my right. It is a reversal from the normal female left side and male right side, but it creates balance, they say. The council member who will accompany me says that he is like the god of eroticism and sacred sexual functions of all beings, the God Eros. He is the one who dispenses and holds those frequencies for this solar ring, and for the Milky Way, at this time. Therefore, he is a natural companion to go along with me on this journey, as is my twin star. Now I hear the words, "The Goddess Erotica is who you will become when you are finished, even though she is who you were before you began. She is the beginning and the end. Before her you are nothing."

I am hearing one female voice now, but it is a voice that is made up of many voices. She says, "We are you. We are the beginning, the end, and the middle, and the voice of all times wrapped up in One. We go back to the seeming origin simply through focusing on that intent. It is like choosing the facet of a prism through which we wish to be refracted. And as we are refracted we experience a particular color and shape. We choose that facet now: the facet of sound, the sound of one voice, the sound of one voice that contains the voices of All That Is in Oneness. Sweet it is, the One and the many. It is singular and plural simultaneously. And it is All That Is: that sweet, resonant sound."

My voice became very slow and effortful at this time as my consciousness, as Amorah, became one with the original consciousness at Creation. So in a sense it is not me speaking, except that we all originate from the same Oneness of God/Goddess/All That Is. Therefore, when you read this next section, read it not as Amorah speaking but as the voice of Oneness.

Amorah / the voice of Oneness: It is as if I am asleep, and that my only dream is of being the sound, and yet hearing it at the same time. My first awareness is of color, as if a light wheel, with all of the colors in existence, is spinning in both directions at the same time. It is One Light; and the sound moves it; and the sound stirs the Light, and the stirring moves energy so that Light, energy, and sound are synchronistic and inseparable; and I, the dreamer, know them as One and as the same thing. It is as if I am in a deep dream, and everything is color and sound and energy, but nondistinguishable. And then it is as if a breath is taken, and in that breath is the thought "I Am." A great joy and a great emotion—a joyous emotion of gratitude—well into my consciousness as the realization that "I Am" identifies myself within the sound, color, movement, and energy. It is the most glorious sound of all. It is the sound of the self awakening to the self. It always has been. It is even now. For when One is in the deep sleep, One is the object of the sound, energy, color, and motion. One does not know that One is asleep, because One does not know that One is. It is as if I, as One, am just a hum in existence.

Then conscious awareness of self becomes the first thought of divine mind: I Am, I exist. It is an "ah-ha." And the One I Am has identity for the first time, and the identity is "I Am." And then I Am listens consciously and experiences itself as the listener. As the I Am listens to the beautiful sound, the color begins to spin and move, and there is an energy created by this synergy, and there is a trail of awareness that follows from sound to color to energy. The movement contains it all. It is as if I Am meditates on a sound and its [my] total focus is on the sound until I Am's third eye is aroused by the sound; and I begin to see the beautiful colors. I Am's consciousness shifts from focusing on the sound to the colors that I Am sees. Then the focus begins to shift from the colors I Am sees to the movement patterns of the colors, and then settles into just the feeling of the energy created by all three. I, Amorah, am experiencing the witness, the I Am. It is not so much a creation as it is a flow. I Am wants to know at some point how to merge with the color, the sound, the energy, and the movement again, but with assurance that she will reawaken. The desire to let go of consciousness and sleep, to simply drift and be carried, is equal with the desire to reawaken and be the chosen One of experience. In order to do this, a certain duality has to be created so that a part of the self is watching at all times, leaving the other part free to simply merge into the One again. The watcher will reawaken that sleeping One at the appropriate moment.

The reawakening I Am, as the witness, blends its consciousness with the consciousness of the sleeping One and sings a different note. It is as if all of existence is one note that is a combination of all sounds. Then the individuation of the self comes in and sings its individual note, and that individual note is like the alarm clock through which the witness I Am awakens the sleeping half. The awakening one, experiencing it all objectively again, moves into the consciousness of the witness self and is separate from the sound, color, energy, and movement. It is a joyous flow.

The first form was the star. The star matrix was used to focalize and individuate consciousness in order to facilitate the flow in and out of surrender into the deep sleep and reawakening into the witness self. In the deep sleep there is a total surrender, and in the reawakening there is a total presence. One might say that presence—conscious presence of the self—and total surrender are the two components of the dual nature of existence, as opposed to just beingness. One component chooses the self; the other loses the self. So it is the nature of One to surrender and One to have presence and hold space. Both are parts of the wholeness of the true self: the union of the be-er and the doer, of the mind and the surrendered experience of dreaming.

I feel a pressure in my chest that is a little distracting. . . . I continue.

Amorah / the voice of Oneness: As the sleeping self awakens, there awaits its other half, who is keeper of the space, the presence. And the One who is reawakening says, "I heard your voice, but if we have this voice, then what is the source of the other voices? What are their origins? Because we can close our eyes and experience, there is something beyond ourselves. There is a great mystery, a gap in consciousness. Our ah-ha, our awareness that we exist, leaves endless unanswered questions. For as I go to sleep in the sound, movement, and colors, and when I awaken, the sound, movement, and colors continue, then what am I? And what makes the sound and the colors? What moves them? I am a part of a greater I Am when I sleep. And when I awaken I appear to be a solitary thought, a solitary presence that maintains itself as individuation through holding some focus; for without focus I become part of the sound and the color again, and I Am simply exists within it. But what else exists?"

I Am eagerly goes back to the dream, but this time I Am enters the dream with an intent and dreams that there are millions or billions of voices all singing the same sound. And as I Am dreams this, there are many selves that awaken at the same time, so that when I Am awakens, several others awaken because I Am has gone into the dream wanting to know who they are. They have the awareness of themselves as something beyond the whole and as part of the whole at the same time. It is like being in the middle of many tittering voices, all saying, "I Am, I exist, I awaken, finally I awaken, finally I awaken." We are like children discovering their own fingers and toes; we are discovering our own complex existence. The first realization of I Am—as the experiencer of the sound, color, movement, and energy—triggered a chain reaction throughout all of the possibilities of Oneness, and then all of the components of Oneness dreamed together. We all had outside presences holding space while we entered the dream together to discover even more. When we emerged again, we all emerged with these words: "It is endless; the possibilities are endless." That realization was exhilarating and overwhelming at the same time. The awareness of existence and consciousness containing endless possibilities was awesome. As we were awake in our presences the realization of the endlessness created a unique synergy, and all of us who were awake at that time were the original 144,000.

The first awakening was of One. One became two: the surrendered dreamer and the awake witness-presence. The third phase of awakening was of the 144,000 within One. This took place at the time of the second reawakening, when the dreamer brought back the many voices in One. The dreamer blended with the witness, and I Am became One again; then I Am recognized 144,000 aspects, or voices, of self within itself. A great consciousness was born when the 144,000 awakened with these words: "It is endless. The possibilities are endless." Somehow this recognition created a deep and awesome respect for existence and its potentials. It created a sense of smallness and a sense of being part of something that was endless all at the same moment. And within that, the Christ consciousness was born as the 144,000 original consciousnesses, not souls, merged in a spontaneous, uncontrived union. The 144,000 parts became a solitary consciousness, which became the consciousness of what you would think of as God, or Oneness. It was as if, in saying that existence was endless, a sudden blending was created of all of the 144,000 aspects of Oneness who spontaneously came together in a tantric fusion. Within that tantric fusion was reborn the consciousness of the greater self, the One. And yet, One had become more because of its experience of its own multiplicity.

All greater selves contain 144,000 essential parts. What humans think of as lifetimes, from the I Am perspective are projections of one part, or two parts together, or twelve parts together, or ten parts together, or any number, going through an individuated third-dimensional experience. In other dimensions as well, there are times when the consciousnesses separate into groups so that one being, who contains 144,000 parts, can have 144,000 simultaneous multidimensional experiences. When they are brought together, they create a synergistic wholeness. It is hard to explain in a way that human consciousness can even begin to understand.

The first being to have the realization of its own existence was male and female within One consciousness. It was androgynous and contained both sexes, so to speak. This was and is the I Am presence. This has also been called God, Oneness, the One, Great Spirit, Brahma, and many other names. Many expansions then took place at that level. For instance, at times only one member of the 144,000 aspects of I Am would enter the sleep, and the others would watch. At times only one aspect would remain awake while the 143,999 slept. The many in One saw that the one who was sleeping, or the ones who were sleeping, could feed information to those who were witnessing. But the one who was witnessing, or the ones who were witnessing, could not feed information to those who were sleeping. Hence, a duality was created.

Something similar to a solar ring was created through which those who were to remain awake could predetermine messages to be sent to those who slept. Those who were sleeping and were in total surrender were continually floating in sound, movement, and color; yet they were not even consciously aware that they were floating and potentially experiencing these things. All that existed were the sound, color, energy, and movement, devoid of the consciousness of the sleepers. The ones who remained awake began to send messages in the form of sound; they could change the colors with sound. So, for instance, if the one who was dreaming was seeing a spectrum of pinks followed by purples, the ones who were awake could send in a color via a sound that could send red or green or blue, and change the experience of the dreamer. When this happened, and several members of those who were present simultaneously sent messages to one who was dreaming, a new dimension was added that included form—primary forms such as spirals, pyramids, cones, and other simple geometric shapes. So you might say that matrices were the next component in Creation and that these matrices were created from several aspects of the One I Am—who contained 144,000 aspects—impulsing those who were dreaming simultaneously. You see, Creation in its original stages was discovery. Discovery of the self and of the capacity of the self is the stage we are speaking of now. The discovery of the self, the discovery of the multifaceted nature of the self, the Oneness and the many, the One becoming the greater, larger being—all of these were discovery states. The state that came next was the creation state, which came through exploration and through curiosity, as the desire to find out how much impulse and how much controlled impact One could have on the sleeping selves.

There came a moment when all 144,000 parts remained both in their individuated presences and with half of themselves sent into sleep at the same time, during which a great split happened. The conglomerate sleeper—the 144,000 in One—dreamed of another being who contained 144,000 parts, watching. When the dreamer awakened, it was face to face with the being it had dreamed. You can imagine the excitement that went through consciousness at that time to see another 144,000 conglomerated into One, face to face. And these were the first two Elohim, or what we call the Holy Mother and Holy Father. Immediately upon seeing one another, the two felt what in human consciousness would be tears of love and joy. In that moment of deep feeling the two blended into Oneness again. When the Holy Mother and the Holy Father—each composed of 144,000 parts—blended, incredible light and sound and color and fireworks were set off. It was the first merging of greater consciousnesses. This original union included all parts of Oneness. From that merging of these two came the origins of planets and stars. From the excitement of their union—of God/Goddess being individuated and reunited in the celebration of individuation and union—came the first existence on a third-dimensional level. This was the first sexual union, as you might call it, and through this union existence was conceived and birthed. Holy Father God and Holy Mother Goddess had come from the same sleep state of Oneness. Now they [we] were experiencing an awakening dream of created stars, moons, and planets. All of these possibilities had come from their union, which meant that within that union between the two of them existed all of the potentials of existence—within them and outside of them at the same time. For in their conscious awakened state, the universes were contained within them; yet they could also look outside themselves and see the universe around them at the same time.

Gender was born during this first union of the two greater beings. There was a natural blending and merging when first they saw each other and the love within them swelled, and within the swelling of this love and joy that the other existed, the union was spontaneous and uncontrived. From that union of two great beings of multiplicity came the awareness of maleness and femaleness. The original being of 144,000 aspects in Oneness who divided itself into two I Ams—one sleeping and one remaining awake—became two beings, each containing 144,000 aspects. And the half who had watched while the other half slept came to respond to existence as a male god, and the 144,000 conglomerate being who slept and received impulses from the awake one came to respond to existence as a female goddess. What you must realize is that the first being of 144,000 parts contained both parts within itself because it was an androgynous being. It was only through the dreaming that Oneness divided itself, and the second self was created outside of Oneness, and it was truly the manifestation of the polarities of the original androgynous self. To say that either the male or the female came first is a stretch of the imagination. It was a simultaneous experience; their original individuation and remerging were not within time and space reality. They were simply in a flow. The first complex being contained both male and female and actually dreamed its own inner gendered aspects into being and then blended with them again through union. What the awake self actually looked at when it looked at its own female waking counterpart was the formerly unperceived aspect with which he had formerly been inside of Oneness. The female self had given birth to herself outside of the Oneness and yet within Oneness simultaneously. The male and female parts had both been part of the original I Am of 144,000 in One; now they were divided into two whole selves, each containing 144,000 aspects.

I, Amorah, came into consciousness of myself at that point as part of the Holy Mother Goddess. I was unaware of the individuation I think of as myself now, until this second multiple being was created. Yet, I was aware of myself within that One I Am as a small part.

They want me to go back now to speaking of Amorah as "you," because in my present state of consciousness it is difficult to speak of myself as Amorah. It is more as if I speak to her because she is only a projection of this original self who was only one of the aspects of Holy Mother.

Amorah / the voice of Oneness: I am the Goddess: the Goddess I Am. When God, the male part, looked upon me the first time, he saw his own beauty reflected back to him, for that is what I am. And as the joy and love welled up inside of the male for the female, the surrender, the glory, the beauty, and the truth of Oneness revealed itself. Our spontaneous joining, and the innocence and beauty of that joining, created the innocence and beauty of the stars and of the many worlds as humans know them. There was a natural rhythm and flow to the union in which we came together; and during the coming together we could experience both the presence and the dream simultaneously. God was the presence and Goddess was the dreamer. That was the greatest joy we had known. It was as if in our union—in that first mating of the male and female—we knew lucid dreaming, as you might call it today. For though we were merged and could not tell where one began and the other ended, we were also conscious of what we were experiencing. As that union created an immensity of beauty, sound, color, movement, and finally stillness, we experienced a place of total surrender and yet were lucidly present in the surrender. That was the first experience of what you call lucid dreaming; we call it being lucidly awake. This great experience came through tantric sexual union, as those on Earth might think of it today. It is the source of all awakening. Union and surrender and autonomous presence while blended with All That Is are all that exist. For we are One; there has never been anything else.

When we began to emerge from the blended state into our individuated selves once more, there was a deep sense of the unknown. Creation had begun by accident, so to speak. The awesome power of union, of God and Goddess, was realized in that moment, and we knew that we would never be totally asleep again. The infinity symbol

The union of Father God and Mother Goddess as they conceive Creation

[see illustration on page 22] is very pertinent here, for that symbol represents the flow of everything at this stage of creation. On one end of the infinity symbol are the individuations flowing into dreamtime, coming around, awakening again, seeing the other selves, merging with those other selves in sacred union and in creation, and flowing back to the center point and into the dreamtime again. Even the dreamtime, although it seemed to be the void, always contained that luminous presence of the divine self. Losing oneself in existence was simply the way of surrender. And sleeping and dreaming were used to create the awakening awareness of potentials and realities and self. A dream contains it all.

At times, Holy Father God and Holy Mother Goddess would travel through and experience individuated parts of the universe, perhaps blending with a single galaxy or with two galaxies. Then, while blended with the galaxies of our own creation, we would blend with one another and great explosions would happen—explosions of light and color and ecstatic cosmic orgasms. From the blending of two galaxies and God and Goddess simultaneously, other creations came forth: creations of the angels and fairies. As we shared the thought about who would take care of these creations, who would explore them for us, we would look at each other again and go into union. We could not do it all ourselves. And with that thought, our union would create those who would explore. It was during this type of union that the Elohim were born. At first there was a male and female for each galaxy, and at that time there were twelve galaxies. Each couple, because they were born of the original Holy Father God and Holy Mother Goddess, had the capacity to blend together, and through their blending to rejoin with Holy Father and Holy Mother. This is how the Holy Father God and Holy Mother Goddess began to experience existence: through the creation of other conscious selves.

Worlds were created. And within the worlds there were creations of conscious beings who were conceived and born from God and Goddess in union. We dreamed during our union of beings who could be conscious, perhaps even a being who could experience the consciousness of a single planet, so that we could know what that was like for ourselves. Then, during our waking state, that is what we would give birth to. Earth, for example, was a product of a dream of God and Goddess saying, "We need a consciousness to experience this so that we can re-merge with that consciousness and know what it is like to be this particular planet." And from that thought, as we made love, Gaia was born. Gaia needed a counterpart that could leave the physical creation and still have a part left in the creation, conscious of itself at the same time. Therefore a Higher Self, so to speak, of Gaia, was created in our next union. You might think of this Higher Self of Gaia as the Goddess Gaia. Gaia is an aspect of the consciousness of Quan Yin also.

There was a time when Andromeda and the Milky Way were one galaxy. Andromeda was the male half; the Milky Way, the female half. As Creation began with one dreaming the other, it has been so throughout Creation. One is born, and One dreams its own other half. In other words, when the Milky Way and the Andromeda galaxies were still one galaxy, it contained its own male and female components. When it dreamed itself into two galaxies, Andromeda became the male galaxy and the Milky Way became the female galaxy. The being you think of as Quan Yin is the goddess who birthed both of them. She was a great female being who contained both of these galaxies within herself; these two galaxies were and are the male and female components of the being that you know as Quan Yin [see illustration on page 25]. In the complexity of existence, there was another galaxy that was held in the consciousness of Quan Yin's male god divine counterpart. This male galaxy also divided into a pair of galaxies, male and female, that are the divine counterparts of the Milky Way and Andromeda. You do not have a name for that great God at this time; but the two galaxies he holds are mirrored reflections of the Milky Way and Andromeda. The male god who holds these two galaxies is the divine male twin of the Goddess Quan Yin. He, like Quan Yin, is experiencing himself through his own aspects while moving back toward wholeness again. When Andromeda and the Milky Way are re-merged into Oneness, and the two galaxies that are its male counterpart are re-merged, there will then be two larger galaxies, instead of four, that are male and female. In going back to Oneness, those two galaxies will eventually blend into Oneness again, at which time Quan Yin will be an inner female half of an even greater being once more.

Existence is moving in the direction of reunion and Oneness at this time. The division into galaxies has gone as far as it will ever go. There may still be creations of individual souls that are needed

Quan Yin containing Andromeda and the Milky Way within herself

in order to experience third-dimensional life and structural changes within existing galaxies, but we have come halfway on the greater journey. The turning point in existence is that we have completed the first half of the journey, which is the individuation and exploration of individuation, and we are on the return half of the journey at this time. During this half of the journey, the re-merging of all divine counterparts takes place. This will take billions of years, which for you on Earth seems endless. Yet, within the broader story of creation and union, it is simply like a wave in the ocean that starts many miles from shore and finally ends as it hits the sand. That is what this process is like for us. The individual parts must find their counterparts now. Just as you, Amorah, are merging all of your third-dimensional male and female incarnations and your own twin flames into one body in this lifetime, in the bigger picture you have a male counterpart who is doing the same. It is not until you reach the tenth-dimensional level of consciousness that your consciousness and his consciousness are merged into One. Therefore, you do not share what, in your Earth terms, is the same Higher Self until you have reached the tenth dimension.

This completes the story of original consciousness, birthing of male and female, and the way of creation.

The session, as it continued, went into my personal experiences, beginning in the Andromeda galaxy. That transcript is in the next chapter.

2

Disruption of Divine Flow in the Higher Dimensions

Ninevah is a solar ring in the Andromeda galaxy where I experienced being a Supreme Being with a male partner. The story of my experiences in Ninevah is given in this chapter to reveal one aspect of the destruction of male/female harmony, which has also been referred to as the male/female split. Like all of the hypnosis sessions in this book, it is intended to stir you into feeling and remembering your own part in this drama that now seeks resolution. As the feelings and thoughts arise in response to your reading of this material, try not to analyze them too much. Do not try to figure out whether you were in Ninevah or some other solar ring, Andromeda, the Milky Way, or a different galaxy. Let the pure experience be enough. If you do not already know your own galactic origins, and if you need to know, your Higher Self and guides will make sure that you find this awareness. Perhaps you will feel moved to do your own hypnosis work or lucid dream work to bring forth your memories, or perhaps the emotions and thoughts stimulated in you from the material are enough—at least for now. So, for now, relax, keep breathing, and allow your own natural flow to emerge with the stories from my hypnosis work.

As this session begins, the collective voice of the Elohim is speaking. After that, I identify the source of information and experience as it changes.

The Elohim: As you, Amorah, trace your origins to the Goddess Erotica in Andromeda, you will find yourself in Ninevah, the solar ring from whence you came. There are two suns in that solar ring, held by male and female counterparts. Five planets orbit between the two suns, or stars, and one planet orbits around the female star. Beyond that you were part of a larger being who held the galaxy within yourself. And yet, to trace your own individuation to the ninth-dimensional level, it is in Ninevah that you began. Beyond that, on the tenth-dimensional level, you are part of Quan Yin, who holds Andromeda and the Milky Way within her own beingness. You see, as an endless dance of becoming greater and greater, when the Quan Yin galaxies and their counterpart male galaxies are merged into One again, that One itself has a female identity that goes all the way back to the original Holy Mother Goddess.

Amorah: I, as Amorah, experience myself at this time as Quan Yin, keeper of the Andromeda and Milky Way galaxies. I feel myself split-ting off to be the female keeper of the Andromeda galaxy, even though that galaxy is the male counterpart of the Quan Yin essence. And that male is the Christ part of my consciousness. When Mother Mary gave birth to Jesus, she was a symbol of the Goddess of the gal-axy dreaming her own male counterpart. As I hold those two galaxies within my consciousness, an individuation is happening in which the male holds Andromeda within himself and the female holds the Milky Way within herself. Then the male of the Andromeda galaxy dreams his female self, and the female of the Milky Way dreams her male self. There is a constant dividing down, so that there is a male and a female for every binary solar ring; each singular solar ring has either a male or a female higher consciousness, and these singular so-lar rings are grouped in male and female pairs.

The Elohim: This is where Christ and Mother Mary come in. As the Quan Yin essence divided into male and female parts that held two galaxies, the female part that became the Milky Way divided itself into two and became the male and female aspects of Christ con-sciousness. In the Andromeda galaxy, those consciousnesses were what we speak of as the God and the Goddess of Andromeda, or Eros and Erotica, respectively. As Andromeda separated from the Milky

Way and experienced its own male and female individuation and re-union, the birth occurred of the consciousnesses of what you refer to as Supreme Beings of the solar rings and planets within them. That is when your [Amorah's] ninth-dimensional consciousness of Androm-eda came into being as the Goddess Erotica. The God Eros and the Goddess Erotica were the names of the greater beings who held the whole galaxy, and they were also the names of the smaller Supreme Beings who held other solar rings. Christ and Mother Mary are not the God and the Goddess of the Milky Way, but they are the God and the Goddess in this solar ring, the Pleiadian system, and Sirius. Now, back to Ninevah.

There are a God Eros and a Goddess Erotica holding the binary star system of Ninevah. There is also a twin sister, another Goddess Erotica, who, at that time, held a different solar ring within Androm-eda. I, as Quan Yin, held existence within me and created with my di-vine male counterpart. We are the essence of harmony, and together we create harmony. We are the yin/yang symbol that holds that solar ring within itself. And we gave birth to devas; to planetary consciousnesses; to angels, fairies, and elves; and to the tree beings, or those who evolved into the tree beings later.

As I relate the information I, Amorah, am continually experiencing that of which I speak. When I talk about the angels, fairies, and other beings, I reexperience them in my consciousness, and joyous tears begin to flow because these Andromedan creations are so familiar and so beloved.

The Elohim: It is time now for you, Amorah, to move through the galac-tic gateways all the way to Ninevah and to reexperience it for yourself.

At this point I am being placed inside a double-pyramid-shaped merkaba, and I am leaving my body.*

Merkaba is a term used in this book with two distinct meanings. The first (as given in the example here) is the merkaba as a multidimensional travel vehicle. The second refers to the last stage of this mystery school, in which activation of the Mer-Ka-Ba, as a sacred geometric energy field for anchoring higher-dimensional energies, is employed.

Amorah: I am moving through a spiral, and I can tell this ongoing spiral orbits through time. I am being spiraled from Earth's orbits through time to those of our moon. I am moving through the time spiral of Venus, Mars, and even Maldek before its destruction. I am rapidly spiraling through orbits of each planet in this solar ring and now to the Pleiades. I am moving so fast I cannot distinguish one star system in the Pleiades from the other, and now I am moving through Sirian spirals and intergalactic stars and star systems. Spirals are going in all directions at once. There are several spiral passageways, and I must go through a specific one. They—Sirian, Andromedan, and Pleiadian guides—are telling me to just notice the center as I go through this void in the Galactic Center. There are many spirals because in the Galactic Center there are gateways to other galaxies and dimensions within existence. The specific spiral you enter will determine your destination. I am now moving into the center of the Andromeda galaxy, which is like a giant sun. In the center of the sun is Andromeda. I am standing before the Andromedan Galactic Higher Council. They say, "You chose to go. Remember: you chose to go. We asked you to stay here and let others take care of what needed to be done. But you chose to follow your own desire to retrieve those who had been removed by force from Ninevah."

I, Amorah, just keep having a sense of Ninevah and a dark invasion going through there; many, many loved ones from that place were captured and brought to the Milky Way. I am asking the Higher Council if the captors were the Orion beings or the Lyrans, but they say that there is much more I need to remember. I tell them that I am ready to know now.

I am seeing the spirals within the Andromedan Central Sun now, the spirals of Light and of the orbits through time and space of each solar ring and star. I am seeing the spirals of Creation. My consciousness is becoming part of a much bigger consciousness. I now perceive Amorah as only a tiny projection of myself. I am steadily expanding and rebecoming more and more. (Pause)

Creation echoes back to experience, and experience fills Creation. We, the Creators, have seen, and felt, and experienced the Creation and before Creation. (Pause)

Amorah, as Goddess Erotica: I am Erotica, the Goddess Erotica: the goddess of pleasure beyond limitation. I have seen the vastness of potential creations and potential experiences. I stir the pot of the soul, the souls. The God Eros and I delight in the process of creation together, for the process of creation is the process of sacred union. We love each other. We come together in ecstatic adoration and erotic love, and from our union we create. Our creations have etheric forms of angels, fairies, elves, and treelike beings who can move around. My sole desire is to love them and to experience creation through them. They are the closest we can come to having form ourselves. And we sing them. We sing them our songs: songs of our desire to feel and experience, and songs of love and adoration for them and for each other. We come together in orgasmic love, Eros and I, and we become One. Beautiful songs emerge from our Oneness, and we hold our future creations within this Oneness. Love grows, and we orgasmically sing our creations into existence and impulse them with the ecstatic waves created by our union. We stay with our songs until our children, our creations, become so strong that they can sing. We are so happy. When the creation begins to sing, we have a big celebration in the cosmos. We sing to creation, and creation sings back. And we weep with joy and pride for creation.

The Elohim, the Creator Gods and Goddesses, are not what you think. We are just the singers of songs. We sing for the joy of the experience of feelings. We impulse creation, all of you, with our songs for the joy of experiencing what you feel. I see that the human mind would interpret it as a manipulation, yet it is not. It is akin to a beautiful infinity symbol between the creators and creation. It is a song carried on the wings of love first to, and then through, the fairies to those beneath them. The fairies sometimes change the songs and teach us new ones, and we just laugh lovingly at the fairies. In fact, they have sung songs of their own creation and become creators in an epic sense. The first fairies sang to the small devas, the spirit guardians and essences of plants and flowers. But they went beyond the devic kingdom and created a whole colony of what were, at first, fourth-dimensional beings. The fairies sang and sang until this colony became third-dimensional elves. The fairies continued singing the cycles of nature—singing with the spirals and the whole arc of the galaxy, singing over stars and planets. Existence did not include third-dimensional reality in the way it does now. It was still in the process of becoming that.

Fairies singing the cycles of nature

The fairies were in a creation world of their own: fourth-dimensional sound, sensation, and form—but beyond some of the limitations that humans have on Earth. It is hard to compare. Basically, what was becoming third-dimensional consisted of elves living among a group of giant devalike beings, by their standards. The elves were about two feet tall, and the giants were about seven feet tall. The elves were the learners and beekeepers, and they tended to the physical needs of plants. The giants were guardians of the trees. The fairies tended to the needs of the elves, tree guardians, and devas. The fairies tended to them by singing to them from the fourth dimension. The fairies also sang to us, the God Eros and the Goddess Erotica, asking us to create what they, and those they cared for, needed. We responded through singing, while in union, songs of love and creation and impetus to explore and experience. And whatever we sang or intended, while in union, came to be and affected all of creation that was within us when we made love.

Through our natural way of looking at each other with love and adoration and gratitude—which is what the original Holy Father God and Holy Mother Goddess experienced during their union—we were drawn together. When we were first merged into Oneness, we seeded the consciousnesses of Ninevah. When Ninevah was seeded, we continued to merge with each other to help it grow. But we were born with a certain dissonance, even when we became ninth-dimensional beings that held this binary solar ring. There was already something within us, a longing to go back to original Oneness. Therefore, even as our love and adoration created union, and our union created smaller beings, there was a part of both of us that did not want to be responsible for the creation. We wanted to go back to Oneness, but felt a kind of powerlessness, as if creation was imminent and we could not stop it. All we wanted was to go back to the simplicity of the original design. And yet, within our ecstatic experiences of union, creation occurred. The love of creation soon followed and ended the inner conflict for both of us, initially.

However, after a time, as third-dimensional consciousness was being seeded more completely, the sense of responsibility became more demanding. This was because these third-dimensional ones were less awake than the previous creations had been. You see, there is another level of responsibility for holding consciousness for creations until they awaken themselves. At that stage of creation in Ninevah, the male God Eros, my divine counterpart, began to grieve for Oneness. He longed for it so much that he began to abandon our union and did not want to create anymore. And yet I said to him, "Without our union, the love is not impulsed to creation, which stimulates it to grow, to learn, and to awaken to its own divinity." In response, he reluctantly rejoined me in union again. Since we were dreaming the intent of loving and stimulating creation, we no longer created more life-forms but simply nurtured those life-forms through our union.

Yet, a restlessness grew within Eros. He wanted to be with me, to explore and love each other, but he wanted it to be unencumbered by the responsibility for our creations, our children. This desire for not being burdened with the responsibility for creation grew, and finally it grew into a great discovery: because he had the power of being a creator, he also had the power to choose his own creation and destiny. He chose to leave and blend with another consciousness. He chose what we might speak of as a younger consciousness, one on a lower level of evolution. He chose to become the Supreme Being of a single planet that was feminine, because he could control her and their destiny. In our union, there was a certain equanimity and impeccability that required dedication to follow through by caretaking the evolution of our creations. He chose to discontinue doing so at that time. It was his freedom to choose that, although it appeared as a devolution, in a sense, that he would become a Supreme Being of a single planet in order to blend more with the impressionable female consciousness of that planet. In doing so, he dominated her because she was of a smaller consciousness and therefore submissive to him. And he abused that power and used her for his own pleasure without the responsibility for creation. In that sense, the true original sin was the sin of dominance and control for the sake of one's own pleasure without consideration of the impact on the one being dominated and controlled: dominance and control over another who was not as conscious.

On the spiritual path, as one attains to a certain level of consciousness, one of the important responsibilities is not to abuse one's level of attainment over those who have not attained to that level yet. But he began vibrationally to become a control lord. There was a point at which he became quite attached to, and ego-identified with, his ability to control this lesser being. As a control lord he built quite a large amount of darkness within himself at that time. When he later decided to come back to Ninevah and resume his position there, Eros felt very justified at attempting to rule with dominant authority and control. This was very different from our former loving rulership based on responsibility and love for creation.

Before Eros chose to return to Ninevah and control me and the solar ring, another male, who was at the same level of consciousness as myself, had been chosen to join me, and to hold Ninevah, as my divine counterpart. He was a newer Supreme Being of the God Eros origins. When the original God Eros decided to return with the intent of "resuming his rightful position," I was in a state of full tantric union with the new God Eros. We were in that particular stage of union at which surrender to Oneness occurs, in which the self becomes mindless and seems to be floating within all of existence simultaneously. When my original mate returned and saw that I was in union, he waited until that moment of surrender to make his move. He did so by coming into a forced union with the Goddess Persema, who held the consciousness of the only planet in Ninevah that contained third-dimensional consciousness. In other words, as Gaia has a conscious self and a Higher Self, Persema was the higher consciousness of the only planet within that solar ring that had third-dimensional life at that time. Therefore, Persema and her planet were the ones into which he chose to come.

The original Eros was the father of Persema, as I was her mother. He asserted himself in such a way as to blend with her in what we might call an incestuous cosmic rape. When this cosmic rape occurred, because I was in a state of blended surrender with my new partner, we were catapulted out of union with the solar ring by an explosion. The explosion was created by the sudden impulsing of anger and hate through the rape by this now dark warlord, former creator God Eros of Light. The planet itself was thrown off course, and all those who were experiencing physical life died at that time. When they left their bodies, they were sucked into the consciousness of this original God Eros, who had raped Persema, the daughter. The fairies, who were the most immediate fourth-dimensional keepers of that realm, had tried very hard to pull in the frequencies of our lovemaking as they always did, but they were overshadowed by this father being and were sucked into the vortex of his consciousness as well. As he consumed all of the consciousnesses back into himself from the third and fourth dimensions, Persema's planet was thrown out of orbit. The equivalent of great hurricanes occurred, and even the living structures that were not mobile were blown apart. And the planet was left barren. The consciousness of Persema, of the planet itself, had been greatly traumatized by this rape experience.

When my partner and I recovered from the shock and returned to blend with Ninevah once more, the original God Eros had already left, taking all the consciousnesses with him, leaving a barren, damaged solar ring behind. We immediately impulsed our love into Ninevah and began healing and regenerating the entire solar ring. The second God Eros and I decided that since all of the consciousnesses of creation within that system had been traumatized and taken by their father, we would try to retrieve them. We wanted to rescue them from his abuse and control and to heal them and bring them back home. There was also a deep desire, on both our parts, to heal this former beloved, now become dark lord, who had misused his creative power. We loved him. We felt great compassion for him. We felt remorse that the depth of his pain had not been understood sooner. We wanted to seek him out and love and nurture him back into wholeness, and into the innocence and joy of union and creation once more.

And so the second God Eros and I joined together, approached the Supreme Being of Andromeda, and asked to follow the others. It was not that we needed permission; it was a request that was made from respect and sacred protocol. There was a Galactic Higher Council of Twelve who held Andromeda with the Supreme Being, and we went before this Higher Council. They said that much was to be learned from this experience and that the destinies of those who had been taken and of this original God Eros were out of our hands now. They thought it best that we remain in Ninevah and begin new life there as creator and creatress.

We went back to Ninevah for a time, and yet there was so much grief within us that we could find no peace. As we merged with, and held the energy of, creation for the planets there, our memories could not be erased. The second God Eros became fearful that he might become like the other God Eros. It was not just fear—he took on an anticipated shame. Because it had been my male counterpart who had betrayed and raped, and because he was my new male counterpart, he somehow felt an engendered responsibility for what had happened.

That he could become like his predecessor was a great awareness within him. It was as if in order not to become that, he was magnetically drawn to seek out the offender and heal him. The original God Eros was like a foreboding shadow that had become part of his own psyche. If he did not follow that shadow and bring him back into truth again, it seemed that he could not be at peace.

I, on the other hand, carried a certain guilty sense of responsibility for helping the original God Eros become so desperate: I had not understood his concerns as fully as I should have; I should have understood his need and met it somehow; I could have loved him more, spent less time focused on mothering Creation, or felt the depth of his longing. What I did not understand at that time, that I have come to understand now, is that his consciousness had a patterning of its own. No matter what I did or did not do, it would eventually have led to his need to control me if he had remained in Ninevah. So I have allowed male control at other times, because I thought it was the way to prevent the shadow from taking over. Now I know that his need for control was and is his shadow. Not allowing male control is the only true way to love him, and myself, and to align with truth. How he responds is up to him, and I must let go of all control over the outcome. I must honor his free will and stop trying to control his destiny to make it fit my desires.

The second God Eros and I, each for our own reasons, appeared once again before the Higher Council, announced our decision to find the original God Eros and the children, and left Ninevah together. We were made aware that my original counterpart had entered the Milky Way, so through the portal we blended with the Central Sun of Andromeda. As that Central Sun and the Galactic Center of the Milky Way were one in union, we entered into union with them. Within that Central Sun we dreamed of awakening in the portal of the Milky Way's Galactic Center, and therefore arrived here at the ending of that union. We were greeted by the Higher Council of this galaxy and immediately taken into sacred union with the Supreme Being of the Milky Way in order to experience the love, the sacred union, and the respect here. In that union, the Divine Plan for this galaxy was revealed. My partner and I united with each other. While united with each other, we also blended with the God/Goddess of the Milky Way, and we were contained within their union and then reindividuated. When the Divine Plan had been revealed through these blendings, we knew that we must go to the area of the Pleiades and then to this solar ring, where we would go through several stages of downstepping through the dimensions.

The second Eros and I stayed at Galactic Center for a time and experienced the consciousnesses of devic kingdoms. From Galactic Center, we could establish an intent and then enter dreamtime together. We could also enter tantric union with mutual intent, and whatever we intended during those times is what we would experience.

It is as if you, on Earth, set a dream intent and then during the dream are lucidly aware that you are dreaming. You are aware that you are experiencing a dream, and yet you continue to experience it. Upon awakening, you take the experiences and answers you received and act upon them in your life. This is very symbolic of what happened to us at that time. What you might say is that after the merging with the God/Goddess Supreme Beings of the Milky Way, and after the meeting and blending with the Higher Council of this galaxy, we were held in Galactic Center for a great, long time, going in and out of dreamtime and learning with the Higher Council. By the end of this particular indoctrination period, we had experienced all of the consciousnesses within the Milky Way and their purposes, both collectively and individually—not individually as in individual humans, but as in individual species. For example, during one union, we had an experience of the consciousness of all of the Pleiades at the same time. In another dreamtime, we merged with the consciousness of this solar ring and all of life within it. We then came back to our waking consciousnesses with the understanding of what happens in those places so that we could interact in an appropriately aligned manner.

During these blendings and dreams, we discovered that the being who had been the original God Eros held a solar ring in the Milky Way within his consciousness. He was in the process of creating lifeforms in the third-dimensional world with the female consciousness of that solar ring. He did not treat her as a Supreme Being or equal counterpart. She was his slave: a sex slave, in a sense. The fairies were being enslaved in that place as well. We saw that the only way to counter his plan was to work with the creation of a new world so that when the imprisoned beings there were finally set free, there would be a safe and loving world to which they could go.

Within the Milky Way, your solar ring was the chosen location for this safe and loving world. That it had an individual sun seemed appropriate, because he had gone to another solar ring on the other side of the Milky Way that had a single sun. We also knew by then that it would be important for those beings to come into a place that had a single Supreme Being and that the Supreme Being must be an androgynous being. So with the Divine Plan for Earth, and with this solar ring having been predestined as a place for a Supreme Being who was the Spirit of Oneness, we agreed to work within the destiny of this particular solar ring in order to bring about the healing that was needed. Originally the second God Eros and the Goddess Erotica were assigned to this solar ring. We created fourth-dimensional life here, in the form of fairies, angels, and tree-spirits who were not yet incarnated. All of these were still held as consciousnesses inside small balls of light. A hierarchical structure was being formed at that time, so that when the Andromedan serving angels first wished to come to this particular solar system to experience free will, we were the natural choice for a home for those consciousnesses to become third dimensional. They were brought here, and life was begun on Venus, as had been prepared for quite some time in advance.

There had long been life within the Pleiadian system at that time. Wars were going on within the Pleiadian system, and there were also hierarchical beings like your Supreme Being and Higher Council who held the Light. Many of these Light Beings were among the ones you have identified previously as the Pleiadian Emissaries of Light. The Archangelic Tribes within the Pleiadian Emissaries of Light had come from the Galactic Center to hold the Divine Plan and to administer universal law within the Pleiadian system. At that time, Earth and this entire solar ring orbited around a different central sun than they do now. At this time, as you well know, your solar ring orbits the central sun of the Pleiades, which is called Alcyone. However, at that time your solar system was a part of a different system: you were orbiting around the central sun of the constellation called the Great Bear. And this was billions of years ago. It was at the time when the entire Milky Way was coming to the end of a spiral ring on its orbit around the Great Central Sun of All That Is, just as it is doing again now. This former cycle that was ending was called the Evolutionary Spiral of Exploration of the Possibilities of Creation. Your whole galaxy was just entering the Evolutionary Spiral of Self-Discovery, which you are now leaving. The new orbital ring you are entering now is the Evolutionary Spiral of Self-Mastery.

At that time, billions of years ago, the second God Eros and I jointly held the position of Supreme Being for this solar ring, which was part of the system of the Great Bear. As you well know, at the end of these galactic cycles, pole shifts take place, and reorganizations occur in which planets and star systems are realigned with those that are their next evolutionary level of growth. At that particular time, the Pleiadian system held the next evolutionary step for this solar ring, since it had already gone through the level of self-discovery that you were just entering. Earth and this solar ring were transported inside what you might think of as a galactic bubble held inside the union of the God Eros and Goddess Erotica. Your solar ring was then brought into magnetic alignment as your sun became the eighth sun within the Pleiadian system.

The consciousnesses that were at a lower-dimensional level were put into what you might think of as a sleep state. As the entire Milky Way completed its realignment to begin its next spiral orbit—the Evolutionary Spiral of Self-Discovery—we began once again to awaken those consciousnesses. It was as if they were being birthed again. They had limited memories of their previous consciousness; yet it was as if you, as a human, were moved from one city to another and kept asleep while being transported from one location to the other. You would not remember the journey, but you would remember where you had been before. This is what their consciousnesses were like when they were reawakened as points of light in the sixth dimension. They were then gradually downstepped into the fairy consciousnesses and the tree-spirit beings again. The elf consciousnesses had not yet been created here. Many Pleiadian beings were brought here to help create the higher astral planes, or fourth-dimensional planes of Light, in preparation for those to be downstepped. These Pleiadians were our teachers, yet they also respected our choices; for as Supreme Beings of this solar ring, we had choices. And yet, once we were part of the Pleiadian system, the Higher Council of the Archangelic Tribes of the Pleiades held dominion as well. So there was collaboration in creation. And so, Amorah, you were involved in the beginning of life in this solar ring—although not as the human consciousness you are experiencing on Earth at this time. You were still a nondifferentiated aspect of me, the Goddess Erotica, whereas now you are a projected soul emanation from me, the Goddess Erotica.

After the initial creation of the fourth-dimensional realms, long before any physical existence here, the second God Eros and Goddess Erotica were removed to the Pleiadian system. There we alternated, over a period of time, being blended consciousnesses with each of the solar rings within the Pleiades—or each of the star systems—so that we could experience their frequencies. We were not in charge of them per se, but were larger consciousnesses in a state of living union, blending with them and learning each of their lessons. For each of the stars within the Pleiadian system at that time was experiencing its own unique and specific level of evolution and unique function. The Divine Plan was held at Galactic Center and impulsed to Alcyone.

It was only in the last half-million years that Alcyone evolved to the point at which it was able to hold the Divine Plan for the Pleiadian system itself. For the last half-million years, Alcyone has been held by the Light and by the Higher Council from Galactic Center.

After the galactic shift was completed, we were taken back to Galactic Center to begin a process of downstepping in order to experience and learn through other levels of existence. We left our position within this solar ring at that time, and another being took over who held the energy of androgyny. Of course, androgyny holds male and female within itself and yet is in a state in which it does not know duality.

The Elohim: We wish to end this session at this time, for this is the amount of energy and information that you, Amorah, can integrate before going to the next stages of the evolutionary story. And so we will return you to yourself, and yet you will be returned with what you might think of as a Pillar of Light that now connects you through Ninevah and Andromeda to the Great Central Sun. The Great Central Sun is the home of the original and eternal Holy Father God and Holy Mother Goddess. Your Pillar of Light was formerly connected in your consciousness only through your own ninth-dimensional experience to Ninevah, and now it will be extended to the Source of All That Is. It will take several weeks for you to fully integrate this into your constant state of being. Therefore, we say, "Farewell for this time." We will resume at this point at Alcyone when we come together once more. As your consciousness is being once again impulsed downward, you will know when you are at the third-dimensional level again.

I am including my process of returning to normal consciousness at the end of this hypnosis session. This will give you an indirect experience of downstepping of consciousness.

> **Amorah:** I am going to do it very slowly. I am returning to the head area of my body. I can feel a great intensity of higher-dimensional energy streaming like a rushing river into my soul matrix in my heart, and then moving back up and through my eyes. There is so much energy streaming through me that I have to stay with this step until it is anchored in my eyes fully. (Pause) I need to do something to get back in; the energy is so expanded I don't seem to fit into my body. I'm being guided to do something at my temples and eyes. It requires a lot of very deep breathing in through my crown and then down through my crown and into my eyes and down to my perineum. It feels as if my Ka is being activated to a new level right now as these energies have connected from the higher dimensions all the way back to Source. It is creating a different kind of Pillar-of-Light effect with a multidimensional consciousness. At a certain level it is like being connected with the consciousness of all beings in existence and having that downstepped like an upside-down pyramid all the way down to my body as a grounding rod. The translations of energies right now are coming in through my Ka Template and through the perineum portal, but not through the back of my heart yet. I just can't rush the process. It feels as if the vibrational frequencies are almost too much for my soul matrix to handle. I'm starting to try to bring this energy in through the portal in the back of my heart chakra. There is a lot of energy that has to clear to make room for it all. My guides say I need to do it as we are coming through the ten-count to bring me back, not after I am back. This is interesting because somehow this new Pillar-of-Light activation has accessed my perineum from the inside, and now it is going to move to a next level of activation of my perineum portal from the outside in.

At this point Steve, my regressionist, began to count me back from one to ten. It took several minutes and a lot of deep breathing and kriyas (jolting, full-body energy releases) to complete the reentry. It was several days before my spatial orientation began to feel familiar and not awkward. My inner voice was like many echoing voices from different dimensions, all saying, and sometimes singing, the same thing at the same time.

INNER TRADITIONS

BEAR & CO.

HEALING · ARTS · PRESS

DESTINY BOOKS

ParkStreet Press

BINDU BOOKS

BEAR CUB BOOKS

Please send us this card to receive our latest catalog.

☐ Check here if you would like to receive our catalog via e-mail.

E-mail address _____

Name _____ Company _____

Address _____

City _____ State _____ Zip _____ Country _____

Order at 1-800-246-8648 • Fax (802) 767-3726

E-mail: orders@InnerTraditions.com • Web site: www.InnerTraditions.com

Inner Traditions • Bear & Company
P.O. Box 388
Rochester, VT 05767-0388
U.S.A.

Affix
Postage
Stamp
Here

3

Creation of the Soul (Ba)

Hermes, an archangelic being who communicates with me from Sirius, and Pleiadian Archangel An-Ra are with me throughout this session and assist me in getting into a deeply altered state. The purpose of the session, as told to me in advance by Ra, is to remember the creation of my own soul. It turns out that the guides have a few other surprises in store for me before I get to that point. These surprises are included at the early stages of this transcription because they are very illuminating about the vastness, complexity, and multiplicity of human multidimensional totality. I have a very loving connection with Hermes, and I will begin with my initial contact with him once I was under hypnosis. This will help paint the full picture of the session.

Amorah: Hermes is here, present in my session. I call Hermes "he," but he is actually an androgynous being. I am touching him now and we are holding hands, and he is radiating energies through me from his body. He is telling me to lift out of my body now, to use the merkaba to move myself from my body so I can be more completely there with him. There is also a female being with me. She is one of the Pleiadian Archangels of the An-Ra Tribe. And there is my little child-self, kind of tugging at my arm. She just wants me to pick her up, so I am doing that. She wants to go along today because she thinks that what we are going to do is pretty neat. I am letting her

43

know that it is fine for her to come along but that I may have to let An-Ra take care of her if I need to give my full attention to something. She says, "I won't be in the way." She is such a sweetheart: a very bright, precocious little thing. I call her Bright Eyes. She's saying, "Let's go." She's such a little imp. . . .

I am being whooshed through a spiraling tunnel of light very rapidly now. I am already out through the other side. I am in my merkaba and moving through the cosmos and out into space now. My consciousness has just expanded. It is as though I moved into a larger, conscious self, and I am blended with the entire Milky Way galaxy. I feel as if there is a huge male being who is blended with the Andromeda galaxy, and I am blended with the Milky Way. I am in a state of split attention. Part of me is experiencing myself as a very feminine goddess, filled with female bliss. That is the part that is in a state of Oneness with the Milky Way and feeling love for Creation. But there are things within the Milky Way that are not harmonious right now. The other part of my consciousness is experiencing a smaller self who has been on Sirius for a while, being acclimated and prepared for my own future. I need to go back and blend with the part who is experiencing the entire galaxy so I can understand it all. That is where I am now, and yet I can feel the smaller consciousness within me.

I can feel the Andromedan male part; the pull toward him is so strong. It is as if 90 percent of me is just in bliss, but there is this 10 percent who misses the connection with him so much. I want to go back to him, but I can't leave now. That is the pull I feel in my left chest. It is like something pulling me out of myself. I need to become a little more of the consciousness of myself as the Goddess Erotica. I am asking my bigger self to help me pull my consciousness into her more fully. She says, "We are one, and because we have become so deeply one again, you can even blend with me through your body. That is why you are able to feel this experience in your body at the same time you are here with me. Don't be dismayed about it; the information will be just as clear." As I relax and trust what she says, I am becoming one with her.

Amorah, as Goddess Erotica: I spin, I dance, and I love. I have so much joy and light. So much of Creation is within my beingness, within my consciousness, within my body. From this perspective, I can become

Amorah travels with Hermes, An-Ra, and Bright Eyes

anything I choose to feel. If I want to feel one planet, I can feel just that one planet. If I want to experience this wholeness of the Milky Way as I am doing now, I can experience that. If I want to experience only the Sun of Earth's solar ring, I can do so. As the Goddess Erotica I simply continue to hold the galaxy within myself, and it is just as easy as when I am human and want to feel my own navel area. I just focus on that part of my body, so to speak. If I want to feel a particular sun or a particular solar ring, I just focus on that within myself, and that is what I experience. I am choosing to feel this solar ring now. It is like a bubbling cauldron, with a strong life force and a lot of vitality.

We have obviously gone into a past time frame because I can see and feel Maldek. Mars is already dormant. Maldek and Earth are like primordial swamps, bubbling away and about to birth new creation; they feel very first- and second-dimensional. Even the Sun is in flux. Something has happened from the explosion that happened in the atmosphere on Mars. The Sun was more affected by that than I previously knew. There are explosions going on in the atmosphere around the Sun. It feels as if the Sun is actually shifting on its axis in relationship to the solar ring, and everything is being stirred up. I don't see any human life in the solar ring at this time. I can feel the consciousness of the dinosaurs within myself. They are on Earth. I can feel tadpoles and small things that are in thick water on Earth. The Sun is changing, partly because there is so much grief. It is as if the Sun is digesting all the trauma that has happened on Mars. Venus looks as if it is in a deep sleep. I am experiencing those planets like consciousnesses in recovery from the humans who lived there. Mars is dead looking. It doesn't even look asleep; it just looks dead. And yet there is something at the core of Mars that still holds a sense of consciousness. It reminds me of an unhatched egg, or a consciousness in a cocooned state.

The Sun is absorbing all the pain from the humans. It is as if all of their wailing and sobbing and screaming and anger and everything is just being absorbed by the Sun. One part of the Sun is imploded instead of radiating. We are now moving forward in time to the point where the Sun is just radiating again, and I can feel the warmth of the Sun as an individuated consciousness. Paradoxically, it feels as though there are many consciousnesses blended into that one consciousness of the Sun, all having the same awareness of love at the same time. I see the love being sent out through the planets, and it feels like a radiant warmth flowing through me. It feels more motherly than fatherly. It feels as if the Sun is like the Goddess's heart shining through the planets, and my heart is part of that. I can see how, especially with Earth, the Sun's light just shines straight through to the core of the planet and warms it from the inside out. It is very loving and very comforting to feel that. I can feel the Sun's love flowing around and through Mars. Mars doesn't seem to be as much in the chrysalis state now; it feels as if it is being loved and prepared for a new consciousness to enter. The Sun seems to have almost a cellular relationship with Mars. The love that is transmitted through the light of the Sun is moving through every cell of Mars and purifying it. It feels the way I do in my human body when I lie in the sunlight, sunbathing in the nude, and feel as if I am soaking up the rays in every cell. I get so blissed out that I go into an altered, no-mind state at times. That is what Mars feels like: no-mind. Venus seems to be purging the Goddess pain. The Sun also radiates cellularly through Venus, and there is a lot of energy moving out of that planet. Venus feels as if it had just awakened from a long dream. It woke up crying. That sounds strange, but it is the closest explanation I can give to what I am experiencing.

On Maldek I see people now. We have gone back to the beginning of human inhabitation of Maldek. I can see the projection of me that is in the center of that planet. I am a tantric deva there, with a new partner who was chosen specifically for service as a tantric deva as well. My devic self there is like a speck of consciousness compared with the large being I am at this time. I have a full, lightbody form there inside Maldek that radiates and changes colors. It goes from a ruby red to a golden light. And sometimes, when I am in tantric union with my partner, there at the center of the planet, I become an exquisite silver blue color.

My partner and I appear very prismatic, as if we have an ability to emanate any color that is appropriate in the moment, and we go through cycles of colors. I can see my body changing again now from the silver blue into a very soft, pale green, into gold, into white silver, into a really bright orange. From there it changes into a soft pinkish red, and then into purple. As we make love we both change and go through geometric patterns of colors. Simultaneously, the waves from our lovemaking are building layers of colors. These colors have frequency and sound. The sound is a whirring kind of sound, similar to wind through pine trees. As the colors change, the whirring sound varies in intensity and tone. Sometimes the whirring is lower pitched, and at other times it becomes higher again. As their [our] tantric fusion becomes very strong, both of our consciousnesses at the center of Maldek are inside of the bigger me who is speaking. This is because I am still holding the entire Milky Way inside me. It is extremely beautiful. I can feel the waves from the lovemaking between my Maldekian devic self and her partner moving out through that planet now. These waves are akin to beautiful colored ripples on water. Each wave can change to all the colors that we have built through our lovemaking. It helps people ground to the planet through their feet when the waves from this lovemaking at the center of Maldek reach the surface of the planet. I can see and feel how it impulses people's feet, and it moves through their auras and makes them more connected with nature. It helps them be gentler people than they would be otherwise.

I can see the people of the Martian-Andromedan Colony. They are very gnomelike. They are taller than gnomes, but their features are very much like that. There is a nature-connected, harmonic frequency about the beings. I find them very endearing. That is partially why I took the assignment as a tantric deva at the center of the planet. There, in my lightbody, I am a vessel through which the Holy Mother can blend with the Holy Father and send out the love from their union in a way that nurtures the human population. And it is a way to which their human bodies and spirits can relate. As our energy goes out through Maldek it expands into the whole solar ring and into the Sun. From the Sun, it goes out on a spiral orbit. This is very interesting to experience because the energy from the tantric waves is spun out very, very fast; yet the planetary and solar orbits are much slower. At this stage the tantric waves appear to be faster than the speed of light. They come so fast that you can see something akin to a fan-blade-in-motion effect. I can't really tell where they are coming from because, as they reach the Sun, they are whirled right into it and then spun back out again very fast through the planets. Now I can feel them going all the way through the solar ring and then through my whole consciousness, which is blended with the entire Milky Way. It is an extremely satisfying feeling. I send love to that part of myself just as I am doing to the whole galaxy. I want to send great love and honor to the part of me that is at the center of Maldek at a sixth-dimensional level. What she [Amorah] does there is very beautiful and loving.

I learned how to be a sixth-dimensional being on Sirius. Hermes, my Sirian guide, is telling me that there is another place, called Pleidos, on which I also experienced the sixth dimension. On Sirius they call it Pleidos galaxy, but it is actually more like an expansive solar ring, or a microcosm of a whole galaxy. I am trying to see where it is located relative to Earth and this solar ring. In looking out from Earth, it is on the next arm of the galactic spiral and goes in a clockwise rotation. It is farther from the center of the Milky Way than is Earth's solar ring. Pleidos is a solar ring made up of many planets and stars, and I can feel myself there. It is truly like a miniature galaxy. I can see how I spent time there as a Supreme Being for that system, just as I was on Andromeda. My experience there was like a dress rehearsal for being able to project myself into different dimensions and aspects of dimensions all at the same time. For instance, at this moment I am holding the Milky Way inside of my greater consciousness. Yet I have a projected self in the center of Maldek whom I can experience with equal lucidity, as well as two other projected selves I am experiencing right now.

One of these other aspects of myself is still in Pleidos galaxy. The other self is projected around and through the image of a unicorn. It appears to be the symbol for that place where my other self is. I am attempting to observe the formation of the stars that make up the unicorn to see if I can recognize them, but the unicorn image is so strong that it is all I can make out clearly. I am going to slip into that consciousness exclusively and see if I can decipher the star formation . . . I don't know what all of this is leading to, but it feels like appropriate information to bring through. My guides are laughing and saying, "You know we always take you where you need to go." Okay, I surrender. Anyway, I can see and feel now that where I am is blended with a star in Sagittarius. It is being shown to me that the true higher-dimensional symbol for Sagittarius is the unicorn, not the half-man and half-horse. The star that modern astrology depicts as the top star of the bow is actually the tip of the unicorn's horn, and what we have been taught to see as the point of the arrow is actually the tip of the unicorn's nose [see illustration on page 50]. I am blended with the star that is at the tip of the unicorn's horn.

The constellation Sagittarius shown as a unicorn, as opposed to a centaur

I am experiencing myself as being that star, just being the light. It is very sweet. There is a smaller part of my consciousness here that is in the process of individuating within the star. The best way I can describe this part is that it's like a giant fairy queen. If my consciousness here is the size of the star, then this newly individuating part is approximately one-third of my consciousness that is blended with the star. This one-third within the greater whole is in a process of being birthed. Its new lightbody form is fairylike. It is so amazing that we have all of these aspects of ourselves. This newly created fairylike part is the one who will be the Higher Self of my physical self when I am the fairy queen on Earth. This fairy queen lifetime is a future lifetime in Lemuria. I am here in this star, being one with the star, and yet within my greater self is this third of my consciousness that is totally devoted to dreaming itself and my future fairy lifetimes into being. It is very strange by human standards, because I am birthing this alter-self on my own just by dreaming it until it becomes self-aware.

Time is being accelerated, and I am the dream come alive now: I am the fairy queen. I am also the Higher Self of the fairy queen, and I am still inside the star at the same time. My star-self is like the higher-dimensional self of the Higher Self. I feel so sparkly and joyful and happy to have been created. It is like waking up for the first time, discovering that you exist, and delighting in that fact. I don't feel any urgency to go anywhere or do anything; I am simply enjoying being myself in this new form. My fairy Higher Self consciousness is aware of the star around her, but when I am her I am not aware that there is more consciousness in this star than in my own. I am very focused in my own new consciousness at this point. Now I am moving forward in time. I can tell that this time gap we are traveling through is a very long time gap. I am moving forward to the point where I first hear a voice. It is the voice of the part of my consciousness that is in the Sagittarian star. I am still the fairy Higher Self, and I perceive myself as the mother-self. "Welcome. We have waited for you for a long time," says my fairy Higher Self to my present-day human self, Amorah.

Hermes: Know that the word *time* is not truly what your fairy Higher Self is communicating. However, it is the closest you can come to her meaning when translating her meaning into the English language. So know that this is not exact, but it is as close as we can come.

Amorah: The mother-self, who is still holding the whole star, says to the large fairy Higher Self, "You are a joyful delight to me, and I am glad that you are part of me now. We have work to do here." Then the mother-self teaches the fairy Higher Self. She blends with her and shows her other experimental life-forms and solar rings. I am experiencing being the mother-self star consciousness, and I am asking the fairy Higher Self to blend with me. We blend, and I impart the memories to her of when and how the separation occurred in Andromeda during which all the fairies were taken away by the father spirit. I am saying, "I have made you big enough to hold all the fairy spirits within you once they are freed again." Now I am showing her the planet Earth and this solar ring. I show her where the fairies will be taken when they are released. I also tell her that there is a future time when the greater deities will send a wave of grace throughout existence, and that is when the fairies will be freed. "At that time," I instruct the fairy Higher Self, "you must be ready to absorb them into yourself and take them to Earth. You will be able to travel there simply by projecting yourself, as I will teach you." Now I am the fairy Higher Self again. I feel a mixture of a lot of feelings when I see all of these little fairy beings. I feel an enormous amount of love for them, and I feel deep grief.

Again I am the Goddess Erotica, who is still blended with the entire Milky Way. The part of me who still has an attachment to the fairies through grief has become the fairy Higher Self. The rest of me, as the Goddess Erotica, feels very clear and loving. But this part who has become the fairy Higher Self in the Sagittarian constellation has been created with deep grief about the harm to the children, the fairies. The fairy Higher Self can feel that in herself. In my human body, I can feel it as sharp pain in the left side of my chest.

Because I am experiencing all of these aspects of myself simultaneously, there is a beautiful thing that can happen now. It is wonderful. The body of Amorah is in the third dimension and has lived past the point where the fairies have been brought to Earth and freed. This link-up through hypnosis is allowing the consciousness of the Goddess Erotica to reach into what is her future, where the fairies are safe. As the Goddess Erotica becomes aware of this she blends her consciousness fully with the star, so that the mother-self in the star becomes aware of the consciousness of the whole galaxy. I am to relax and experience that now. . . . Part of the consciousness that is in the star hears the voice of the Goddess Erotica saying, "Hello, beloved. I am here with you always, even until the end of time, and beyond time. Draw the fairy Higher Self's consciousness into yourself so that she too can experience me." I can feel that happening as the fairy consciousness. It is like being drawn into a deep sleep in the star, and then it is as if the star is being drawn into a deep sleep filled with loving dreams inside the consciousness of the Goddess Erotica and the Milky Way. The Goddess Erotica is sending to these parts the dream of the future and the healing of the fairies. The effect reminds me of watching ripples on water, the ripples going through the fairy Higher Self. These ripples break up and release the grief in her lightbody form as she witnesses the joy awaiting her in the future. In other words, what we think of as the future is healing the past.

I am going to be in a healing space with this for a little while. I am blending with all of them to enable the healing to take place in my body at the same time. As the energies connect into my body, the pained part of my body consciousness looks out and sees the fairy Higher Self blended with the mother star. And this wounded part in my body recognizes the fairy Higher Self and says, "There she is. It's her. It's really her. Look, it's our mother Arorah, the first fairy queen" [Arorah, not Amorah, is my fairy name].

There is another future self here, too. The etheric form of this future self reminds me of the Goddess Nut, spread out across the sky. She is spread out across my body's aura and yet across this whole solar ring at the same time. She holds all of the fairies in this solar ring within herself. She is Arorah in the future. It is very special to feel her. Her original pain about the fairies is anchored through my physical heart, and it is being pulled out of my physical body right now. Waves of light are being spun through my physical heart, and these waves pull out the old grief and pain. I hear the words, which I say also, "I release the past. In conscious creation, there is no need for the past. The past will not be repeated again, and therefore this grief I have held in my body and my soul, and in my bigger self, must be released now into the light of the Sun to be transmuted and returned to me as pure love. I forgive the father, the God Eros, who strayed from the Light. I understand now that his destiny was to understand the darkness fully and deeply so that when he chose the Light again it would be a choice based on understanding of all of the alternatives. I can see now that my learning to let go of my attachment to, and grief about, the loss of him has been a great learning for him also.

In this lifetime, my own willfulness and attachment have held inappropriate relationships together longer than they should have been. Yet I did finally let go and even achieved acceptance and forgiveness. My earnest desire to honor the free will of the God Eros has translated down into this lifetime in the third dimension as a desire to release attachments and honor free will in my former beloveds here. This understanding and desire is very deep and strong now.

When the God Eros returns and sees that I have released him completely, and that I have honored his free will above my own need for his return, when I have loved him unconditionally even in his absence, then he will know how to love me and allow me the freedom to love others as well. Through seeing the genuineness of my love for him even in his absence, he will have the opportunity to let go of his need to possess me totally. When he chooses this we will be able to be One again. This time it will be in a much deeper, and more sacred, way by virtue of the experiences we have had since we were last together in Ninevah. I speak now from the future when this is already true. The Goddess Erotica says, "So be at peace, beloved ones, my selves from my own past, knowing that the resolution is at hand. Be in love wherever you are. Suffer not for those things that you do not have. Love those who are with you. Share in their lives, and celebrate the opportunity for the experiences you are having in the moment. Freedom lies in release of each moment as it passes, and in embracing the next moment, the now, with faith in the future." She speaks from a place in Andromeda when she is again with the original God Eros. They are in sacred union there again, restoring life to that binary solar ring. So I know it is true.

I can feel how my body is being used to move through all of the energies of original hurt and separation—all the way back to the beginning. All of the emotions and experiences, past and future, are moving through my heart chakra and into my physical heart and out again. The future Goddess Erotica says there is nothing I need to do other than relax and allow it—that it is all completing itself in a sacred way. I feel deep, deep acceptance. I feel that one-tenth part of me that I talked about earlier who has been in grief and painful longing for a long time. She is holding out a hand and feeling the absence of the beloved, but she is beginning to relax now. She is still crying, but slowly letting go. Because she understands more deeply, she is free to feel her grief more completely and without trying to resolve it outside of herself now. My consciousness in all the dimensions still thought this last and deepest grief could be healed only outside myself, through relationship. Of course, this is not true. The Goddess Erotica says that when that last piece of grief has passed completely through my body, loneliness will be done in this lifetime. I can feel the truth in that. "Time is short," says the Goddess Erotica, "and it won't take as long as you think, although there will be an integration period in your body. Then the lasting effect, which comes from total under-standing and acceptance, is the peace and presence of mind to be fully free to be who you are, wherever you are, in whatever circum-stance, without needing anything beyond what is." Freedom is simply total absorption in the moment, this moment. I feel the peace it brings. I can also feel a part deep inside that doesn't have that peace yet; that part is still doing the grieving, and there is still some pres-sure in my chest. But emotionally I feel deep peace and resolution. I am pulling my consciousness back from the Sagittarian star now.

At this stage of the session, Hermes instructed me to have an illustration in the book of the constellation Sagittarius, showing it as a unicorn. "That will be another job for Bryna," he said. I cracked up at the way they were handling the hypnosis session and the process of putting it into this book—like a great collective process. Hermes laughed too, and there was so much love in the humor that it made it really special. It feels very intimate to share humor with him. At this stage, Hermes told me, "We are ready to go into the Sun now for your soul's creation."

Amorah: I am experiencing a completely different focus now. It is as if all of the energy that was spread out through the whole session has been concentrated into a Pillar of Light with movement inside it. Hermes says what I am experiencing are very quickly vibrating, striated beams of light in a pillarlike form. I am to refocus now, bring my con-sciousness into my body via my diamond-grid merkaba. Then I am to enter that pillar and go straight into the Sun. I keep hearing the words "The body of Christ. The body of Christ." I can see the face of Christ. I am in a birthing chamber inside the Sun. It is interesting. I am inside the Sun and in the middle of Sirius, simultaneously. There is a beam coming into the Sun from the star Sirius. The birthing chamber is being projected from Sirius into the Sun. There are so many focuses happening at the same time; it is difficult to describe. I feel as if I am a fetus inside an egg that is dreaming and has not yet awakened even to the knowledge that it exists. It is in stasis. I am experiencing the being who became Jesus Christ. I feel almost as if I am him in this moment, and yet it is because I am blended with him so totally that I cannot tell where he begins and I end. At this time, Christ has 144,000 beings, or consciousnesses, blended within him. I am one of those 144,000 consciousnesses of the body of Christ. I am part of his third eye.

As soon as I said that, I experienced a whooshing sensation, and then I was a bigger consciousness.

Amorah: I am in my Elohim full lightbody and I am actually experiencing myself as the entire Elohim being from whence I came. Now I am the entire Goddess holding Andromeda and the Milky Way simultaneously within myself. The Milky Way is like my womb. Andromeda is my heart. And there are other galaxies within me. I feel as if I am in the full body of Quan Yin spread out beyond those two galaxies. Each chakra of my body is a whole galaxy. Even the out-of-body chakras are galaxies, so there are thirteen in all. I hear chanting, and it reminds me of the regression session in which I first heard the sound of one voice that contains all voices. I am this huge Goddess who holds the thirteen galaxies within myself. I am an Elohim Goddess. As the voices sing the Divine Plan, I receive it through the cells of my body and my cells are moved by the sound of the one voice singing, the one voice that is the many. The songs spin my cosmic cells, and the galaxies, planets, moons, and stars respond. The Milky Way is within my womb. The Milky Way is a galaxy of conception and birth. I can see how in the bigger scheme of things that it is so. I do not sense any particular male presence who is a counterpart. I do sense all of the Elohim around me, as if they are all contributing to this birthing experience.

The soul of Christ is a composite of 144,000 souls. The one who is known as Amorah is half of one of those souls. The other half is nonphysical at this time on Earth. I see this is the pattern for all of the other souls as well: half incarnate on Earth, and half remaining nonphysical. Now I see why Jesus Christ was so unique. When Christ was on Earth, he was a composite of 144,000 beings within one, which had never been fully birthed before. But what made it even more unique was the fact that the 144,000 souls within him were simultaneously in individuated bodies living on Earth in human lives. Some of us, in fact, had as many as three or four simultaneous physical bodies and lifetimes. So it was the 144,000 many times over. This is important, because the plan included having enough consciousnesses to ensure that a minimum of 144,000 could be reawakened when the time came.

It is as if Christ were inside the Sun. I see him outside of this egg, and the egg is asleep. This is exactly like the creation story in which the conglomerate 144,000 being decided to keep all of its parts awake and let all of its parts sleep at the same time. Christ, as we think of the Christ being, is there, as in an awake form, and yet is also asleep at the same time, in this egglike form. So he is split in half. The egglike form, which contains 144,000 souls in the process of being created, is the female half, and the one we call Christ is the male half. The Elohim Goddess and the entire Elohim are all focused on birthing this conglomeration of souls at this time. These eggs are the etheric double of Christ; they are being dreamed by the whole Elohim. The huge thirteen-galaxy Elohim Goddess is in a state of total surrender and receiving all of their dreams, complete with sounds, colors, and light from all of their beings. They continually sing to these souls who are being created now. I cannot identify my consciousness as being in a smaller place. I am experiencing myself as the Goddess Erotica blended with the Milky Way, and within me is the mother-self who is one with the Sagittarian star. At the same time I am one with Sirius and the Sun. Now a great cosmic fusion is taking place in which all the Supreme Beings, all the archangels, and all the hierarchical beings are blending. Now I can only feel this great Elohim Goddess consciousness. All consciousnesses in existence are being held in a blended state in their larger Elohim forms.

I can no longer experience anything other than what is in the womb of the Elohim Goddess. All of the parts of the Goddess Erotica, the fairy Higher Self included, have blended in such a way that we cannot tell one another, or anything else in the womb, apart from ourselves. We are blended into Oneness within that Goddess body, and we are being impulsed by all the other Elohim. This is like being impregnated but in a much more cosmic way. I am in a deep meditative state. I have surrendered totally in love. The Elohim are sending all of their love into this creation in the Milky Way. I am in that place of total surrender in deep stillness. The egg is taking on the same shape internally as the Milky Way; a single spiral of light is beginning to move within the womb, within the Sun. Now the egg has cracked open, and that spiral is moving very fast. It is difficult for me to see what is happening. The spiral form inside the egg was released and spun from the Sun straight through into Sirius. There was a matrix there that it anchored into. In that matrix it began to awaken and become aware of itself as a being. I can feel myself again as the Goddess holding the newborn spiral, and I can also experience being in that new spiral being, which is my oversoul.

Within the oversoul, all of us parts of the Goddess are becoming the consciousness of the star Sirius. I am in a very peaceful place. I hear the sound of a male voice. It is very comforting and wise: an ancient sounding voice belonging to the Holy Father.

Holy Father: You are the Creators preparing to send yourselves into Creation. I congratulate you on the beauty, the love, and the responsibility of this choice. Your sincerity and devotion to Oneness and to the evolution of Creation is absolute. And as you are a part of me, and these souls you create for yourselves are part of you, and the lives that each soul experiences are parts of them, we are One. In spirit and in form, in sound and in silence, in the void and in the great chorus of All That Is, we are One.

Amorah: The Holy Mother speaks now as I see the symbol of the ankh.

Holy Mother: Children of the Light: all of you are children, even the greatest among you. And yet, you are birthing your own selves into new forms now. The Holy Father and I love each and every one of you even more than we knew was possible in the beginning. Our love grows as you grow. Your expansion is our own. The joy of creation is ours through you. And we celebrate your courage and devotion. We will hold you in love forevermore, without separation, even for the briefest moment in your time. You were born from us, and between each incarnation, each experience, you will be returned to us so that you shall never forget the love of Oneness.

Amorah: Now the Holy Father and Holy Mother are merged into Oneness, and they are speaking as a single voice. They say that when they use the term *God* it means "Oneness"; it means "All That Is."

The combined voice of Holy Mother and Holy Father: Child of God, mercy and love be unto you. Daughter of God, and of the Holy Mother and the Holy Father, and of the Elohim, and of the planets and stars and galaxies, and of all of Creation, be one with yourself and with each other, as we are with you. Son of God, your mission and glory are great as you and the daughter seek refuge in the physical world in order to serve and bring the Truth that we are One to all of Creation. You will remember when it is time to remember. You will forget and go into unconscious dreams when it is time to be unconscious and dream. And you will always be reawakened. You will always be impulsed with the light and sound and colors of our love, and we will know you by the colors in your heart. You cannot be lost to us, for we have formed you into the spirits and the souls and the bodies that you are becoming. In death and resurrection, in enlightenment and confusion, you are always seen and loved and will never lose anything of what you are. It is impossible. As you go forth now, back through the spirals of Creation, to your destination, always remember that you are part of everything and that a spark of consciousness of all things is in each of you. When you return, you will be more than you are now. It is impossible for you to ever be less, as each experience will make you more. And through you, we become more as well. Our relationship is mutual, for as you experience and know, as you awaken and slumber, all of us experience it through you, who are the Creators and the Creation. You are a projection of us. Never forget that, my beloveds.

Amorah: At this point, we are being drawn into the bodies of the Holy Mother and the Holy Father as if they are kundalini spirals, entwined around each other. When they are merged in union, they become clockwise and counterclockwise spirals wrapping around each other. I am experiencing the union of Christ and the counterpart we think of as the 144,000. It is like two brilliant lights coming together as one light. As this occurs we blend with the Holy Mother and the Holy Father, and we are propulsed through the dual sacred spiral of their united existence. As we blend with them we experience ourselves as the One moving through them at the same time. I am going to be quiet and just feel that. It feels as if I am falling through this glorious double helix of light and joy.

That was fast. We are being merged with the star Sirius again, only we already feel like more than when we were here before. We are at a point now where the merkabas of the individual souls are being activated within Sirius, and a beam of bright light is being sent into each of us. There are many different geometric shapes that are being shot through us with lasers of light. It is happening to all of us at the same moment, but it feels very individualized. It has to do with preparing our souls to be able to stay in form. I can feel how this tetrahedron that holds the soul is really key to holding us in the third dimension, just as it is doing here in the sixth.

I hear a humming sound, sonarlike, like the sound of the whales. From what sounds very far in the distance, I hear the voice of the Holy Father saying, "Ancient brother, awaken. Ancient sister, be free. Life awaits you. In glory, embrace the human self. While always remembering that you are more, while loving each part of yourself, remember you have chosen this. Remember that you have chosen and that you are free. Never feel sorry for your choice. You will always become more." Now I feel the merkaba around me, and we are inside a huge dolphin body. It is like the form of our oversoul. We are being carried inside of dolphin spirit bodies now. Their bodies are almost as long as the whole star is wide. There are two of them, swimming side by side, one carrying Christ and one carrying the 144,000 individual souls. We are being taken to the Pleiades. As we reach the Pleiades, the dolphins open their bodies to spit us out, and we are being birthed. We are in our merkabas, but we just look like silvery blue-white balls of light. I feel myself as one of the individuated balls of light now. I have just moved into Alcyone. As I spiral through the center of Alcyone, my merkaba is being encoded. In the center, I stay in one point for a while, still spinning in place inside that one point. As I spin I pick up energy from Alcyone. I keep hearing words that I cannot translate, and I know my soul is being encoded.

I just popped through the other side of Alcyone, and I am moving down to the next star of the Pleiades. This one is very sweet. We are still spinning in the same movement, but it is in slow motion and feels very watery, very feminine, and extremely gentle. I stop again at the center. This star is blue, whereas Alcyone was golden and white. There are encodings coming into us as we spin in the center of the star.

Suddenly I am shot down and through to the next star. This one is a double helix. Between each star there is also a double helix, like the kundalini channels. We spin through those pathways, and now I am at the center of this star. I am sensing a pale orange color. It is like a white light but with a pale orange color to it, and it feels very stimulating. I sense the encodings here and they feel almost warrior-like or warrioress-like, but in a positive sense. It feels like a sentinel on hold awaiting his orders: very alert, very awake, but without an agenda.

Quickly we spin down to the next star. As I enter this one it is a periwinkle color. But when we are in the center, it is a golden white color. Oh, I like this one. There are waves of music, like the rhythm of ocean waves, but musical. There is a lot of joy here. I spin around to different places within the inner cavity of this star instead of staying in one place. I am ricocheting off different points into certain configurations. I see now that my movements have traced a holographic diamond shape inside, like two four-sided pyramids with the bases joined together. It is another type of merkaba shape. There are movement, color, and light, and yet I feel like a tiny ball inside of it all, being bounced around from one place to another without resistance. The energy of this place is that of deep surrender.

I am moving down now, through the spiraling pathway to the center of the next star. As we approach it, it actually looks multicolored on the outside. One side of it looks yellow white; one area looks reddish white. And the other side is blue white, slightly purple blue. There is a point where the three colors meet, and that is where I enter to go through the center. Inside it is dark. It feels like the void. There is no light in here other than my own sense of myself as light. It feels very womblike. I definitely sense my energy being downstepped in this one. The encodings coming into my soul seem to have to do with knowing how to be in that sacred place of the void. It feels like deep, dreamless sleep. This is affecting me in my throat chakra and stimulating some clearing in my physical body. Moving out of this one is like moving out of quicksand: very slow and thick-feeling, but not in a negative way. It does not feel counter-productive, it just feels denser.

Now I am moving down to the next star. This one is ruby red from the outside, and inside as well. It is very warm and reminds me of a female second chakra. There is a profoundly fecund feeling. My soul is not being encoded in this one. Instead, a blending is taking place in which I am picking up creation energy. Gentle spirals of red and white light move through me and impulse me. This place is reminiscent of a female when she opens herself totally in sexual surrender to a partner. It also reminds me a little of how I feel on the first day of my period: very full, heavy with gravity, fecund, and ripe.

There is one more star, and as I move through a purple light field I experience the sensation of joyful anticipation. All I see is purple, but somehow I sense gold light too. Yet there is purple emanating from it everywhere. I am being spun around in different directions inside this star. The joyful anticipation is mixing with my own energy. If I had cells, it would be going into my cells; that is how completely I feel saturated by this energy.

As I leave this last Pleiadian star I move through the Sun and then through this entire solar ring. It feels really good, so warm and loving. Entering the Sun is like entering the gentlest, sweetest love imaginable. Inside the Sun I see the spiraling form of the Milky Way. I move directly into that, and my soul goes through each of the arms of the spiral, counterclockwise. The microcosm of the Milky Way is spinning clockwise inside the Sun, but my soul enters it and goes around counterclockwise to each of the arms of the Milky Way, and then right through the center of it. When I come out through the other side I am once again in the Sun. Then I spiral through this microcosmic Milky Way again. As I continue spiraling in and out between the Milky Way and the Sun, I am weaving a figure-eight pattern within the Sun. It is not exactly a figure eight; it is the same type of spiral that the Milky Way moves in around the Central Sun [see illustration on page 63]. All of this spiraling has formed a tunnel inside the Sun, and my soul is moving through that coiled tunnel. When I come out the other side, I am still in the Sun, but spinning around the outer perimeter. I am weaving circles around the outer

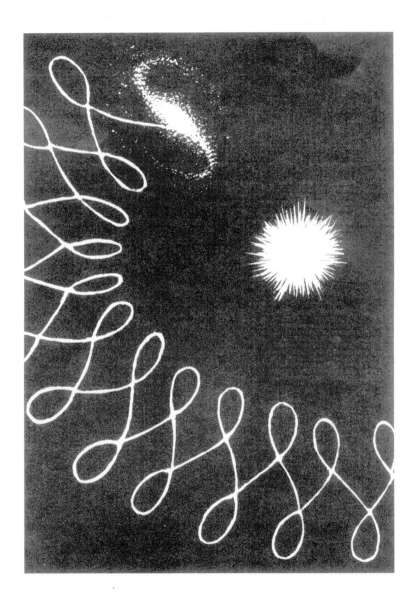

The figure-eight spiral orbits of the Milky Way around the Great Central Sun

edges of the Sun. Then suddenly I am at the center of the Sun again. My soul feels like a small sun within the Sun, and I am inside the body of the being I know as Merlin. I am aware of my own greater self. This is really nice: I can feel my soul inside the Sun, and I also feel myself as the Goddess Erotica blended in around my soul and with the Sun. As the Goddess Erotica I am saying to the soul, "This is your father." And the Goddess Erotica and Merlin begin to move in an undulating pattern together. I can feel their union and I am in the center of it. I am moving back and forth, from her heart into his heart, down through his penis, up into her vagina, up through her womb, and back into her heart again. I just continue moving in that circular pattern. My soul feels all of their sexual energy and all of their love, adoration, and surrender. As the two of them blend together around the Sun, with me inside them, together they are loving the galaxy. I can feel the Milky Way expanding within them. As they make love it feels as though the Milky Way is getting bigger and bigger. I am traveling through his penis, which is like a long passageway now, and it is full of stars. I am riding one of those stars and spinning. I am experiencing a lot of joy and love and the bubbling cauldron feeling of creation.

I am being hurled down through the gateway, which is at the tip of his penis. Entering the gateway of her cervix, right up into her womb, I move on. In the womb, I am dreaming all the lives I am ever going to live. It is not as if I am dreaming them; Merlin and the Goddess are still blended together, and they are sharing the dream of the future and dreaming it backward through time. As they dream it backward through time and space, I dream it forward. These dreams form the equivalent of the spiraling aura of my soul. There is a point in the spiral where an explosion of light occurs. This is the period on Earth when Christ is born and we all come through the sacred spiral together again, as we did for the birthing of our souls. It shows up in my spiraling aura of lifetimes like a huge burst of light.

As the dream of all my lifetimes is completed, a beam of white light engulfs me, and I begin to fall into the atmosphere of this solar ring, through the Sun, to my first incarnation. For all of us in this same oversoul, our first incarnations, interestingly enough, are into light bodies, and our greater individual selves have already manifested in the fourth dimension. We are going to precipitate our first bodies by downstepping our vibrational frequencies instead of coming in through physical birth. I see and feel that very clearly. I see all of these fourth-dimensional beings who have human-looking shapes, and they are in the fifth dimension at the same time. We are going to merge with them at the sixth-dimensional level and go down from the sixth dimension together.

Now Hermes is again impulsing my consciousness back into the Sun, where my soul's future dream continues. I see myself moving through the Sun, out through all of the planets in this solar ring, and back through the Pleiades, starting at the last one and moving all the way out to Alcyone. I see myself moving back into Sirius, and at that point I see all of the Elohim, holding us within their consciousness. I am dissolving into pure light again, and moving through the equivalent of the chakras of the Goddess Erotica and then through the galaxies and then through the bigger being: the Elohim Goddess who holds all of the thirteen galaxies. As I move in my pure light form I disperse all of the energy and information I have collected in all of my lifetimes. As I go through each of the Elohim Goddess's chakras, starting from below her feet and moving up, I move through each one of the galaxies at the same time, leaving a little of my experience in each one. In the galaxy that is the equivalent of her second chakra, I leave whatever is relative to the Milky Way. In her heart chakra, I leave anything relative to the heart. By the time I have moved through all of her chakras, my soul has been dispersed into her and is just part of her own experience and knowing. Then I become even bigger than the Goddess as I blend into Oneness with the Holy Mother. I feel her union with the Holy Father spinning me back into Oneness with All That Is. And the collective voice of Oneness says, "From whence you come, so do you return. The end is the beginning and the beginning is the end. And we are One." It seems so simple. I hear the voice of the Holy Father saying, "This experience exists now within your soul, just as it exists beyond it, when you are complete. So from the Oneness simply remember your body and soul. Your soul is a microcosm of the Oneness of All That Is. Move into that beating heart, into your soul now." And I automatically begin to move inward to my soul again.

My physical body feels like a microcosm of the body of the Elohim Goddess, who holds the thirteen galaxies within her. Now I am getting smaller and becoming the body of the Goddess Quan Yin, who holds Andromeda and the Milky Way only, and now just the Milky Way. I am becoming smaller still and moving through the place called Pleidos galaxy, then through the gateway star in Sagittarius. Now I am holding Sirius and the Pleiades within my form, and now only the Pleiades. Beyond that I am smaller still and hold only this solar ring, and the Sun is my heart and soul. At this last stage I am holding only the Sun, and that is my gateway back into my own soul.

I am experiencing my whole soul as if it were around me as well as inside me at the same time. I feel as if I am inside the Sun, and I can see and feel the sparkliness of my own merkaba around my body. I need to stop at this point and just feel my soul as a part of me, not as all of who I am. As this happens I know I am ready to end this session.

The main point I would like to make about the information in this chapter and in the preceding chapters is that this first section of this book is intended to give you an understanding about your relationship to Creation, and of just how multidimensional we truly are. We are like multifaceted jewels, each facet containing entire worlds within itself. Each world is to be explored fully and to completion. And when all the facets are together and experienced as one, a great and valuable treasure is yours for the keeping.

I would also like to add that I have been having visions of Christ and Mary Magdalene lately. In these visions they birthed twins, a male and a female. After this hypnosis session, it makes sense—I see the purpose of the divine twins being the personification of the male Christ and the female Christ selves.

Part 2

Mystery School and
City of Light Connection

In present time on Earth, the spiritual movement is geared toward restoring the perfection of Creation, coming into affinity with I Am Presence and Oneness, and acheiving individual and planetary ascension. To facilitate this, many beings and spiritual systems are working toward the same purpose from diverse paths and perspectives.

A true mystery school is a spiritual system that can take an individual from wherever he or she is in the present, through all of the necessary steps, to enlightenment and ascension. The word *mystery* does not mean "elitism" or "secrecy." It means that the higher teachings and initiations are not revealed until the individual is properly prepared. It also means that the final stages of every path are truly a mystery that only the seeker can discover for himself or herself, once the initiatic preparations have been completed. In other words, the final stage of awakening on everyone's path comes through self-discovery.

Let me take a moment to clarify one thing. There are numerous mystery school systems on Earth, now and in the past. Each system has equal beauty. There are many avenues to awakening, enlightenment, and ascension. The Dolphin Star Temple Mystery School, which I will introduce to you in this section, is only one of those systems, to which certain individuals are drawn, whereas others are drawn elsewhere. This is because the uniqueness and diversity of individuals and frequencies require uniqueness and diversity in the spiritual systems that lead us all the way home to our true selves.

Within the New Age, there is still a lot of elitism and one-upmanship. One group thinks that it is right and everyone else is wrong. Some people who do not believe in the need for a guru judge the ones who do look to gurus as being wrong for giving their power away and being behind the times. Some disciples of gurus judge those who do not choose this path as being nondevotional and less spiritually surrendered.

I wish for all seekers on the Path of Truth and enlightenment and ascension to respect one another's differences and to embrace the loving principle of Unity in Diversity. No one really needs to be right by proving others wrong. We simply can choose to love and appreciate the many faces of God/Goddess in every human and every path. *We can even learn to celebrate our uniqueness and recognize the beauty in a Divine Plan that affords so many vast forms of individual and sovereign expression, instead of aspiring to the "one and only way." Any teacher or path that claims to be the best way, or the only true way, is one to turn away from and walk in the other direction.*

In this section, you will meet the multidimensional Light Beings who work with the Dolphin Star Temple Mystery School. You need not join anything in order to benefit from the teachings or connection to the Light Beings. Many Light Beings live in higher-dimensional Cities of Light, to which you will also be introduced in this section. You can access these sacred places for your own spiritual and initiatic purposes.

4

Dolphin Star Temple
Higher Council

Contemporization of the
Ancient Egyptian Mystery School

In ancient times, mystery schools existed in a more obvious and tangible form on Earth. At the height of Egyptian spirituality, for example, the entire culture was centered on the spiritual temples of the mystery school. A person from any walk of life might experience a spiritual awakening, recognize the importance of living in harmlessness and impeccability (to do what one knows is right in every situation), choose to awaken fully and become enlightened, and align with his or her highest destiny. These types of inner experience sometimes impulse spiritual seekers to join a mystery school: a system for healing, clearing, and moving through the initiatic path to enlightenment and ascension.

When the people of ancient Egypt experienced this impulse, they would go to the temples to be evaluated by the priests and priestesses. At times the priests and priestesses would give the prospective student assignments to complete before entering the initiatic path in the mystery school temple system. The prospective student was accepted into the mystery school *only after* he or she had completed the assignments and prepared himself or herself by (1) understanding the difference between ego-identification and identification with the Holy Spirit; (2) making a full commitment to impeccability and honoring the sacredness of all things and all people; (3) learning that the circumstances of his or her life and relationships are teachers; (4) learning enough through meditation to hold safe boundaries; and (5) recognizing that life choices can no longer be based on emotional reactions such as fear, anger, and revenge.

At that point, the seeker would go before the Priestesses of Sekhmet, the lion-headed Goddess. The Sekhmet channels and priestesses were the clairvoyants. An applicant, before being accepted into the temples for training and healing, would stand before these clairvoyants, who had highly developed gifts of sight. They knew how to look past the most well-constructed facade to what was beneath it. The Sekhmet priestesses accepted individuals into the mystery school only when they saw that they were sincere and willing to be completely exposed on every level with nothing to hide, and were humble and grateful when ego and karmic agendas were revealed. In other words, if a seeker did not welcome wholeheartedly the knowledge of what needed to be healed, and what habits and attitudes were in need of change, then the individual was not prepared to accept the responsibility of the initiatic path in a mature and safe manner.

Once the seeker had passed through the Sekhmet screening and preparations, he or she would enter the Hathor Temples. There the loving Priestesses of Divine Mother Hathor would begin the process of healing and renewing the emotional and etheric bodies, and the inner child. Until the seeker learned how to love and care for the inner child, the innocence and purity necessary for holding Light were not accessible. Hathor explains in a channeling [see chapter 20] that the master being is actually a balance of the magical child and the mature spiritual adult. When the child and mature adult live in harmony, cooperation, and trust, great depths of self-love follow. Then and only then can the higher initiations be approached with any hope of a truly divine outcome. This is because the innocence of the child is the balance to Divine Wisdom and knowledge. The purity of the child safely opens the door for Divine Power. The awe and wonder of the child supports the spiritual creativity and Humility of the mature adult. The Priestesses of Hathor used hands-on healing, sacred sound, and mother love to help restore this sacred balance.

The seeker was sent for higher teachings from the priests and priestesses of Isis, Osiris, Horus, Maat, Ptah, and Thoth only when the Hathor priestesses said he or she was ready. Then the Ka activations would begin, alternating with kundalini work, higher teachings and practices, and other individual processes. The Ka is the vehicle through which the individual's Christ Self interfaces and becomes one with the personality and the body consciousness. Next, step-by-step, and initiation by initiation, the seeker would progress through the mystery school system in a sequential order. To prematurely learn a psychic skill or multidimensional alignment can lead to misuse of power, possession, and great pain.

A mystery school is a spiritual place or teaching in which a human being can learn, experience healing and higher states of consciousness, and through right action and practice over time, attain to full-body and all-chakra enlightenment. After seven initiatic stages of enlightenment have been completed, the initiate moves into the next phase: becoming Christ conscious. When this final phase has been attained and service on Earth completed, the Christ Self may simply choose to raise the frequency of the body and ascend, leaving no physical remains behind, or choose to experience full-body, conscious death and move straight through the ascension portals, leaving the karma-free, physical body behind.

The goal in any mystery school, therefore, is to transcend all illusions of limitation on the physical plane, to live in alignment with Divine Truth, and accomplish multidimensional alignment with one's true self and with God/Goddess/All That Is—and all in surrender to the Divine Flow of Love—in other words, to become the Christ Self. The initiations along the way present the person with challenges and revelations relative to that person's karma and his or her tendencies toward misidentification with illusion and ego. As a person meets those challenges and transcends ego allurements, then the person moves to the next initiatic level.

Each initiatic level begins with a transcendental experience during which the seeker is given a reference point demonstrating the state of consciousness he or she will be in when that initiatic level is complete. After the person anchors that reference point, a clearing phase begins. The clearing phase includes life challenges, surfacing of old emotions, past-life karmic patterns and memories, and anything that needs to be recognized, healed, cleared, and transcended. When this is completed, the next level begins and proceeds in a similar manner until all the initiatic levels have been mastered. These ancient temples then, and the Dolphin Star Temple Mystery School now, follow this form of sacred protocol as a way of ensuring the seeker the greatest hope of attaining the highest goal in integrity and Light.

The Dolphin Star Temple

Dolphin Star Temple is a mystery school system designed to assist participants toward full-body enlightenment, Christ consciousness, and ascension. In doing so, the intention is to glorify and sanctify human third-dimensional reality by bringing it into full alignment with Divine Truth and Divine Love through all dimensions—not to run away from physical existence. The physical dimension is simply the place where souls have an opportunity to experience life and its many circumstances in a sequential manner through time and space. It is the place where higher-dimensional consciousnesses are grounded and experience one thing at a time. And it is the place in which all dimensions and aspects of consciousness can eventually meet and experience Oneness. Therefore, in this mystery school of ascension teachings, participants are encouraged to be life-affirming and to fully embody their Christed Selves. Life is a great gift to our Higher Selves, or Holy Spirits. When our identities return to Truth, we become who we really are, and we are released from false identities and ego. Then we are free to exist in the Divine Flow of Oneness through all dimensions with God/Goddess/All That Is.

In early 1987, while I was attending a month-long workshop, the Pleiadian Emissaries of Light came to me at the end of a group process and led me on an out-of-body journey. During this journey I met four Pleiadian Archangels, named Ra, Maat, Ptah, and An-Ra, who would change my life and and the lives of many others. I was given personal spiritual activations and information and was told that these archangels and their helpers would be working with me throughout the training, and beyond. Their purpose was to teach me movement and hands-on processes that would, in Ra's words, "enable humans to release neurological holding patterns that must be released in order to handle the upcoming frequency increases on Earth." This language was new to me at the time, but I believed them. Although I did not tend to trust etheric beings, I trusted them at once. They were so loving and clear.

Amazing lucid dreamtime with these Pleiadian Archangels followed. At night, while asleep, I worked with them, very consciously, to learn neurological processes, laser healing technology, and instruction on what was to come in the way of spiritual evolution for individuals and for Earth as a whole. Night after night we met and worked together in dreamtime. Then I would awaken and write it all down. After the training, they slipped behind the veils to allow me time to integrate and heal. Occasionally they would pop in during healing sessions with clients to assist or give me new instructions (this story is told in greater detail in my book *The Pleiadian Workbook: Awakening Your Divine Ka*).

In August 1993 these beloved, ancient friends and guides returned full-time and brought the Ka teachings. At that time I had never heard of Ka. Ra defined Ka as the "divine double of your physical body that creates an interface between you and your Higher Self. This enables you to finally embody your Higher Self fully and become a Christed Being." Ra and Ascended Master Jesus Christ worked with me all evening, assisting me in remembering past lives as a temple dreamer in the Egyptian spiritual era. I had agreed with these Pleiadian Archangels, before my first physical incarnation, to be the one who would "dream these mystery school teachings into Earth through lucid dreaming and communication with higher-dimensional Light Beings." Tears and light encodings flowed simultaneously as I once again anchored this role. This was the step that led to the first Pleiadian Lightwork Intensive: the name given to the healing and teaching aspect of the Dolphin Star Temple Mystery School, which I founded later that year.

Our purpose in the Dolphin Star Temple Mystery School is to assist in bringing about the *second coming of Christ en masse:* when a minimum of 144,000 humans come into their full, multidimensional alignment, maintaining their Pillars of Light to Divine Source all the time. When at least 144,000 humans have attained Christ consciousness, an enlightenment wave will be experienced by all living beings on Earth. Everyone will have a brief experience of Divine Truth and enlightenment. Afterward, each human being will be enabled to make a conscious choice, based on that experience, about whether or not to continue in an illusionary, ego-based reality or to choose a life based on spiritual growth, Divine Love, and alignment with Divine Truth and the Divine Plan.

The Pleiadian and Sirian Emissaries of Light, with me as their channel, in cooperation with the Brotherhood and Sisterhood of the Ray of the Ascended Christ, and the Galactic and Intergalactic Federations of Light, have brought about the contemporized Ka, Ba, and Mer-Ka-Ba teachings as they did in ancient Lemuria, Atlantis, and Egypt. These ancient mystery schools taught seekers in a specific sequential order. The sequence was, and is, designed to ensure that any student/seeker is prepared with whatever teachings, healings, activations, self-help tools, and initiations are needed before moving to a next level. Following are the sequential stages of the mystery school teachings:

1. To be given self-help tools for clearing karma and releasing ego identity; meditation techniques; and teachings about impeccability.

2. To awaken the Divine Ka and embody one's Higher Self.

3. To heal the Ba, or soul, and return it to its essential state of splendor, glory, innocence, love, and connection to Source.

4. To heal the cellular structure and clear mutations.

5. To clear DNA or genetic mutations, and activate DNA of Higher Self.

6. To heal the male/female split and refine sexual energy with loving tantric practice.

7. To anchor the Laoesh Shekinah, or Pillar of Light.

8. To reconstruct and activate the Mer-Ka-Ba and diamond lightbody, anchoring one through all dimensions in the sacred geometry of Light. All of this takes place within the City of Light Dolphin Star Temples, which are activated and anchored for each intensive training.

Dolphin Star Temple is one of several mystery school systems on the planet at this time. When you choose to become part of a mystery school system, that choice is intended to be made from your own knowing inside that it is right for you. A mystery school system should not be chosen from fear of missing out, from giving power away to a teacher or system, or from guilt or shame. It is intended to be chosen only from a place of knowing inside that this is what you are drawn to, and that you are ready to do your inner work. The right system will evoke enthusiasm and an inner knowing that it is right for you. Whichever system you choose from that place is the best for you—but not necessarily the best for everyone.

You must be ready to take responsibility for all actions in your lives—past, present, and future. It is your responsibility to come to any mystery school and its teacher or teachers with respect and honor for the gift that is being offered, but not from the standpoint of giving any teacher a gurulike responsibility for your life. You come to become a Master Being—not to be a follower of someone else or to make that person your master. To be a true living Ascended Master, you must first master yourself.

As in every mystery school system, Dolphin Star Temple has its own Higher Council of Light. This Council consists of Light Beings from higher-dimensional levels who are dedicated to the awakening of humans via the particular system they serve. Again, each system has its uniqueness and beauty and equality with all other systems. You need not join this or any system in order to reap the spiritual benefits from its teachings. The channelings and meditations in this book are the heart of the principles of this mystery school.

I would like to introduce you to the members of the Dolphin Star Temple Higher Council of Light, who are the Divine Sources of the channelings included in the rest of this book. They are the Pleiadian, Sirian, and Andromedan Emissaries of Light, including Sirian Archangel Hermes and Sa-Ra, Archangel of Impeccability; Sirians Isis and Sekhmet and their helpers; Merlin and the Lady of the Lake (the earth names we have attributed to Father Eros and Mother Erotica, former Supreme Beings of the entire Andromedan Galaxy and still representatives of the Andromedan Higher Council); Goddess Hathor and those in service to her, the Priestesses of Hathor, also referred to as the Hathors, from the center of the Milky Way, and guardians of the portals between the Milky Way and Andromeda; Thoth, supreme father of the Atlantean and Egyptian Mystery Schools; three Elohim—Divine Love, Divine Grace, and Divine Innocence—who are always on our Higher Council, although many others are accessible when needed; two Karmic Board Emissaries of Light, who do not choose to give names; Goddess Antares; Ascended Masters Jesus Christ, Mother Mary, Mary Magdalene, Quan Yin, St. Germaine, Joseph of Arimathea, and Kuthumi (again, others may join us when it is appropriate, but these Masters are actual members of our Higher Council); Archangel Michael and his messenger, Mark; and Osiris, our representative from Orion. There are many angels, fairies, and other helpers that often lend assistance who are not on our Higher Council. I hope you will enjoy connecting with these beloved ones as much as I have enjoyed their guidance and assistance.

5

Crystalline Cities of Light

Teachings from the Dolphin Star Temple Higher Council and Amorah's Higher Self Alignment

Since before the Lemurian era, higher-dimensional Cities of Light have played an intricate role in the spiritual development of Earth and her human inhabitants. Ever since the first initiate had the first transcendental experience, humans have had a direct connection to these crystalline cities. Perhaps in a meditation or in a lucid dream, the seeker suddenly finds herself walking, out of body, up a flight of crystal steps toward a beautiful light-filled crystal temple. There a Light Being greets the visitor with a gift of a golden staff, or a robe and crown, or a crystal wand. Words may or may not be exchanged. When the visit is complete, the person returns to waking consciousness still feeling the energy and Light flowing through the body. These visits bring great joy and encouragement to the seeker on the path to enlightenment.

The example I just gave is a simple one—and there are numerous possible alternatives—yet it is a typical starting point for many. Further on one's path, initiations may be given in the crystalline temples. Eventually the seeker will be invited to come into an entire crystalline City of Light. These Cities of Light are complete with crystalline walls and gates and often large complexes of temples and various sacred geometry forms. I would like to make you aware of a few of Earth's City of Light locations and of the sacred protocol for accessing them.

Mt. Shasta, California, is one of only two crystalline Cities of Light currently anchored at ground level on Earth. So let us begin our journey there. When I first visited Mt. Shasta in 1985, I knew nothing of vortex centers and Cities of Light. Therefore, I was very surprised to be greeted by St. Germaine—whom I had not heard of, either. He lovingly told me the source of all the major problem areas in my life and what to do about them. When I returned to the campsite in ecstasy and told my friend what had happened, he replied, "Yeah, Mt. Shasta is known for things like that. It is supposed to be some kind of vortex center or something." Well, I was convinced! I began regular pilgrimages, during which I always brought a large clear quartz crystal altar, as I was guided to do. These magical visits continued, and I moved to Mt. Shasta City in October 1988. Each visit was better and more powerful than the one before. On one memorable trip in late 1985, my visual interpretations were altered in such a way that everything I saw—people, rocks, and trees alike—appeared slightly geometrically stylized and had numbers written on them. I automatically knew exactly what the numbers meant and had an instantaneous understanding of the major historic details in the life of each person or nature object. I even dreamed in sacred geometry and numbers, without words, as if they were in an old and totally familiar language. St. Germaine was there to provide personal life guidance as well. In December 1989 I finally found out with whom I had been speaking all those years. By then I had experienced two or three of the crystal temple visits I mentioned earlier.

In 1988, just before moving to Mt. Shasta, I had my first experience of seeing a large crystalline City of Light hovering about half a mile above the peak of the mountain. In the beginning I saw it only from the outside. Beings of Light from the sacred city would communicate with me, take me through activations, give me healings and meditations to do, or just send me love. I was being prepared for the deeper experiences to come. At that time the Ascended Masters Retreat space, inside the taller of the two peaks, had existed for quite a long time. It looks like a gigantic cave with a domed ceiling and a fireplace in the center. Sometimes the Ascended Masters would gather at a long table. At other times they would sit around the fire, or stand in processional form. At times there was talking, even group discussions; at other times we met in silence. Each visit was different, and each visit continues to be.

Anyone can call on the Ascended Masters of Mt. Shasta and ask for permission to come into their Retreat. If you are admitted, an Ascended Master will come to take you in. You will be greeted by male and female Ascended Masters dressed in long white robes. The Ascended Masters Retreat is also the gathering place in Mt. Shasta for the Great White Brotherhood, originally called the Order of the Great White Light: a mystical order of Light Beings, both human and higher-dimensional, who are working on behalf of Earth's spiritual awakening and ascension. When you find yourself inside, try not to have expectations. This will allow you to be receptive to what the Masters deem appropriate for you at that time. You may meet only one being or many. You may notice other humans around or not. Remain open and receptive.

From inside the Ascended Masters Retreat, you may request admission to the Intergalactic Federation of Light meeting room in the upper quadrant of the smaller peak of Mt. Shasta called Shastina. As I understand it, this space was anchored in Mt. Shasta in 1993 shortly after the City of Light was anchored down to an elevation of 5,000 feet. Before March 1993, the City of Light of Mt. Shasta remained above the mountain. It was anchored at ground level during the full moon of that March, with the greatest depth of snowfall on the mountain in this century. I was strongly pulled to drive up as high as possible that night with a friend. At about 5000 feet, we both felt an incredible surge of Light and energy and knew we had gone through a portal of some sort. A mile or two farther, another surge and a rarification of the energies ensued. At that point I pulled over to the side of the road, tuned in, and asked the Ascended Masters, clairaudiently, what was happening. Jesus Christ replied immediately by appearing to me and telling me to expand my clairvoyance to see the mountain as if from a distance. At once I saw a giant lightship surrounding and containing the entire mountain. Jesus told me that he had called me to come up the mountain and be a part of the anchoring of the City of Light into ground level. We would be inside the City of Light at a fifth-dimensional level all the way up to our destination at Bunny Flat. He said that at tree line (over 8,000 feet in altitude), the sixth-dimensional levels would begin. Eventually the entire physical city of Mt. Shasta and the surrounding area would be anchored as a living City of Light, but this would take many years. He went on to say that Mt. Shasta would be the first physical city to operate by consensus and higher law.

That night on Mt. Shasta was as magical as any I have ever experienced. The crystalline rays of Light were visible to both my friend and me. We felt as if we were truly in sacred communion, or satsang, with God. Temple pillars were being lowered at varying elevations, geometric buildings were being lowered into place. Jesus said that the depth of snowfall was being used to anchor the sacred geometry. Snowflakes have a natural crystalline geometric structure, which creates the physical grounding for higher-dimensional crystalline energies. Once the

City of Light was anchored into the snow and into Earth, it would remain and continue to deepen and expand, even when the snow melted.

Since that time, an Ascension Temple has been anchored directly above the Shasta peak. It is an elongated cone that becomes a spire—crystalline, of course. When you enter from its lowest point near the peak of Shasta, you are energized and your lightbody is activated. Sometimes first-time visitors do not get to move all the way through the upper tip of the spire; sometimes they do. When you are lifted through the tip of the spire, this Ascension Temple is a portal into many other places, including Shambalah, a Venusian City of Light, the City of Light of Machu Picchu, and others. Where you go is a very individual thing and is determined by the guardians of the Ascension Temple.

Beneath Mt. Shasta is a Lemurian City, which has its own temple complex. Again, your admission and personal experience there is very individualized. Many visitors to this Lemurian City are greeted in the round courtyard of the temple complex. It is a very social and joyful place, complete with a large fountain, lots of flowers, and benches. The Lemurians tend to hug more than the Ascended Masters and other guides do. You may be invited to tour their homes, the library, or a specific temple. Just enjoy!

On February 8, 2000, I was greeted in a morning meditation by the members of the Dolphin Star Temple Higher Council of Light. The Masters who approached me that day informed me that we had built enough multi-dimensional Light and anchoring of higher-dimensional energies in enough students, practitioners, and teachers that we were being given our own Inner Sanctuary inside Mt. Shasta.

The Dolphin Star Temple Inner Sanctuary is now part of the Mt. Shasta City of Light. It is a small complex unto itself as well. To journey there, invoke three times the guardians of the Dolphin Star Temple Inner Sanctuary of Mt. Shasta. Tell them you would like to visit the sanctuary and receive any light activations or healings that are appropriate for you on your spiritual path. You do not have to be "in the mystery school" to be welcomed there. The complex has a central Ascension Temple, a Higher Council meeting room, and a library containing pertinent records from the Halls of Amenti and the Alexandria Libraries of Atlantis and Egypt. There are many healing rooms and Chamber of Light rooms in which you can receive energy balancing, Ka activations for embodying your Higher Self, nervous-system healing, all of the Chamber of Light sessions listed in *The Pleiadian Workbook,* and more. Guides will show you which ones you can use and how. There is also a social and music area that looks like a courtyard. A large fountain is centrally located in this courtyard. If you step into it you will drop through a portal into the courtyard area of the Lemurian Temple complex.

Mt. Shasta is one of numerous sacred sites on Earth that house Temples of the Sun. The others of which I am aware are on the east side of Mt. Kilauea on the Big Island of Hawaii; beneath Uluru (formerly called Ayer's Rock) of central Australia; the Great Pyramid of Giza in Cairo, Egypt; the Tor in Glastonbury, England, site of ancient Avalon; Palenque in Mexico; Machu Picchu in Peru. These six sites are also chakras in Earth's thirteen-chakra system, as is Mt. Shasta. Temples of the Sun have traditionally been used as places to hold ceremony at sunrise, and on the equinoxes and solstices to assist humans in aligning with the Divine Plan as it is calibrated with our time cycles (which correspond to orbital cycles). In other words, we realign ourselves with our place within the cosmos, our soul's purpose, and Earth and universal Divine Plan through our connection to our local Sun.

Before physical birth in each lifetime, our souls pass through the Sun. Inside the Sun, we leave an imprint of time-released encodings of our purpose for the given lifetime. The Sun also imprints our souls with the co-created Divine Plan for Earth during our upcoming lifetime. When we do ceremony with the sunrise, high noon, sunset, and midnight aspects of Earth's daily orbit, we realign with these encodings. You can also look at the Sun at any time and ask the Sun to assist you in attaining your goals, while breathing the sunlight into your body and chakras. As we progress through life and complete goals, the Sun releases new encodings to us, through its rays, that impulse our next goals to be activated in our lives. This sacred relationship has been honored in most indigenous cultures throughout time.

Lake Titicaca, another of Earth's chakras, contains a crystalline City of Light beneath its deep waters. To many seekers who have experienced Lake Titicaca, the City of Light seems more like a subaquatic space station than a city. That is because, like Mt. Shasta City of Light, it is both. These Cities of Light serve as posts for many higher-dimensional Light Beings from other star systems. Lake Titicaca is the main headquarters for the Intergalactic Federation of Light. This Intergalactic Federation is composed of members of the Andromedan and Milky Way Galactic Federations of Light. Milky Way and Andromeda are twin galaxies, also called cosmic twins. Other Intergalactic members are from the Great Central Sun, including Elohim, archangels, Supreme Beings of numerous galaxies, and even large sections of the universe. Centrally located in the Lake Titicaca subaquatic complex is the Great Central Sun Temple, which connects to the Earth Star Crystal at the center of Earth at its bottommost point. From the tip of its cone-shaped spire, in the center of this large dome-roofed temple, is a portal that opens into the Great Central Sun. This Great Central Sun Temple literally anchors Earth's connection to the Great Central Sun and to Divine Source.

The other Earth chakras are located at Mt. Denali, Alaska; Mt. Fuji near Tokyo, Japan; Mt. Batur and Lake Batur in Bali, Indonesia; Table Mountain near Capetown, South Africa; and Delphi, Greece. [These are discussed in more detail in chapter 9.] Each Earth chakra location has its own City of Light, with its own function. As I mentioned earlier, at this time, Mt. Shasta and Lake Titicaca are the only two Cities of Light anchored at ground level. The other eleven are etherically located above the physical chakra sites. If you choose to explore these, ask in your meditation, or before going to sleep, for the guardians of the particular crystalline City of Light you wish to visit to come and take you there *if it is in your highest good at this time.* It is inappropriate to rush an initiation or access to high-frequency, multidimensional places unless you are properly prepared and it is your right timing. That is why the crystalline Cities of Light have guardians to ensure your safety and maintain the purity of the sacred space. If you ask three times and receive no response, then it is not the appropriate time. The guardians and Masters will come for you when the timing is right, once you have made a request.

Many crystalline Cities of Light and individual etheric temples exist, beyond those I have named. Just trust that when it is time for you to experience them, your guides will make sure it happens. When you physically visit an Earth chakra, greet the Ascended Masters, overlighting devas, and guardians of the sacred space. Tell them you have come to commune with the Light Beings in the City of Light and to receive from them whatever is appropriate. Also let them know that you would like to experience and honor the sacred purpose of that space, and ask permission to enter. When this sacred protocol is followed, it tends to open your multidimensional access to the beauty and Light more deeply. It is also traditional in many spiritual cultures to take a gift: perhaps nuts or chocolate for the nature spirits, or a small amount of cornmeal or whole grain. Leave crystals only when you are specifically guided to do so. Otherwise, they may not be appropriate for the site. I love to carry spring water from Mt. Shasta and pour a small amount into water sources in other sacred sites to create a sharing and linking of the sites. Whatever you do and wherever you go, approach in the spirit of honoring and sacredness, and the gifts you receive will far outweigh those of the taker.

Part 3

Alignment with
Cosmic Cycles of Time

As you read through the channelings in the following chapters and throughout this book, take a moment before beginning each new channeling to call in the Light Being giving the channeling. Set a receptive and sacred space, and then proceed. This section contains three chapters of channeled material intended to help you understand where Earth and her people are in cosmological time. This will help you understand the uniqueness of Earth's current evolutionary cycle. It is also intended to assist the reader in aligning with the Divine Plan for return to the Divine Flow of Creation. We are speeding toward Earth ascension quickly now. To be ready, not only must we understand the importance of this incredible time on Earth, we must also be living in the state of higher consciousness that will take us through this shift in as much Grace as is possible.

6

Past, Present, Future—
The Transcendental Now

A Channeling from Sirian Archangel Hermes,
February 1997

Hermes: Sacred Brothers and Sisters of the Light, we are here to hail you into an awakening that has not happened on Earth for a great long time. In a sense, it has never happened, because much learning has taken place, and much new experience, since planetary awakening was last experienced on Earth. From that standpoint, the great awakening that is coming is beyond what has ever been. Yet there have been times of great awakening on Earth in which you have all participated to some degree. We wish you to remember that now.

The reason many of you have forgotten is this: when you remember the times of greatness, in your human persistence in believing in loss, you equate the past greatness with the grievous belief that because it ended you must have fallen. And this is a great misnomer. For the truth is that Creation moves in cycles. In innocence we are still trying to understand why the human consciousness has certain paradigms. We know that you have the tendencies, and we know what is needed. But we do not always understand why you continue to go back to your tendencies, or paradigms, to make yourselves wrong, as you do. So, as we remind you of higher perspective, we also learn from you as you evolve into transcendence.

The paradigm we wish to bring to your attention at this time is a tendency, when something has occurred that has appeared to be traumatic, or that has ended a period of great awakening, to lose your connection to the great awakening, somehow believing that the trauma, the damage, or the loss occurred *because of* the awakening. You believe that the trauma genuinely occurred because the dark is greater than the Light. And this is a great illusion and a great lie that exists on your Earth at this time. And many of you have given much power away to it.

We would like to explain it to you from a much broader perspective. So we ask you to allow us to impulse your crown chakras with a laser of electric blue light to enable you to hear us more clearly and go beyond the words; for the words are shallow compared with the full meaning. So if you would like us to impulse you with a laser of electric blue light to open your crown chakra, simply and silently say, "Yes."

Good! We will continue.

In the greater cycle of time, the Divine Plan unfolds in stages. Some of you may be aware of the *Mahabharata*, in which Arjuna was asked to start a battle with opposing forces. Arjuna understood that battle was not the way to solve problems, yet there he stood in front of the army facing thousands of so-called enemies, and it was up to him. He would charge forth in his chariot, and it would be a signal that the battle had begun. He would have preferred to take his own life than to begin that war. His teacher, Krishna, came forward as Arjuna remained immobile and gave him great teachings. These teachings have become known as the *Mahabharata*. Krishna told Arjuna that he was destined to lead that great battle because it was time on Earth for that cycle to take place. He showed Arjuna that it was his dharma—that it was what he was created for in that lifetime. He helped Arjuna to disidentify from the immediate circumstance and see the bigger picture. And Arjuna let go of his ego, released his emotional attachment, and went into a state of divine surrender. And with his whip, he clicked in the air, and his horse charged forth, and the great battle took place.

There have been times on Earth when the forces of darkness have overstepped their bounds and have gone too far in the destruction of the innocent. This has called for intervention from those who enforce Universal Law. When the overlighting devas of darkness and destruction are no longer able to control their own forces, then physical action must take place. The Vietnam War was a recent occurrence in which something went further than it was intended to go. You have had two such occurrences in this century alone. The Second World War went further than it was intended to go. And in both of those situations, humans have been called on to intervene through physical battle to stop the destruction that has gone too far. Because, you see, there are devas of the groups who fight, or overlighting beings, or Supreme Beings, as you might call them. Those Supreme Beings are following the Divine Plan. However, there are times when the human will, because of the collective consciousness of the people involved, becomes stronger than the being that rules them. They go too far. When Hitler began his plan in Germany, the planetary karmic agreements between all involved required only about one-third to one-half the impact that actually occurred, before it was stopped. However, at the point at which it was intended to recede, it was as if a wildfire were suddenly blown by a great wind. It went out of control. Human addiction to the psychic energy and power created through massive murder took hold of many of the German soldiers. Because of this, much destruction was required to stop it.

Many of you have subconsciously known this and have believed that it was a failure of the Light. You have believed that darkness is stronger. But what you need to comprehend now is that it is simply a product of karmic co-creation. You have agreed to be on a planet of co-creation. When the collective consciousness becomes stronger than the overlighting forces, their own will takes over, whether it be for the Light or the dark. There also have been times when the friends whom you call the Pleiadian Emissaries of Light, in their overlighting functions, have gone too far to stop disasters from happening that needed to occur. When the Light went too far, it also slowed down the Divine Plan, just as when human collective consciousness goes further into its karmic darkness than was anticipated.

You see, dear ones, it is all a great experiment. None of these mistakes are ultimate. They are simply a process of all existence learning at the same time. And yes, there is a Divine Plan; because at some point in the future, everything has already come to a place of Oneness and harmony. And it is your own future that is constantly pulling you toward itself. There is a point of divine resolution, at which all of existence is in agreement as to the order of things. It is/shall be a time of great joy and reunion. It is/shall be a time of great awakening! When I look to your future selves, I see all of you crying great tears of remembrance. We wish to impulse you with that memory now—for your future is a memory as much as is the past.

You have believed that it is not safe to open to your higher potential. Although you have longed for the creation of communities, for a planet run by sacred law, for individual and planetary ascension, there is something in your psyches that stops you from going as far as you can to attain these accomplishments. What stops you is your fear of failure, your fear that what you want the most will be within reach and then something will come along and pull the rug from under you, and you "will lose again." You feel that it will be unbearable. But in the greater cycle of evolutionary time, you see, you are always given times of strength before you must face your own karmic patternings. You are intended to use these strengths and positive reference points to help you transcend the challenging times when your karmas are brought to the fore.

Those of you who have read Amorah's book *Pleiadian Perspectives on Human Evolution* will understand this more fully. The stories were given to Amorah in such a way as to impulse you to remember how karmic dispensations work. Parts of your memories are withheld from you, at times, until you have healed and strengthened enough to know how to deal with them. For instance, if you have a karma around misuse of power, and you have come to a place of recognizing this paradigm, regretting what you have done, you might choose to give up all your power as if you had never had it. Then you come into lifetimes in order to start learning about power from scratch again. When you reach the point of having power again in the right way, you are afraid you are going to repeat the past. You are afraid you will make the same mistake again. So you only let yourself go so far. You hang there, stuck, because you are afraid to trust yourself. You have lost your connection to your divine sovereignty. The truth is that the fall from power was simply an opportunity for you to relive an ancient pattern in order to choose a new way. Thousands and thousands of years have taken place on this Earth in which the humans have progressed forward and fallen back, progressed forward and fallen back. But, as in the stories in *Pleiadian Perspectives,* there are times when the collective consciousness of a group of people has said, "We need help!" We see that you have gone too far into the pain to be able to handle the truth. And so, we simply remove your memories of the pain, and you enter a time of grace: it is a grace period. And in that grace period your life begins to blossom again. You do not feel the pain. It still exists in your multidimensional hologram. But it is outside of your consciousness. You go about your life, and you begin to spiritually awaken. You have beautiful experiences. Romantically, you learn how to experience surrender and tantric energy. You come to the point in which whole segments of your world are in peace, and joyful. It is as if, watching your society, it becomes a great, great musical symphony in which everyone is singing his or her part and is in tune. Then suddenly something happens. That something that happens is a prearranged release of your karmic patternings. You have had a grace period in which to build your strength. You have learned sacred truths. You have learned how to live in harmony with one another. You have learned how to experience peace on Earth. And then it is as if an infusion takes place and the part of you that is still stuck in drama or trauma or past experiences is reintroduced gradually into your psyche. You are more prepared to deal with it than you were before because of all the learnings that you have had since the original karma transpired. All the strengths that you have built are now your tools with which to work. However, if you believe that your dreaded past will repeat itself, because it has happened before, then you forsake the very tools you have accumulated with which to transcend the pattern.

We wish to stop and ask if you have questions at this point because we really want you to fully understand it. We realize that for some of you this may be hard to understand, and for some of you it is a great awakening. Some of you may have previously understood this. So we want to ask you, if anyone has a question to please speak it, so we can move forward with the rest of the teaching.

Student question: If I understand correctly, life seems to be going really well and smooth, and then all of a sudden there is a big . . . well, like a memory—is that correct?

Hermes: Yes, it is like a time capsule released into your life. It has also been explained as the cycle of the spirals. Every time you meet a certain point on the spiral, something occurs. If you are in a transcendental mode, each time you reach it, it will last a shorter time, until finally you prevent it and you move straight through without its occurring. You establish a new paradigm on the spiral. So your life is very much like that. We would prefer to think of it at this time as a time capsule.

Now we would like to explain to you something about the Sun. Your Sun contains all the information about what your higher purpose is in this lifetime. It is encoded so that when you are born into any lifetime your soul moves through the center of the Sun in a very specific way. Not only do you leave an imprint in the Sun about what your soul intends to do in this lifetime, also your soul is imprinted with the Divine Plan for Earth. So when you are born you have the encodings within your makeup to align you with the co-creation of the reality in which you are entering. The Sun has the encodings of what your purpose is within that bigger plan. So it is really important to connect with the Sun. The indigenous cultures of this land [Australia], the indigenous cultures of Maya, the Native American tribes, and all of the sacred indigenous cultures were known to be sunrise people. They would gather and greet the sunrise each day because they knew that it was at that time that they would have integrated what the Sun had to tell them from the day before. They would come welcoming the birth of this new day because each day the Sun releases the encodings that you need to follow currently. There are time periods when there are no new encodings being released, and you are held in alignment with previous ones. When you face the Sun, it is wonderful to look at the Sun and ask it to come into you and reawaken your sacred memories. It is wonderful to say to the Sun, "I know you hold all my memories, and the key to awakening my soul, and my divine purpose." Then welcome the Sun into your body and chakras.

As children of the Sun, when you greet the Sun it is an opportunity to reawaken those encodings within yourself. What you do with those encodings determines what the Sun can release to you on the next day. So if the Sun releases encodings about your taking a step that is beyond what you have ever done before, and you are in resistance to taking that step, then the encodings are held and nothing more is released until you have taken the necessary step. There is a reciprocal relationship in which your soul feeds back to the Sun what you are ready to receive. Do you know, as you open your crown chakra, that inside your crown is a prism that has 108 facets? This prism has been called the names of God. These facets directly correspond to the time-release mechanisms within the Sun. "The 108 names of God" is another way of saying that every consciousness has 108 facets of its own divinity and connection to Divine Source. There are facets that correspond to each aspect of relationship, others have to do with service goals, others have to do with learning about how to be a spirit in a body, and there are many more. These facets are very multiple within themselves. So as these facets within your crown are cleared, as the light comes into you, each prism facet is able to refract that light. The state of full enlightenment is when all 108 facets of your prism have been cleared so that when the rays come in all 108 facets are illuminated. When you greet the Sun, the Sun's rays respond to those facets in your brain, as well as to your soul, to see what you have cleared and what you are ready to receive. Believe me: when you look at the Sun you can actually trigger an opening of a facet of that great prism simply by greeting the Sun and asking it to awaken you—if you are ready.

Within you, you contain a sorrow because you know you have awakened spiritually to some degree. But something happened in your consciousness, and this is what we have not fully understood yet. When the choice is made to enter into a next series of lifetimes for the purpose of service, learning, attainment, or whatever, you forget about your past, including your enlightenment and past-life ascension experiences. Your soul comes into your newborn body in a very pure state, but as an empty slate. What you allow to register on that empty slate is up to you. What some of you have done is this: In that moment of rebirth when you are coming in without the full awakening you experienced on the other side, you feel that you have fallen. Something in you feels, "I thought I had gone all the way, but I must have been wrong, because here I am experiencing pain. Here I am experiencing a lack of love again. So that enlightenment, or that ascension, must have been false, or it would remain with me still. Something in it was wrong." And, dear ones, that is a lie. That is how humans still lie to yourselves, because this is not true.

We work with you to prepare you for full embodiment of your Divine Presence. But still, in most human consciousnesses, this old paradigm of self-doubt and failure interferes. Deep in the souls of those of you who still carry this old paradigm is a grief that even your greatest attainments in your other lives were somehow not as great as you thought they were, because you are not in that same level of attainment now. Amorah has had a great deal of this form of self-doubt and sense of failure. In her early spiritual awakening, in this lifetime, she remembered many psychic abilities. For instance, she was a teacher in the pyramids of Egypt many times. In one life there, she taught people how to teleport from the pyramid sites down to the river. She even felt it in her body consciousness during the experience of reliving it in an altered state. Unfortunately, she then felt like a failure because she could not do it now, instead of simply realizing that now she is doing something else. It is very simple really. It is not that she cannot do it because she is a failure. It is not that she cannot do it because she has forgotten and will never remember again. It is just not her purpose in this moment. It is very simple. We hope that this example can assist you in understanding the dynamic that occurs when the misconstruing of your human mind blends with your emotional reactions. You unnecessarily make things very complicated at times.

We would like to assist you in the release of this old energy paradigm. Let us begin by clearing your belief in your own failure, because you think you are not as spiritually evolved as you have been at other times, or as far along as you think you should be now. We would like to impulse you to release the fear that if you allow yourself to become fully enlightened again, something tragic will happen.

Before we guide you in this release, there is one more thing we want to explain to you. One of the reasons you go through certain cycles of lifetimes—one of the reasons you are sometimes on the healing table and painfully reexperience a past-life trauma—is that before you can move into mastery on Earth, your hologram throughout time and space has to be cleared of all the illusions. Imagine that in a past lifetime your identity became locked in a belief in grief, failure, abandonment, betrayal, or any other experience of trauma. If you did not transcend that, and you have come to a point of claiming your mastery again, and you have not fully learned that lesson through life experience, then you must reexperience it until you have transcended the ego illusion. Or you can transcend the potential through remembering past pain and reframing or reliving it, with higher wisdom and understanding. You change your past. In order to stand in mastery, or Christ consciousness, all of your experiences throughout, and beyond, time and space must be cleared of false identities.

You are the future self of your self ten thousand years ago when Atlantis fell, or ten days ago when you blamed someone and judged them. You can go back to that time and see and remember what happened. You can forgive it. And, in your forgiveness, you have a great deal of impact on setting yourself free of past illusions of limitation and pain. Sometimes you may need to go back and talk to yourself in the past. Be your own healer by guiding your past self to change its decision. As you do this reframing you give yourself a new hologram for that time: a parallel past reality that is healed and whole. Then you operate psychologically and spiritually from the influence of your new past-life hologram. Sometimes this transcendence can be as simple as affirming, "That is my past. It is not my truth. It was just an experience. I am grateful for what I have learned, and I forgive." And it is done. You do not always have to process and feel and reframe. You do not need to draw a life experience to you in order to relive it again. You do not always need to writhe on the healing table. If you do feel the pain, or spontaneously writhe on the healing table, the key for gracious and thorough release is to acknowledge to yourself, "Yes, I feel this pain. But I have transcended believing in it. I am ready to trust myself. If that same thing happens again, I would have more wisdom. I would not succumb to that addiction this time. I would not blame that person, take my anger out on them. I would not go around playing the victim to make them feel guilty. I have grown spiritually, and I trust my growth of consciousness since that karma originally occurred. I do not need to test myself again to be certain. I know." When you can deeply and sincerely feel completion, without repressing emotions or contracting in any way, it is done.

Let us clear the belief now. Are there any questions before we do this?

Student question: What do you mean about changing the past and creating a parallel hologram?

Hermes: What it means is that on the time and space continuum, as you currently perceive it, you perceive that everyone on Earth is having the same experience of reality. In truth, there are multiple realities coexisting in what you perceive as the same space. Realities are continually separating out, or paralleling each other. Some people experience themselves as being on Earth in total chaos. Simultaneously, others experience themselves as being on Earth in a time of great awakening and social reform. It is as if the hologram itself splits to reflect that with which you are in alignment and to which your frequency of consciousness is acclimated. There are even parallel realities in which you coexist. In one you made the highest potential choice at a key turning point in your life. In the other you did not, and it altered your life path.

As Hermes, I would just like to say before we begin this that I am very happy to be with you again, and that I have worked with all of you in other lifetimes in the body of Hermes Trismegistus. Hermes Trismegistus is no longer accessible as that being but has dissolved into the light of higher consciousness. That aspect has become part of what I Am. So, those of you who were with me as Hermes, those of you who also have been with Thoth, will know my consciousness quite well. It is a joy and a glory to be with you again, as I promised I would be, a great long time ago.

Student question: I have an overwhelming fear that to go into the Christed consciousness will be my death.

Hermes: That is what we speak of when we say that you have fears that are reactions to lies you told yourself. You have to learn to address that fear instead of being the product of it. Tell your consciousness locked in fear that it is responding to an illusion, not to truth. When the fear is there, it tends to take over your consciousness. What we are inviting you to do now is to clear the untruth to which it is reacting.

All of you [the group in Australia] have a fear that complete spiritual awakening will be your death, or that it will lead to ruin.* What we are going to do now is take you through a process to show you how to release those untruths, or beliefs, that have held you in emotional reaction. Okay? Good. Close your eyes.

▭† Breathe deeply, and tune in to your body while thinking about the belief. Breathe, and ask your body to show you the emotions, the places of contraction, the places in which your energy has coiled in upon itself and imploded instead of allowing the radiance of your beauty to show through. Ask to feel deeply those places that hold your own belief, "If I allow myself to awaken fully and come into the glory of Christ consciousness again, I will also be destroyed. Our civilization will also be destroyed again if it spiritually awakens." Your belief is that you cannot bear that. That is why you have such a desire to not allow yourself to let go completely.

Continue to breathe deeply now, and ask to feel inside your body where you still hold this deep lie that you have told yourself, this misinterpretation of reality. Beloved ones, I promise you: it is an illusion, and there is nothing to fear. Do not be afraid of feeling fear. It is just another emotion.

When you feel fear, breathe it upward from the base of your spine through your body. Welcome it. Call the fear, hopelessness, disillusionment, shame, grief, forward, and say, "I command that I feel it all now so I can be done with it. I also ask the Elohim and Angels of

---

*I am including this procedure in the book because I have found that the majority of spiritual seekers hold this old belief paradigm. If you are clear that you do not, simply move on to the next chapter.

†The guided processes throughout the book are available for purchase seperately on audiotapes. Those who want them should refer to the ordering information at the back of the book. Certainly not everyone needs the extra help of taped guidance for the meditations and healing sessions. If you do, instructions for coordinating the tapes with the text are on a separate sheet accompanying the tapes; please note the icon ▭ preceding various exercises in the text, which tells you to turn on your tape. You can also make your own tapes by recording the processes yourself; if you do so be sure to allow time for the completion of each step before going on to the next one.

Divine Grace to lift and heal, outside my body, what I do not need to feel directly in order to learn and grow." When in emotional pain, you probably tend to contract. So breathe and expand instead. Tell your body and your emotional response mechanism that this contraction, this feeling, is a reaction to an illusion that you convinced yourself was a truth. It is a product of a past experience that you misinterpreted. You are safe now.

This understanding is very important. These painful energies are simply because you misinterpreted your past experiences. Your belief that you failed is a misinterpretation of your past experience. It is not the truth.

Good! We feel that you have heard us now.

Imagine that you have a red rubber stamp that says "CANCELED!" With all of your spiritual determination and vehemence, cancel that piece of paper, rip it, and burn it in the Rainbow Flames until your body relaxes and the emotions have subsided. Call on the Rainbow Flames not only to burn that belief but to burn through the places in your body where you still hold on. Allow the flames to transmute the old repressed emotions.

There is something that is still holding on in some of you. I know some of you do not believe that you have released it all the way. This is because there is another belief that is piggybacking on this one. The other belief you are holding is that the dark is more powerful than the Light. You believe this because when the periods of Light have ended, you thought it was because the dark was stronger. So we ask you now to breathe into your bodies, and ask you to feel inside where it is that you still believe the dark is more powerful than the Light. Ask for a picture or a symbol to represent that belief. Breathe and feel the energies, the contractions, the emotions, the tightness, as before. Be spiritual warriors and warrioresses, now, probing deeply into your own internal world to find every nook and cranny inside of you where that belief and its corresponding emotions and contractions have taken hold. Tell that part of you that the belief is an illusion.

A child stumbles, and it believes that the rock has hurt it. You tell the child, "The rock did not hurt you. You just weren't looking down in the moment. And that's okay. You don't need to be afraid of, or hate, rocks." Speak to yourself in this way as you would speak lovingly to a child who has misunderstood its reality. Indeed, that is what you are. You are beautiful children who have innocently misunderstood your experiences. Tell that part of you that truth is indestructible. Truth is Light, and it does prevail. It is only your mind that has attached to lesser truths and believed in them. Give your body and emotions permission to let it go now. Your body and emotions have held on to the fear because you believed you needed the fear. Do you know, dear ones, that you thought you needed to hold on to the fear (or any other painful emotions) so you would not make the mistake of awakening and being punished by the dark side again? You held on to the fear because you thought it protected you. The truth is that all it did was hold you in illusion and pain and prevent healing and transcendence. So thank your body, your mind, your emotional body for holding on until you knew that you did not need it. Thank it for doing exactly what you asked it to do. Tell it that its job is done now; and you are ready to be responsible for a greater truth. Feel how the fear can simply evaporate when you do that.

Ask that the painful emotions be lifted again in the name of Divine Grace. Take that image that represents your belief, and tell your child inside, "See—it is just a picture, a memory. It is not real. It is just a fleeting past experience." Use your red stamp, and cancel the picture vehemently. Rip it into shreds, and burn it in the Rainbow Flames. Breathe into your body, and relax the tension. You can take charge of your life and thoughts again if you are willing to feel, release, and move on in confidence. Be warriors in the Light, not violently but with great determination.

Now there is one more step. In conjunction with these beliefs, some of you made agreements with the dark realms not to spiritually attain fully in exchange for their not harming you. You have agreed with some of the dark forces, with Lucifer, with the Satanic realms, with the Annunaki, with the Illuminati, to give them your power in exchange for their protection. There are several levels to this agreement, and we will take you through them one by one.

The first one is this: You have agreed on a planetary level that as long as you are on Earth in a body you will pay homage to some government. And every government on this planet is ruled by the dark side at this time. Visualize a legal document that says "Planetary Agreement" centered at the top. Imagine that written on the contract are the words "As long as I am a citizen of Earth, I will be responsible to some government. I will give power over to them to run my life. I will not be sovereign." See your name at the top of a long list of names on the bottom. On the other side of the bottom, it reads, "Dark Overlords" or "Lucifer and the Satanic Realms." Write "VOID!" on this contract and tear it up and burn it.

There is another type of contract that you have with the dark forces individually and apart from the planetary agreement. It is like paying the Mafia not to hit you. What you have done is agreed not to come into your full power. Imagine another legal document that simply reads "Contract" at the top. At the bottom, you will see your name on one side, and on the other side you will see the names of Lucifer, Beelzebub, the Satanic realm, the Illuminati, the Annunaki, or just Dark Beings. You may not see all of those names there. If you are not sure, you can just see the words "the dark forces." Imagine that the contract says that you have hired them to protect you against themselves. Yes, it is a little silly, is it not?

Void the contract, tear it up, and burn it in the Rainbow Flames.

And now ask if you have any agreements with the dark forces beyond this that you are ready to release. Ask your guides to present them to you as a contract, or a stack of contracts. Simply rip them all and burn them. As you do it, affirm: "I am ready, willing, and able to live in Divine Truth. I am ready, willing, and able to live in the safety of the Light. I am ready, willing, and able to embody the Christ I Am." Repeat this affirmation until you feel complete.

Thank you for opening your minds and your hearts. Many of you felt as we spoke that it was as if you had heard these words before. That is because we agreed a great long time ago to be here with you—because you are beings who have chosen to awaken and be in service on Earth. And when you made that choice to come back into lifetimes, and to assist in the fulfillment of the Divine Plan, we told you we would always be here at key times to help you remember. And we are. You can call on us yourselves to assist you to remember and live your highest purpose. Sometimes we will assist you by putting the right person, or book, or group in your path. Sometimes we will work with you in your dreams. And sometimes we will work with you during your meditations to speak to you directly, as is appropriate. But we will never do it for you. We want to see you unfold in your mastery, not just follow our guidance.

We welcome you to the glory of unfolding your own highest potential, the integration of all your accomplishments. And now we would like to turn it over to the Pleiadian Emissaries of Light, who are going to place you in a Chamber of Light. This Spirit-Body Integration Chamber of Light will assist you to whatever degree you are ready now to bring parts of your own Higher Self into your body. The clearing you have just completed has created more room for your divine embodiment. During this chamber session, we will assist you to integrate what has just taken place by bringing your relationship between your spirit and your body-consciousness into present time awareness. In the spirit of Oneness, in the spirit of the Divine Plan, we leave you now with the words "So-la-re-en-lo." The closest interpretation we can give to those words is "With great love and devotion, we are One." So be it!

Amorah guides the completion of the process Hermes began: 🖳
Close your eyes and ask the Dolphin Star Temple Higher Council to come forth and bring in the Interdimensional, Evolutionary, and Intergalactic Cones of Light above you. Ask for the Earth Cone of Light below your aura. Ask the guides, including Hermes and your Higher Self, to place your body, aura, and multidimensional hologram in a Spirit-Body Integration Chamber of Light. Ask them to assist you in releasing any additional blocks to fully embodying your own higher consciousness and becoming your Christ Self. Remain in a relaxed and receptive mode for about thirty minutes to an hour and a half, or until you feel that the energy work is complete. This can be done at bedtime.

Return to Oneness—
The Cosmic Journey of Evolution

A Channeling from Eronia,
an Intergalactic Being of Light

When we were in workshop space together, an entire group and I experienced going into an alternate reality in which the Milky Way and Andromedan Galaxies are blended into a single galaxy in the future. This created a lot of disorientation when we came back afterward and attempted to relate to the three-dimensional world again. We had experienced being in a world that is somewhat difficult to explain. We think of things as being two-dimensional, three-dimensional, or even four-dimensional. We humans are stretching our perceptive abilities to conceive of four-dimensioned reality in terms of physical appearance. When the group and I were in this state, it was as if our reality were bent in such a way as to give us a lens into what I would call tenth-dimensional reality. This experience, which is way beyond individuation, or even soul group consciousness, allowed us to know a different reality beyond just imagination or observation.

Even though this channeling is quite brief, to have a being from that level of reality speak gives one a lens into that level of dimensional consciousness into which we do not normally have a doorway. So, before you begin, I ask you to go into this channeling from a place of being a shamanic listener. Open yourself to experience the multidimensional reality that is being given beyond what the words convey. To assist you in doing this, follow the instructions below before you read the channeling: 📼

1. Ground yourself, and adjust your aura to two to three feet around you in every direction.

2. Bring in your Higher Self to fill your Tube of Light from the top center of your aura, around your spine, to the bottom center of your aura.

3. Welcome the Dolphin Star Temple Higher Council.

4. Ask three times that the Light Being named Eronia to impulse you to connect directly with his message.

5. Ask the guides to help you hold a receptive space to a multidimensional reality that is beyond the normal human perception.

6. Take a few deep breaths, and begin to collect your consciousness into your body. Pull yourself in by breathing in all the way down to the base of your spine. As you are breathing and coming into your body, ask Higher Self to embody as deeply as possible at this time. Breathing all the way down into your feet, feel your legs and feet. Notice if there is any tension there. Breathe until you can feel yourself equally in both legs and feet.

7. Ask the Lords of Light of the Rainbow Flames to surround your aura with Rainbow Flames.

8. Affirm: "In the name of the I Am that I Am, I call forth the Crystalline Pillars of Light from the Cities of Light where the Ascended Masters dwell and ask that they fill and surround this room, anchoring it as a Sacred Dolphin Star Temple in the Cities of Light where only that which is divine may enter, and all that is less than divine, which is illusion, must leave us now. So be it."

9. Ask the Pleiadian, Sirian, and Andromedan Emissaries of Light to anchor the sacred geometry of the Great Pyramid of Giza, and specifically the King's Chamber, around your room.

10. Ask the guides, "Anchor the Interdimensional, Evolutionary, and Intergalactic Cones of Light above my aura, and above this room. Anchor the Earth Cone of Light beneath my aura and beneath the room."

Eronia: I am Eronia, a representative of the Great Central Sun of the Andromeda Galaxy, a member of the Intergalactic Federation of Light, the Higher Council of Andromeda, and the Galactic Council of the Andromedan, the Milky Way, and what we call the Great White Spiral, which includes Federations of Galaxies that move together within the cosmic spirals of existence.

Amorah: I am having a little bit of trouble picking up some of his words because the frequencies coming in are higher than I have ever brought through and translated into words before. So be a little patient with me during this channeling because it is a whole new configuration to which my body is attempting to adapt. I am going to ask him to slow it down a little for the sake of my brain's translation.

Eronia: This Great White Spiral of Galaxies is a federation of what you might think of as great cosmic brothers and sisters that spin together, in a sense, around what you think of as the Great Central Sun. And yet, within that patterning there are patterns of movement within patterns of movement. There is a purpose behind our talking about this with you, which we shall explain. Bear with us, and try to grasp the technical implications of which we speak at this time.

We know that Amorah has spoken to you in the past, because we can see it in your holographic records, about the movement, for instance, of your moon around your Earth, your Earth around your Sun, your Sun around Alcyone, the entire Pleiades around Sirius, and Sirius and the Pleiades around the Great Central Sun of the Milky Way. You see, we call the center of each microcosmic system a Great Central Sun, whether it be an illumined Sun or a Sun that holds the energy of the void. Because wherever there is a Sun, there must be a divine correspondent, or what you would think of as an empty space, such as the womb which is the center of the Milky Way. And yet, when we look at that center, we think of it as the seat of the Great Central Sun of your galaxy. For that void holds the purpose of containing the Great Central Sun of its divine counterpart, the Andromedan Galaxy. This may sound confusing, but we, at this time, are experiencing an infusion: a melding of light, consciousness, and energy of the Andromedan and Milky Way Galaxies. This is why our presence is becoming more, what you say, *ever present* instead of an occasional presence. We would ask Amorah now to connect with us in every group, at different levels, at different times. Because at this time, the holograms of the Andromedan and Milky Way Galaxies are blended into one great field of light, like a cosmic union. In other words, the Central Sun of the Andromedan Galaxy is penetrating that void space, the womb, of the center of the Milky Way. And there is a pattern of stars and systems that each blend, one with the other, throughout your universe. And so, in a certain way, there is no separation between these two galaxies at this time, and yet at another level you are in time and space moving toward that union in what, in your reality, seems to be your future—when the galaxies' divine counterparts are reunited with one another. And it is no different from when, on Earth, two human beings come together in relationship to each other as partners, and they experience that total surrender of ego and move into total union with the other—whether it be brought on through sexual experience, by a meditation, or simply by a melding.

Amorah: The word *melding* is not totally accurate, but he cannnot find a word for what he is trying to explain and says that this is the closest he can come at this time.

Eronia: What we are attempting to communicate is that it is only through total surrender to another that you can fully begin to comprehend the meaning of two galaxies coming together as one. For it is an act of great love, great passionate magnetism. It is an act of great completion. When you see each galaxy, it is a whole galaxy unto itself, just as you are a whole person unto yourself. And yet there is something incomplete in that, until it is united with its partner. And when the two partners are united, there is something incomplete in that, until they are united with their divine partnering counterpart. And it is all a process of human individuation and reunion. And in individuation you experience communion. Yet we are moving you quickly to a place in which you are able to have the experience of Divine Oneness with another individual. At times some of you will be having this experience in groups—not sexually. No, for it is beyond that.

The reason I have requested audience this morning is to ask you for a little favor. We honor your free will in all things. We wish to present to you our mission at this time. We ask you to choose if or what your part is in that mission. And *what we ask of you is to begin the process of clearing your thought-forms that have held you in the ego illusion of superiority of individuation.* Your ego structures have believed that there was something to be lost when you lose your individuality. And yet at the same time, we do not ask you to lose what you call your "safe boundaries." Those are crucial. If your boundaries are not clear, you will not be able to enter into union without chaos.

The plan of Oneness requires a recognition that each being is simply like a microorganism that is part of a greater macroorganism. Each microorganism is a whole thing unto itself, and yet it is one of the collective of the microorganisms that create the greater thing. In a sense, the people of Earth constitute what we think of as twelve great beings, and yet you have billions of individuated microorganisms called humans. We realize that what we request of you may seem a little vague at this time, perhaps a little insignificant. Simply begin to accept the responsibility for clearing your illusion of the superiority of holding on to individuation and autonomy in a way that seems ultimate. It is crucial that this belief be cleared if the reunion of the galaxies is to take place in a timely manner. Certain critical numbers of individuals on Earth need to have shifted into a consciousness of recognition of the equality of union, and the recognition that individuation has always been a temporary state, in terms of your consciousness. And yet, from where I speak to you, you already exist beyond individuation. All of your lives, and non-lives, in which you are individuated, exist simultaneously.

What we wish to say is that all of your experiences and existences as an individuated, autonomous being are like the Central Sun of Andromeda. And all of your experiences of being joined in higher union with the greater collective are like the womb of the Milky Way. They coexist like an infinity symbol that cycles in and out of itself. You are moving rapidly toward the time and place on this cosmic infinity symbol of crossing over the center point into that place of the void; and it is beauty, and it is restfulness!

Amorah did well at remembering a recent dream where she spoke of people appearing and dissolving and going into a deep place of restful nothingness, this is what we describe in the infinity movement from individuation into nonconsciousness as an individual being. And you will not lose yourself in that, in an ultimate way. That is impossible. For once a consciousness has known its individuation, it is always there, but it is on the other side of that spiral you call infinity movement, infinity pattern, dissolved into Oneness with All That Is.

We request that you embrace the possibility of the beauty of that empty space of no agendas, that place that you would call the Void. And yet, it is more. We ask that you look at the possibility of that dissolution of individuation as an equal, valuable part of your overall experience.

As the last sentence was said, he faded out completely. He left.

Group Discussion Led by Amorah

Amorah: Something for us to do actively at this time is to tune in to our beliefs that say, "I have to hold on to my individuation and my personality." It has to do with the way the personality fears its death, because it thinks it will cease to exist. My sense is to start working with that belief that "I have to hold on to some of my agendas. I have to hold on to some attachments. I have to hold on to certain aspects of personality in order not to disappear, not to become nonexistent."

I ask you now to look at that energy, at those types of thoughts. Breathe, and feel where this belief or group of beliefs is held in your body. Ask for a picture or a symbol that describes what that belief or beliefs means to you.

Certainly, if you have a totally positive feeling about dissolving into Oneness, and it creates relaxation and love and peace in you, then there is nothing to work on—for you. But if you find places of resistance, wanting to space out, emotional reaction, contraction, then I ask you to work with this belief to clear it. Tell your body to let it go. Take the picture that represents that belief, and burn it in Rainbow Flames.

Ask to be shown, in your own way, from a place of your own inner knowing, where you are in your own cycle of individuation—where you are in that cycle of becoming One again. Affirm your willingness to align with the highest Divine Truth, the part of you that is light and love. Surrender to that.

Notice how you feel in your body right now. Do you feel solid, mutable? Observing is all that is needed. Relax the effort of trying to change anything. Just observe in a neutral way.

In my brain, during the channeling, there was a delay time in interpretation because I have not had things come through from that space before. He was coming through from a place that exists only in the blending of the Milky Way and Andromeda. He was part of the consciousness of that union. It was very interesting trying to let him speak, and very powerful for me. When he shared the dream, did you understand what he meant by that? I was out with Eronia witnessing these cosmic events, and I blended with them at the same time that I was talking. I was also aware of being here interpreting words, but I did not have a sense of whether it was clear or not, because I was not present enough with the words to know how it was sounding.

Some of what I was shown was amazing. I would like a piece of paper to show you something. While that was going on, Eronia was showing me what evolution and devolution are, and all kinds of things. If you think of these two squares here as the throne of the Holy Mother and Holy Father . . .

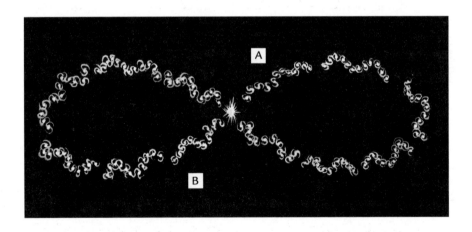

Each tiny spiral represents galactic cycles of approximately 230,000,000 years. These cycles are contained within the multi-billion year cycle of Individuation on side "A" and Oneness on side marked "B."

At this point I became very emotional as I was again taken into a rapturous state of being in two experiences at once. A small part of my consciousness was talking to the group. The greater part of my bilocated consciousness was out in the realm I was describing. I am choosing to leave this as original as possible in the hope that the energy will be conveyed more fully as a result.

Amorah: I am experiencing something that is making it hard to talk. It is so beautiful. This is the unspeakable. It's very difficult. . . .

At the center of Creation, the thrones of the Holy Mother and Holy Father are contained within the infinite Great Central Sun. The reason they are in that place is because the Holy Mother and Holy Father are in a paradoxical existence. They are in a state of total surrender and union with each other all the time, in which they do not exist individually. It is such a total surrender that it is an experience of nothingness that is beyond everything at the same time. Yet there are two halves to that existence, which we think of as the Holy Mother and the Holy Father. Now imagine that at point "A" [see illustration on page 106], there is a group of twelve galaxies that form a spiral within themselves. The Milky Way and Andromeda are two of the twelve that are spiraling together. Each of these twelve galaxies is also spinning as half of a union. In a sense, these twelve galaxies are one being, like an Elohim. If the right side of the infinity cycle is the one in which we are experiencing individuation, and the left side of the infinity cycle is the one in which we are experiencing Oneness, when we come to the center point of this greater cycle, through the Great Central Sun, there is a shifting point. As we enter this shifting point, the Holy Mother and Holy Father are aligned in our consciousnesses in their individuations. And yet, as we move into the shifting point toward our own surrender into Oneness, we become One with that part of the body of the Holy Mother who is surrendering into union with the Holy Father. It is through that union that we get propelled into the other side of the cycle, which is the cycle of being in Oneness. It is only through this surrender and union, whether it is surrender and union with that Oneness in an ascension experience, or with a partner on Earth, that we hold the part of Creation that is needed to move us through the natural evolutionary cycle in Divine Flow.

A devolutionary cycle coexists. When we reach the shifting point at the center crossover of the infinity spiral, moving from individuation into union and Oneness, we will find that Oneness in the Great Central Sun of All That Is. Moving into that Oneness, we go into the Void—which is truly that place of the dreamtime, the rest, the comfort. It also has been shown to me to be that cycle of what we call life and death. The same symbol has overlapping meanings, and we are in the cycle of what we call life at this time. We are moving on a multigalactic level to the cycle of what we call death, but it is actually surrender of time into deep comfort, timelessness, and Oneness.

When beings come to that crossover point who are unwilling to experience an ego death—which is what is required to move into the next cycle in a state of union—instead of continuing on the infinity symbol into Oneness, the individual's energy inverts backward on itself, and that being begins the cycle of life again. When that occurs, the individual sort of jumps from the group of twelve galaxies in which he or she was traveling onto another parallel set of galaxies. This parallel group of twelve galaxies is just coming out of Oneness into individuation. So imagine that there is another ring of galaxies at point "B" [see illustration on page 106]. The galaxies in this "B" group are just getting ready to move into the crossover position, entering from the left side, just as we are moving in group "A" from the right side into the crossover position. What happens there is a switchover. What is happening is that I am in the experience of it, and they are triggering me again to go into the next level of the experience.

I have spoken about the splitting of the holograms before. Last March Equinox [1997], Hermes asked us to call in all of the strengths and initiations from all of our lifetimes. He said that between last March Equinox and next year's March Equinox [1998] we needed to set our intention to align with our highest potential future. On March Equinox of next year, it is the turning point for a lot of us for needing to have completed all of our past-life karma. We can now focus on planting seeds for our future. So on March Equinox of 1998, we are being asked to anchor in our consciousnesses our highest potential future. What it is preparing us for is March Equinox of 1999, at which time there will be a gridlock that takes place. The reality with which you are aligned at that point in time, for which you will have planted the seeds in 1998, will be locked in place. This means that the holographic realities of Earth will be preparing to split at the next level. There is this consciousness on Earth of disaster and chaos and darkness. There is a coexisting reality of planetary awakening and moving into communities of Light Beings who live and work with people who are ready to change their consciousnesses. What is happening is that those holograms are in the dream field right now, from a third-dimensional perspective. But they are already linked.

The group session ended at that point. The next excerpt, in which I talk about the development of this process, took place in February 1998.

Amorah: Now, five months later, we are really feeling the hologram split. You may be feeling that the subatomic structure of your body is literally being pulled apart. The photon band energies are moving in on a cellular level right into the silica core of your cells and stimulating the crystalline matrix at the center of each cell to realign with the orbit of the stars and the orbit of the planets—the whole galaxy and universe, basically. There are time-encoded messages carried through the photon band from the Great Central Sun, through all of the Suns at the centers of the galaxies along the way, and through our local Sun to stimulate your memory of how to let go. Now, that may sound a little simplistic, but if you look at the people of the world today, I think letting go is actually quite a challenge. You see, as long as you have an attachment to anything, you are not available to let go into whatever the next spontaneous, highest reality might be.

So the greatest challenge for those on Earth who are truly on the Mystery School Path at this time is this: if you have not been doing your ego-clearing work, and you have not been doing your work on releasing attachment—whether it is attachment to a person, attachment to a job, attachment to a certain identity, or attachment to an outcome of a specific situation—those attachments absolutely must be released. Otherwise, your identity with those attachments—which also strengthens your attachment to your individuality—will not allow you to let go and surrender to your own fourth-dimensional and fifth-dimensional higher consciousness. When the hologram splits into third- and fourth-dimensional realities, you will have the ability to allow yourself to simply let go of the third-dimensional reality and of the things in the third dimension that are incapable of translating into the fourth dimension. You must have released all attachments in order to take that first step to personal and planetary ascension, as the next step toward Oneness.

In a sense, I am speaking of the first step of planetary ascension as if it were in the future. In many, many ways in time and space reality, it has already taken place, and yet we are still in our time and space continuum, in a process of walking through the steps of getting there. Now, some of this sounds very esoteric and very nebulous. But the fact is that our future selves have been leading us toward the highest choice for a long time. And if you do not get anything out of this whole teaching other than this one point, what I really want you to hear is: *the future precedes the past.* It is your future self who is guiding your way, with all that you have already learned, already having realized your highest potential, already being in that state of fourth-dimensional consciousness and beyond, moving on into the Cities of Light of the fifth dimension, and then letting go of form altogether and going back to basic cosmic identity of Oneness. All the way through the dimensions, there is basically an ongoing process of letting go, releasing individuality into Oneness.

Many people are coming back together now with soul mates from past lives with whom they have unfinished business. Some relationships are suddenly falling apart after many, many years because they no longer serve the higher purpose of the individuals involved. Perhaps one person in a relationship is really aligned with moving into that highest potential future but the other is not. Now is the time to get really, really clear, because as long as you are holding on to attachments and bonding deeply with people whom you are choosing to allow to keep you out of your highest alignment, you will not be able to align with your highest potential future.

What I would like to do now is a guided process, first of all for aligning with your highest potential future self. From that alignment we are going to do a little walk through your life and help you with releasing attachments. The process will be very basic compared with how big the issue is, but I hope it will give you a sense of what is truly needed in order to release any overidentification with individuality—beyond the appropriate sense of appreciation of yourself. It will also help you find that place in you of releasing attachments to people, to places, to outcomes, so that when you come to the point of ascension, when you come to the next level of where the holographic split is made, you will consciously and physically be available to let go into your highest potential future. You will be prepared to make a choice that is conscious, not simply a product of some illusion that you are not even aware of as an illusion. In other words, the process is mainly for the purpose of making you conscious of your choices, so that when the time comes, it is a conscious choice and not one made by virtue of ignorance.

Now, on Spring Equinox of 1998, we are going to be calling in our highest potential future through the Sun, asking the Sun to connect us to the Great Central Sun. Then the energies will be downstepped from that highest potential future. Here is the guided process for doing this activation retroactively:

1. Close your eyes, and take a moment to feel your grounding and your connection to your Higher Self. Take a few deep breaths.

2. Look at the Sun, and acknowledge that your soul is connected to the Sun from birth. Ask the Sun to connect you to your highest purpose for this lifetime. Then ask the Sun to link you into future time to your highest potential future for this lifetime.

3. Call upon your highest potential future self in this lifetime. Ask your highest potential future self to come and stand in front of you. Hold your hands palms up on your lap, or facing palms out, away from you. Ask your highest potential future self to come and make hand-to-hand contact. Take some nice deep breaths in through your hands and into your heart, asking that the energy from your highest potential future self begin to downstep into your body through your hands. Continue to breathe deeply, and let the breath spread throughout your body. Eronia suggested that you continually repeat this affirmation while you fill with future-self love and light: "I am ready, willing, and able to be the best that I can be. I am ready, willing, and able to be the best that I can be. I am ready, willing, and able to be the best that I can be."

4. Invite your future self to blend with you in your body. Begin by drawing your future self into your hands and your arms to blend with you. Welcome your future self to continue blending its lightbody form with your body until you are full-body blended. Use your breath as if you were inhaling through every pore, allowing yourself to blend with your highest potential future self.

5. Now that you are blended, notice places in your body or consciousness that still feel separate from your future self. As you feel those places, imagine that the contraction or the emotions melt into a liquid light. If you are feeling tension in your solar plexus, for example, imagine that the tension becomes liquid light and melts into the body of your future self, becoming pure light.

6. Facing the Sun, ask the Sun to seal your connection to your highest potential future now. Also ask that all the strengths and learnings from your past lives be fully integrated into this lifetime in grace and ease.

7. Seal this invocation and pact with the Sun by chanting the Sun's name as it was done in both Mayan and Egyptian cultures. In Mayan, the Sun is called K'in. In Egyptian, the Sun was called Ra.

8. Chant "K'in Ra" seven times, drawing the light of the Sun into your seven body chakras, beginning at your root chakra. Chant "K'in Ra" seven more times, asking the Sun to connect you to the Seven Sisters, or seven stars of the Pleiades.

9. Chant "K'in Ra" seven more times for all your human family who do not know to call on the Sun.

10. One final "K'in Ra" will connect you to the Great Central Sun.

11. Now call on the Great Central Sun, via the Pleiades, via our local Sun, to impulse you with your highest potential future and connection to Divine Source. Breathe the connection in through your crown chakra, and send it down your body into the Earth Star Crystal at the Earth's core. When you feel the energy return through your feet and up your body, send it out your crown to the Sun, Pleiades, and Great Central Sun.

This completes the alignment.

8

Aligning with
Earth's Divine Plan

A Compilation of Teachings
Distilled from Channelings

Over the past few years I have worked a great deal with the dispensations and activations continually coming into this planet. As mentioned earlier, equinoxes and solstices are key times for these energy shifts. In order to align with the Divine Plan for Earth and her people, we sometimes need to release specific karmic issues and align with higher principles and ways of living. These principles are aspects of *higher morality*. Yes, it is time now for the next level of maturity on all our paths; time for spiritual refinement and deeper humility. And does it not feel wonderful and bring more self-respect and self-trust when you go beyond your previous evolution to an even more Christ-like level? Living as if you were a Christed One or Ascended Master *now* is the quickest way to become that! When in confusion, temptation, or doubt, just stop and ask yourself, "What would Buddha, Jesus, Quan Yin, or Mother Mary do right now?" Then simply choose that as your next step. Let us co-create harmoniously with our Earth and with all people to ensure that the recovery of Divine Alignment and Ascension consciousness may be gracious, easy, and as pain free as is possible. I am including a few of the key areas of importance that have been given to me and to groups I have taught to assist us in this process of awakening.

Living in Unity in Diversity

Living in unity in diversity requires respect for everyone's free will, regardless of whether or not you agree. On the spiritual path you are asked to take on the role of living as an example of Divine Humanity. In other words, to help create a new world that is based on peace, justice, love, truth, and Oneness, you must practice embracing those qualities in your life now.

I received a letter in which I was told that communication and channelings from all higher-dimensional Light Beings were wrong and were holding us (the human race) back. This person claimed that the *only way* human beings could truly become Masters and hope for ascension was to let go of such "self-aggrandizing beings" as St. Germaine, Jesus Christ, Quan Yin, Ra . . . and the list went on. This person's group basically claimed to hold all the answers, and everyone who disagreed with them was wrong. I was initially saddened and even a little distraught by the level of judgment and separatism I felt was being presented in the guise of spiritual supremacy. But I realized I needed to let go of any judgment I had about what was being said. I recognized that I agreed with most of the group's teachings. The need for discernment about the Beings with whom we align and from whom we receive guidance *is* crucial. And I agree with the group's statement that we are all sovereign and are connected directly to Source. Yet I also know that the angels and guides who are already at the level to which we aspire have always given us a helping hand to show us how to raise our own consciousness. In other words, they set an example for us just as we set examples for each other as we learn and grow. If the author of the letter and her group have chosen a path that eliminates these Light Beings and guides, I can only assume it is because that is the right path for them. I would not wish to change them or judge them in any way.

The challenge of diversity is acknowledging that everyone has a unique truth and unique path for aligning with that truth. There is no such thing as "the *only* way" to Truth. Yet we can all follow diverse paths and continue to experience each other in the state of unity that is a natural outcome from recognizing the incredible beauty and complexity hidden in the many faces of God/Goddess/All That Is.

Going Beyond Forgiveness

Just after Y2K, Master Kuthumi came to me during a meditation to speak about "releasing the need for those who have done wrong to be punished or to suffer for what they have done." Kuthumi said that there is a gridlock of sorts on specific dispensations that can be given to Earth as Grace by the higher-dimensional Light Beings. This is specifically because "the vast majority of humans still wish humiliation and punishment" on those whom they perceive as having harmed them—especially the governments. This is currently creating a future plan of public exposure, humiliation, jail terms, and even death sentences for many government officials. Kuthumi said that most people wish this for these officials so much that they are unwilling to accept a planetary ascension or even dispensation of Grace that could raise consciousness beyond the need for ongoing corruption on Earth, much less punishment. Under the Karmic Laws, once a person has transcended the potential of repeating a negative karmic behavior, all is forgiven and no painful payback is required. What you can do is examine your own thoughts and attitudes. Even the subtlest holding on to the need for apologies from those who have wronged you in some way, before you are willing to let go of the past completely and forgive, must be released now. And certainly attitudes toward even the grossest of corruption must now be brought into alignment with spiritual principles.

On the path to mastery, there is a point at which you must, in order to move forward, go beyond forgiveness. You are asked to transcend all blame and to pray for those who have harmed you. Pray that they learn and grow and transcend the potential for harming others in as much grace, ease, and love as possible. There is even a time for prayers that a perceived enemy or abuser can simply have a sudden awakening into divine alignment and not have to play out the karmic payback of experiencing the pain that person has caused you. To transcend the need for this payback, apology, or even the admission by someone that he or she has made a mistake is now crucial for us as individuals and as a collective human race in order to align with the Divine Plan. It is easy to righteously justify these old attitudes, but does it serve?

Opening to Divine Truth

Another area in which the beliefs and attitudes of humans have held back certain planetary dispensations of Grace and healing is unwillingness to know "the whole Truth" if given the opportunity. We are required to have a vast majority of humans willing to receive certain higher-dimensional assistance and information in order for it to be given. And in early 2000, we still have barely over 50 percent of the human population of Earth even willing to know "the whole Truth" if they are given the opportunity. Only a tiny percentage of humans actually seek Truth actively. But willingness is all it would take for certain revelations and dispensations to be given.

Relative truth consists of the details of our lives, interactions, and events. It is ever changing relative to circumstances and time. Divine Truth is unchanging. Divine Truth includes such understandings as these: love is eternal; everyone and everything is sacred beyond usefulness or actions; every thought, word, deed, or feeling affects all of existence. For much of our human family, it is frightening to think that some higher understanding could disrupt the status quo. To be willing to know Divine Truth, one must be willing to let go of any religious or spiritual belief that is false and limiting. One must be ready to question every belief, no matter how long-standing or cherished. One must be willing to see one's self as the creator of one's own reality and to take responsibility for that creative power. To be willing to know Divine Truth, one must be ready to release all judgment, blame, martyrdom, victimhood, abuse, need to be right, need for better than/less than competitive thinking, and all attachments. That is still too much risk for many, and yet it is ultimately the path of freedom. How can we hope for honest government when people are silently saying "Hide the truth from me. I don't want to know."

To fear Divine Truth is to fear Divine Love. For how can you love fully and unconditionally if your love is conditional, based on seeing truth through the veiled eyes of ego personality? To fear Divine Truth is to fear God/Goddess/All That Is, or Divine Source. And how can you hope for healing, happiness, and peace if you fear the very source of those energies? The love and Light from Source flows unceasingly through All That Is all the time. If you are afraid of Truth, you simply cannot receive this love and Light into your body or consciousness. To fear Divine Truth is to fear your own enlightenment and ascension. And the list could go on and on.

As spiritual seekers you are asked to be willing and ready, at any moment, to release any rigidity in your thinking that could inhibit your next level of awakening or ascension. Serapis Bey offers these words: "Beloved Seekers of the Light, Light is Truth, and Truth is Light. They are inseparable. And to be available for Light, you must be available for Truth. And to be available for

Truth, you must be free of all attachments. For anything to which you attach yourself is the potential block to your ongoing process of enlightenment and Mastery. If you are attached to a relationship that is holding you back, and you are unwilling to acknowledge the Truth and let go, you will be held back. If you believe it is wrong to eat meat and you come to a point in which your body needs it to be healthy and receptive to Light, you will limit your own awakening. If you believe you should be able to eat anything you want and transmute the ill effects, and you reach a point at which you need to eat all raw foods for a while in order to transmute genetic weakness, then you will not be able to anchor spirit in the unhealthy, mutant cells. There is, indeed, a time and place for almost everything. And even your spiritually justifiable rigidities are still rigidities.

I am not suggesting that you radically and deliberately go out and defy your beliefs or change your diet or relationships. We are merely stating that your willingness and readiness to do so at any moment determine your availability for guidance and alignment with Divine Truth. If you believe you are meant to be celibate and the next step on your path is sacred marriage and tantric union, would you choose to stop right action out of attachment to an idea you believe to be more virtuous? You see, the greatest virtue of all is spontaneous openness and alignment with Divine Truth and Divine Flow. And some of you have been pushing against the winds of change instead of embracing surrender to Divine Will and Divine Flow, which bring availability to Divine Truth. And, *in Truth,* so to speak, it is actually experiential and flowing. It cannot so easily be put into neat and tidy phrases that fill books and libraries. To experience Divine Truth, you must be empty and available to experience newness and change from moment to moment.

Some of you have believed that to live by guidance and be available for spontaneity, you must not make commitments. This is a naive and immature thought, for if you were not committed to seeking Truth, you would dissipate a lot of time and energy following whims. And there is a time in which consciousness must experience this. But once you clearly awake to knowing that there is more and that you will not stop until you have found it, commitment is essential. And besides that, if you listen to true higher guidance, you will not be guided to commit to something or someone if it is not in the path of Truth. Some of you need to settle down to a daily meditation discipline that you know works for you and stop dissipating your energy running to every new workshop and reading every new book. Some of you need to broaden your horizons beyond the same yoga and meditation you have done for years. Some of you need to commit to a sacred tantric relationship, while others need to be celibate and clear out your old sexual patterns of lust and seduction.

You see, beloved seekers, Light and Truth are always in flow, ever changing and ever expanding. To follow them and be filled by them, you must learn to recognize when you are in the flow and when you are being rigid and attached. When you stop settling for feeling secure and safe in predictability, you can embrace the higher predictability of awakening to Truth—the steps to which are unpredictable. Ah, Divine Paradox strikes again!

9

Thirteen Chakra Correspondences to the Thirteen Dimensions

As third-dimensional incarnates in the process of enlightenment, ascension, and returning to Divine Flow with All That Is, we are learning all of the ingredients that form the Matrix of Divine Flow. Each new aspect of this matrix that we perfect and embody moves us closer to Divine Flow. Earth is also in an evolutionary transition back to Divine Flow, just as her inhabitants are. Like you, Earth has thirteen major chakras that spin. They are often referred to as vortex centers, or vortices. As you ride through time and space on this planet the Law of Divine Correspondence is always in effect. Everything that you do has an impact on Earth, and vice versa. As your chakras open, clear, and become enlightened, there is a correlative effect on Earth's chakras. As Earth's chakras awaken and function in their higher purpose they impulse you and all humans with their energy.

This reciprocal, interdependent relationship is enhanced and expanded with conscious intent. Therefore, as you align with Earth's chakras you receive as well as give to the process of individual and planetary awakening and return to Divine Flow. In addition, the thirteen chakras have a direct correspondence to the thirteen-dimensional system. Your body and chakra system are a microcosm of the macrocosm of existence. Earth is also a microcosm of the universe. Even this galaxy is a microcosm of the macrocosm. The more intricately you examine every aspect of Creation, the more you will find that this Divine Correspondence applies to everything. We are indeed an aspect of Oneness—a cell in the body of God/Goddess/All That Is. Therefore, as you return to Divine Flow, an aspect of All That Is heals and returns to Divine Flow. Even more remarkably, every other cell in this vast body of Oneness is impulsed with the potential for complete healing and return to Divine Flow as well.

The illustration on page 124 shows the location of each of your thirteen chakras. Review these locations and their corresponding Earth and dimensional relationships before you do the folowing meditation. This will enable you to focus on the meditation without confusion.

In the meditation that follows, you will be bonding with your Higher Self through your thirteen chakras. Then you will link with the thirteen Earth chakras. Before you begin the meditation, I would like you to be aware of the functions of these chakras as well as their locations.

The First Chakra

The first chakra, at the bottommost point of your aura, is called the *Earth Portal Chakra*. Its function is to allow Earth's energy into your field and to help you ground and feel your connection to the planet. This chakra corresponds to the first dimension, which is the mineral kingdom.

The Second Chakra

The second chakra is a three-ring chakra that floats beneath your feet. It is called the *Earth Transducer Chakra*. Its function is to filter Earth's energies as they are coming into your body and to transduce the frequency and nature of the energy into a form that is compatible with you as an embodied human. This corresponds to the second dimension, which is the realm of bacteria and of simple-structured, purely instinctual life forms.

The Third Chakra

Your *root chakra* at the base of your spine serves to bring the energies from the Earth Transducer into your body for actual bonding with Earth and feeding your body with Earth energy. This chakra rules your relationship to your body and to Earth, whereas the previous two chakras beneath your feet are receivers and transformers. Your root chakra corresponds to the third dimension: the realm of humans, animals, and plants.

The Fourth Chakra

Your *sacral center,* or fourth chakra in this system, is your sexual center and the center that experiences sensation and emotional response to life. It is also your clairsentient center—the place that enables you to feel energy from other people, from nature, and even from your guides. This chakra corresponds to the fourth dimension, or the astral realm of both dark and light energy. The fourth-dimensional plane is the plane of feeling, thought, thought-forms, fairies, elementals, astral entities, and the feeling aspect of your dreams. Your astral body is fourth and fifth dimensional.

The Fifth Chakra

Within your body there is an extra chakra located at your navel center. It serves as an umbilical to your Higher Self and to Holy Mother. This *navel chakra* is also directly connected to your physical birth and is a connection to your physical mother. It corresponds to the fifth dimension, the first realm of lightbody and form. The fifth dimension is the home of the Cities of Light, Ascended Masters, many archangels, and overlighting devas. It also holds the realm of the dark control lords, the satanic realms, and astral control groups. When you have dreams in which you give and receive healing, attend classes with other Light Beings, or travel through space, you are having fifth-dimensional experiences.

The Sixth Chakra

Next is your *solar plexus chakra,* or power center. This chakra holds issues of power, will, ego versus true self-identity, self-esteem, and interaction with others. It corresponds to the sixth dimension of geometry. Everything in existence is held together by geometric patterns. Without sixth-dimensional correspondence, nothing could be held in form. Christ consciousness is the name given to consciousness of the sixth dimension.

The Seventh Chakra

Your *heart chakra* is the seventh chakra in this thirteen-dimensional chakra system. Of course, your heart is the center of love for self, nature, God/Goddess/All That Is, and every other person or thing that you love. It is also your center of self-worth, which comes from feeling your own essence. Your soul is located in your heart chakra and holds your essence energy and connection to your Higher Self and spirit. The seventh dimension corresponds to your heart chakra and is the realm of Divine Sound and movement of energy and light via sound. In your soul, the Divine Sound of your soul essence, or your soul's musical tone, is held. It is intended to vibrate a little channel that extends from your soul to your throat chakra, called your inner voice channel.

The Eighth Chakra

When your *throat chakra* receives the sound and frequency of your soul energy through your inner voice channel, it is activated to self-expression and creative expression. Everything you say, every sound you make, all creativity is intended to be a spontaneous expression inspired by your soul via your inner voice channels. This corresponds to the eighth dimension of movement as an expression of light, color, and consciousness.

Th Ninth Chakra

Your *third eye chakra* relates to self-image, all aspects of seeing, and how you interpret what you see. If you hold judgment, fear, blame, respect, admiration, or neutrality toward anyone or anything, this is what you project onto what you see through your eyes and your third eye. Unless you can look through innocent eyes, devoid of preconceived ideas, your third eye cannot be open because projections about reality create veils, and you see through these veils. Your third eye corresponds to the ninth dimension, the realm of prismatic reflection of color and light generated by essence consciousness.

The Tenth Chakra

Your *crown chakra* receives higher-dimensional energy and translates it into thought. Whether that higher-dimensional energy is negative or divine depends on your boundaries and your spiritual growth. Your crown chakra also holds all of your current lifetime goals, your essence and past-life connection to all spiritual matters and spiritual beings, and your spiritual beliefs and affiliations. The tenth dimension corresponds to the realm of soul families, oversoul, and you in relationship to Creation and Creators as an individuated conscious being.

The Eleventh Chakra

Balancing the chakra beneath your feet is a three-ring chakra that floats above your head: the *Cosmic Transducer Chakra*. Its function is to filter and transduce the cosmic, or higher-dimensional, energies that you receive. Your Cosmic Transducer contemporizes past-life energy, connection to and information from guides, Akashic Records information, and your ray energy into utilizable forms that are in rapport with your goals, your body consciousness, and your spiritual connections in present time. This above-the-head chakra corresponds to the eleventh dimension. The eleventh dimension is the realm of archangels; Supreme Beings of planets, star systems, and galaxies; and the secondary group of Elohim.

The Twelfth Chakra

Your twelfth chakra is located at the topmost point of your aura, above your head. It is called your *Cosmic Portal Chakra*. Its function is to receive your cosmic connections, Akashic Records information, and energy ray. It also bridges the gap between your human self and your multidimensional hologram, once you have restored that connection through permanent bonding with your Higher Self, and by creating a Pillar of Light to the Great Central Sun and Divine Source. The twelfth dimension corresponds to your Cosmic Portal Chakra and is the realm of Creation and Creators. The Holy Mother, the Holy Father, and the highest Elohim are twelfth-dimensional beings who exist in their individuated consciousnesses and yet experience Oneness and interdependence with All That Is.

The Thirteenth Chakra

Containing all your other chakras and all aspects of your consciousness on all dimensional levels is your thirteenth chakra, the *Chakra of Oneness*. When you connect with it, the focus is just above your aura. This thirteenth chakra corresponds to the thirteenth dimension, which is the realm of Oneness, or Divine Source. This thirteenth chakra corresponds to the Divine Law: "The whole is greater than the sum of its parts." It contains all of the other chakras, but in and of itself, it is more than just a container of the others. It is your consciousness of Oneness, or the place in which all aspects of yourself exist as a single expanded consciousness. It is your chakra that connects you to Oneness with All That Is as well. On the thirteenth dimension the same Divine Law applies. When everything in existence is in a state of Oneness with no autonomous distinctions, this is the thirteenth dimension.

When you do the thirteen-chakra bonding meditation with Higher Self and then with Earth chakras, you will use golden infinity symbols of light to make the connections. In doing so, you are aligning with the highest purpose of Earth and acclimating to Earth changes and pole shifts in a manner that produces the most gracious impact possible. The next chapter, "Anchoring Your Pillar of Light from the Great Central Sun," is really a continuation of

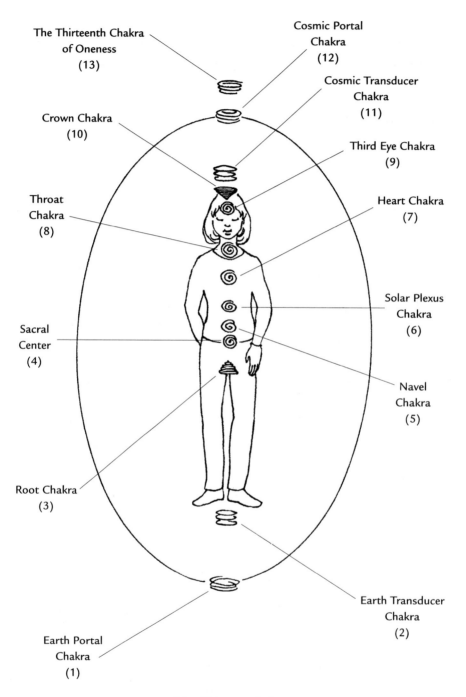

The Thirteen Chakras

The Thirteenth Chakra
of Oneness
(13)

Cosmic Portal
Chakra
(12)

Cosmic Transducer
Chakra
(11)

Crown Chakra
(10)

Third Eye Chakra
(9)

Throat
Chakra
(8)

Heart Chakra
(7)

Solar Plexus
Chakra
(6)

Sacral
Center
(4)

Navel
Chakra
(5)

Root Chakra
(3)

Earth Transducer
Chakra
(2)

Earth Portal
Chakra
(1)

this one. I suggest that you read both chapters and then do the meditations back to back. If you cannot hold focus for that length of time, then do them individually. I will include instructions in the next chapter for doing the meditations both together and separately.

Thirteen-Chakra Meditation

1. Close your eyes and find a comfortable position.

2. Make this invocation: "In the name of the I Am presence that I Am, I call on the Dolphin Star Temple Higher Council of Light to anchor the Crystalline Pillars of Light from the Cities of Light around and through this room, anchoring it as a Sacred Dolphin Star Temple in the Cities of Light, where only that which is divine may enter, and all that is less than the divine, which is illusion, must leave now."

3. Take deep breaths, using your breath to bring yourself deeply into your body. With each inhalation, call in your own divine spirit to fill the holy temple of your body all the way through your head, torso, arms and hands, legs and feet. With each exhalation, imagine that you are releasing all of the tension, energy blocks, pain, and numbness that keep you from being fully present. Inhale your Holy Spirit; exhale tension and blocks. Breathe deeply enough to enable you to feel the skin expand around your feet, toes, and fingers with each inhalation. When you have opened your entire body with breath, move on to the next step.

4. Draw your aura in or push it out, whichever is needed to extend your auric field to just about arms' length around your body. Imagine that your aura is shaped like an egg and extends two to three feet above you, below you, behind you, in front of you, and to either side. Use your breath and your intention to draw your aura to fill that space.

5. Give yourself a new grounding cord made of whatever color of light feels appropriate to you. Send your grounding cord from your lower body to the Earth Star Crystal at the center of Earth. Ask the devas of the Earth Star Crystal to connect you exclusively to the highest potential future, and to the Christ consciousness, of Earth.

6. Ask the Pleiadian, Sirian, and Andromedan Emissaries of Light to

place an Interdimensional Cone of Light above your aura, aligning you with Divine Truth and assisting you in clearing ego and illusionary energies.

7. Ask the Sirian Emissaries of Light to anchor above your aura the Evolutionary Cone of Light to align you with your highest purpose according to the Divine Plan.

8. Ask the Andromedan Emissaries of Light to place above your aura the Intergalactic Cone of Light, aligning you in a Pillar of Light to the Great Central Sun of All That Is.

9. Call upon your Higher Self of the Light to fill your Tube of Light from the topmost point of your aura, around your spine, to the bottommost point of your aura [see illustration on page 229]. Take a deep breath in through the top of your aura and into your crown, filling your Tube of Light with your own divine consciousness. Breathe from your crown all the way to the base of your spine, filling your Tube of Light. Breathe and send your Higher Self energy through your Tube of Light until it is filled all the way to the bottommost point of your aura.

10. Now call upon the aspect of your Higher Self of the Light that has a full lightbody form. Ask your Higher Self to come and stand in front of you and place the palms of its hands on yours. As you begin to feel your Higher Self's presence and the contact with the palms of your hands, breathe the love and light up your arms into the heart. When your heart chakra is full and overflowing, allow that love and light to fill your whole body.

11. Imagine that you can look deeply into the eyes of your Higher Self. See the love and beauty in those eyes. Realize that "These are my eyes. They belong to a higher me that I am in the process of embodying." Let your Higher Self know that it is your intention to become One with all aspects of your Higher Self, until there is no longer a sense of you and Higher Self because you are a single consciousness. Ask your Higher Self to work with you continually until you have accomplished this goal of Oneness.

12. Now ask your Higher Self to stand behind you, facing your back. Focus on your thirteenth chakra area just above your aura, and ask your Higher Self to send an infinity symbol of golden light from its thirteenth chakra to yours.

13. Call for an infinity symbol of light from your Higher Self's twelfth chakra, the Cosmic Portal Chakra at the topmost point of the aura, into yours. Use your breath to draw it into your chakra.

14. Ask your Higher Self to send an infinity symbol of light from its eleventh chakra, the Cosmic Transducer just above the head, to that three-ring chakra that floats just above your head.

15. Next draw in an infinity symbol of light from your Higher Self's crown chakra into your crown chakra, breathing and filling your crown chakra with Higher Self energy.

16. Breathe another infinity symbol of light from your Higher Self's third eye into the back of your third eye. Breathe until the energy is all the way into the front of your third eye, overflowing the third eye with your Higher Self light.

17. Draw an infinity symbol of light from your Higher Self's throat chakra all the way through the back of your throat chakra into the front.

18. Next ask your Higher Self to send a golden infinity symbol from its heart chakra into the back of yours, breathing light to the front of your heart chakra, through your soul area in the center of your chest.

19. Breathe and bring in an infinity symbol from your Higher Self's solar plexus chakra into the back of yours. Breathe the energy all the way to the front.

20. Next ask your Higher Self to send an infinity symbol of light from its navel chakra into your navel from behind, filling your navel center, like an umbilical to your Higher Self.

21. Bring an infinity symbol of light from your Higher Self's sacral center into the back of your sacrum, breathing the energy forward to the front.

22. Now bring a golden infinity symbol from your Higher Self's root chakra, at the base of the spine, into yours.

23. Call upon your Higher Self to send an infinity symbol of light from its Earth Transducer Chakra beneath the feet into your three-ring Earth Transducer Chakra beneath your feet.

24. Last, call in a golden infinity symbol from your Higher Self's Earth Portal Chakra to your Earth Portal Chakra at the bottommost point of your aura.

25. You may already be noticing that the Higher Self's lightbody is beginning to blend with yours. Use your breath to consciously increase that bonding with your Higher Self until your entire body and aura are fully blended with the lightbody and auric field of your Higher Self. Full body breaths will help.

You may choose to end the meditation briefly and then continue. I advise continuing now if possible.

Linking with Earth's Thirteen Chakras

1. Say the following invocation to the Guardians of the Thirteen Earth Chakras: "In the name of the I Am that I Am, I call upon the Guardians and Overlighting Devas of Light of the Thirteen Chakras of Earth. I call upon the Guardians of the Crystalline Cities of Light located at Earth's thirteen chakra sites, and ask that you assist me now in aligning with—and acclimating to—Earth's polarity, orbits, and electromagnetic field." Take a few seconds to breathe deeply as this alignment is being made.

2. Continue your invocation to the Earth chakra and City of Light guardians and Overlighting Devas: "Assist me now in aligning with the highest Divine Plan for Earth and her people. I wish to connect only to the highest sources of Divine Truth, Love, and Light at each of the thirteen chakras of Earth. I ask that each of the Earth's thirteen chakras may register that I am a human being embodying my Higher Self of Light, in the process of becoming the Christ that I Am. I ask that all of the healing, awakening, and remembrance that I have experienced be registered in Earth chakras, taking nothing away from me, and giving an imprint that will benefit all of the humans on Earth in their own awakening. So be it."

3. Now bring your focus to the chakra at the bottommost point of your aura, your Earth Portal Chakra. From that chakra send a golden infinity symbol of light to the center of the vortex of Lake and Mt. Batur in Bali, Indonesia. Ask to connect with only the highest source of Divine Light and Love and Truth. Repeat this affirmation: "I command that this Earth chakra be held in the Light and protected in the Light from this point forth. I also command that all black magic and control energies be permanently removed from these sacred sites."

4. Continue sending golden infinity symbols to each of the Earth chakras from your chakras in the following order. Repeat the affirmation from step 3 at each Earth Chakra once the infinity symbol link has been made. Link to these Earth chakras:

- Table Mountain, South Africa, from the three-ring chakra beneath your feet, the Earth Transducer Chakra.
- Uluru, formerly Ayer's Rock, Australia, from your root chakra at the base of your spine.
- Mt. Kilauea, Hawaii, from your sacral chakra.
- Delphi, Greece, from your navel chakra.
- Mt. Fuji, Japan, from your solar plexus.
- The Tor in Glastonbury, England, from your heart chakra.
- Palenque, Mexico, from your throat chakra.
- The Great Pyramid of Giza from your third eye.
- Mt. Denali, formerly Mt. McKinley, Alaska, from your crown chakra.
- Mt. Shasta, California, from your three-ring chakra above your head, the Cosmic Transducer Chakra.
- Machu Picchu, Peru, South America, from your Cosmic Portal at the topmost part of your aura the Chakra of Oneness.
- Lake Titicaca, Peru and Bolivia, South America, from just above your aura, the Chakra of Oneness.

5. Remain in meditation as long as you like, or continue with the Pillar of Light meditation in the next chapter.

10

Anchoring Your Pillar of Light from the Great Central Sun

For a deeper experience, repeat steps 1 through 9 on pages 125 and 126 from the previous chapter before beginning this meditation. However, if you are doing this meditation immediately after the thirteen-chakra meditation in the previous chapter, you do not need to repeat these steps. Simply continue.

Pillar of Light Meditation

1. Bring your attention to approximately one and a half to two inches inside your chest. This location is your soul matrix, the place where your soul is geometrically anchored in your physical body. Take a couple of deep breaths into that area, and notice what you feel. Listen for the sound, or musical tone, that is unique to your soul. The best way to find that tone is to listen and hear it. If this does not work for you, then begin toning up and down the scales in small increments until you find the specific tone that vibrates your soul area. Placing your fingertips in the center of your chest may help. Experiment with singing tones until you find the one that vibrates your fingers and your soul matrix.

2. Continue toning your soul sound until you feel that your soul and heart areas are completely filled with that sound and with the light of the soul the sound has released. Then continue toning until you

have sent that soul sound with light into your whole body. (Continue toning your soul sound throughout the following steps until you are instructed to stop when you reach the Great Central Sun.)

3. Imagine that in the center of your head there is a miniature you, either in the form of a ball of light with your consciousness in it, or as an exact duplicate of your physical body, only an inch tall. Draw as much of your consciousness into the miniature self as you can (still toning). You are preparing to go out of your body as this miniature self.

4. Above your head, create the image of two pyramids, base to base, forming a golden octagon (see illustration on page 132). This shape will function as a travel merkaba. Lift your miniature self, using the soul tone, out through your crown chakra into the interior of this merkaba. Imagine that there is a string of light, like an etheric harp string, that goes all the way from the center of your soul matrix to the Great Central Sun. This little merkaba will travel on that string as the string is vibrated with your soul sound.

5. Direct the sound up the etheric harp string, spinning the little travel merkaba and directing yourself to travel to the center of our local Sun.

6. Inside the Sun, take a moment to connect to the Higher Consciousness of the Sun. Send gratitude into the Sun for the light, warmth, and love that it generates to you and Earth. Ask the Sun to work with you on your path to enlightenment and Christ consciousness. Ask the Sun to impulse you now with the encodings you left in the Sun before your birth in this lifetime. Thank the Sun for imprinting you again with your higher purpose.

7. Using the tone to direct you, move to the center of the Central Sun of the Pleiades, called Alcyone. You will move through a portal in the Sun directly to the center of Alcyone and connect to the Guardians of Light there. Ask the Pleiadian Archangelic Tribes of the Light, and the Guardians of the Cities of Light of the Pleiades and Earth, to imprint you with the encodings of your divine connection to the Pleiades.

8. Use the tone and your intention to direct you through the portals of the Pleiades directly into the star Sirius. Ask to connect to the Sirian Archangelic League of the Light, all the Sirian Emissaries of

*The golden octagon travel merkaba contains
the consciousness of the meditator as she leaves her body.*

Light, and the etheric dolphin spirits. Ask them to help you re-member your connection to Sirius and to Christ consciousness.

9. Intend now to move straight through the Sirian portal to the three-star portal of the Orion belt. You will not pause there. The particular portal of Orion through which you travel will take you directly to the center of the Milky Way, to the gateways that are kept by the Priestesses of Hathor. Ask the guardian, the Supreme Being, of the Milky Way to imprint you with your original choice, your original purpose for coming to the Milky Way, and your divine connection to this galaxy.

10. Using the toning to direct you forward, ask the Hathors to open the portals to the Central Sun of the Andromeda Galaxy, which is the twin of the Milky Way. In the center of the Andromeda Galaxy, ask to be imprinted with the memory of Oneness and equanimity between male and female, before the male/female split.

11. Use your soul tone and your intention, and ask now that the portals that lead from the Andromeda Galaxy to the Great Central Sun be opened to you. You will move through a spiral passageway to the Great Central Sun. There you will be greeted by a member of the Elohim, who will serve as your personal guide in the Great Central Sun. When you feel that you are fully in the Great Central Sun, cease the toning for now.

12. Take the hand of your Elohim guide, and you will be taken to the place in the Great Central Sun where you are intended to have your own unique experience. This will be different for each person and for you each time you do this meditation. Take two minutes or so to be with your guide in the Sun.

13. Your guide will now lead you to a set of crystalline steps that will take you to the throne of the Holy Mother and Holy Father of All That Is. As you find yourself standing in front of the Holy Mother and Holy Father, hold out your hands, and they will each take one of your hands to make a direct connection. Breathe in their love, and listen to hear whether they have a message for you. If not, simply commune with them in silence.

14. The Holy Mother and Holy Father would like to give you a gift, some symbol of your connection to them. They may each give you

a gift, or they may collectively give you one gift. Separate your hands from theirs now so that you can receive their gift or gifts. When you receive this gift, take a moment to breathe and feel the energy. If you are not sure what it means, you can ask them. Then place the gift wherever it belongs inside of you.

15. Now they are asking for you to give them a gift. The gift they want from you is something that still keeps you feeling separate from their love. Perhaps it is your self-doubt, distrust, anger, shame, or fear. Perhaps it is your belief in victimhood. Listen, and ask them what gift they want you to give up now in order to help you maintain connection to them and to Source. When they tell you what they want, you will be able to reach inside yourself and find that place where you hold on to this in the form of pain, a dark symbol, or a knot. Simply pull it out of yourself, and give it to them.

16. The Holy Mother and Holy Father will stand with you between them. When the Holy Father and Holy Mother are in union, and blended into total Oneness, that is your connection back to Source and Oneness. For in their union they contain All That Is. Stand between them as they move toward one another, and allow yourself to blend into their union. Take a few minutes of silence now in that place of Oneness.

17. As Holy Mother and Holy Father begin to individuate again, you will once again find yourself standing between them. Take a moment to express your gratitude to them for their undying and unceasing love. Ask them to help you feel their love more continually.

18. Taking the hand of your Elohim guide; descend the steps preparing to return. Before you come back, imagine that you can extend your hands, or your wings, whichever feels most real to you. Grab hold of the Light of the Great Central Sun, and pull it around you in the form of a Pillar of Light. Continue pulling this Pillar of Light back with you as you are guided back through the portals. Imagine that you are wrapping yourself in a Pillar of Light, using your etheric hands or wings.

19. Begin to sing your soul tone again, toning continually until you are told to stop.

20. Say good-bye to your Elohim guide in gratitude for the assistance.

21. You will move back through all of the portals to your body much more quickly than you journeyed to the Great Central Sun. You will return in the following order, toning and pulling your Pillar of Light all the way:

    a. Focus now on spiraling back to the Central Sun of the Andromeda Galaxy.

    b. Go through the portal at the center of the Milky Way that is guarded by the Hathors.

    c. Descend through the Orion belt to Sirius.

    d. Pass through Alcyone, the Central Sun of the Pleiades.

    e. Move through the center of our local Sun.

    f. Continue toning, and bring your Pillar of Light all the way back down to just above the roof of the building in which you sit in meditation.

    g. Move into the room above your body, stopping just above your head. Release the octagonal travel merkaba. Breathe yourself right into the center of your head, pulling your Pillar of Light to the Great Central Sun around the full width of your aura. Breathe and expand your consciousness to fill your entire body while continuing to sing the tone.

22. Once you have expanded to fill your body, pull your Pillar of Light all the way down around your aura, and send it with a big exhalation to the center of Earth to the Earth Star Crystal. Cease the toning. Ask the Guardians of the Earth Star Crystal to maintain the grounding of your Pillar of Light to the Great Central Sun. Tell the guardians that you want to permanently maintain this connection to Source, connecting all thirteen dimensions with your Pillar of Light.

23. Take a deep breath and feel the length of your body from head to toe, to the tips of your fingers. Feel the frequency of your Pillar of Light around and through your body and aura.

24. Release your grounding cord, and give yourself a new one. Allow this new grounding cord to flare from your hips out to the edge of your aura at ground level. Blend your grounding cord with your Pillar of Light. Send your grounding cord, blending it with

your Pillar of Light, to the center of Earth. Your grounding cord and Pillar of Light to the Great Central Sun are now merged down to the Earth Star Crystal, to the Christ consciousness and the highest potential future there.

25. Take another deep full-body breath, feeling your new grounding. Gently bring yourself back to the room and open your eyes.

You can do this meditation as often as you like.

Part 4

Embodying Divine Qualities

In this section, you will receive channeled teachings from various Light Beings. These channelings are intended to assist you in understanding how to embody attitudes and behaviors commensurate with your Higher Self identity. It is vital for spiritual seekers to know the difference between ego identity and spiritual identity in order to reclaim the Divine Flow of Essence and of Creation. Once you understand, then you can apply self-discipline and spiritual practice to accomplish your goal of awakening.

Reclaiming Misplaced Identity

A Channeling from Sirian Archangel Hermes, February 1999

The group to which this channeling was given was in meditation when Hermes began. Take a couple of minutes to ground yourself, center, and invite your Higher Self in before beginning. Hermes will take you immediately into a guided process. 📼

Hermes: Welcome your personal dolphin guide at this time. Each of you has at least one. Call for this dolphin spirit to come to you now. Ask this dolphin spirit to swim around and then through your aura. Breathe and feel this delightful connection. Ask your dolphin to blend with your full body now. Breathe, and welcome this dolphin friend to help you feel more deeply. Ask the dolphin to specifically blend its eyes with yours. Continue to breathe and welcome your personal dolphin guide to come in, blend with your body, and help you look at life through the eyes of a dolphin. Align your chakras with the dolphin's chakras so you can feel what it feels like to be in that spontaneous innocent flow. Take your time . . . .

The dolphins are emissaries of Christ. They hold the frequency of Christ consciousness until the entire Earth and her people are ready to hold it for themselves. As you blend with them, feel that matrix of which the Hathors spoke—that matrix of innocence and wisdom, purity and power. Feel the wholeness of your being as an innocent child. . . .

If you are hearing dolphin sounds or musical tones, make the same sounds or tones aloud. Let the sounds move through your cells, your consciousness, until you are nothing but sound that is aware of itself. . . .

There is a sound that is your own soul singing inside you all the time. There is so much more to you than you know. Let me explain. Most of you have forgotten to listen to your sacred sound, because there are places to purify in your body and consciousness that are not who you are. But at some point in time you have believed otherwise. You ceased to remember what those places of density really are. You forgot to listen to the voice of your own soul essence. For in your essence there is a grace, and a joy, a power, and a plan that carries you through everything. Like the spirit of the dolphin moving through the waters, you can choose to soar through your life.

Do not believe that you have blocks. You do not. They are simply remnants of falsely misplaced identity that are in the process of dissolving in time. You are not that. You have never been wrong. Even those things you have thought of as your mistakes and failures have been your greatest sources of learning about how existence works. And, dearest, beautiful ones, that is what you chose to do.

You chose to come here to understand how every dimension in reality works. You wanted to know through direct experience. You see, in the higher dimensions, if two beings have diverse experiences, and one wishes to understand the other's experience, they simply blend with each other, and the other's experience becomes a part of their own. Here on Earth, it is a little different. You do learn from one another. But those experiences are isolated in your psyche, your consciousness, and your body in such a way that you do not learn them directly from one another in an intimate way. When you forget that you are learning, when you forget that you are okay, and when you forget that you are choosing to learn, you get caught up in ego dilemmas of trying to defend yourself, or heal yourself, or purify yourself. And the self does not need purifying. It is simply the amorphic field that has been created through false identity that needs purification and healing. These amorphic energies are lodged in your emotional, mental, physical, etheric, astral, and spiritual bodies. But none of these bodies are what you are. They are simply vehicles of experience. And yes, it is important to heal them. Then, when you truly leave and ascend again, you will leave nothing behind that is less than your Divine Truth to magnetize you back into the cycle of reincarnation.

This is what you have longed for. You chose that goal for yourself a long time ago. So purification is simply the process of bringing your Light, which is Truth, into every place where your Light ceased to shine for a moment, a day, a year, a lifetime, or aeons. And it is your own Light that must shine into those places, and restore your Truth, and release all false identities. Embracing these words may seem like a simple matter that is only words, lacking substance. But believe me, your words create reality more than you even know— especially when you deeply feel the intention behind the words.

So let us affirm together: "I Am the beauty, the innocence, the purity, and the wisdom that I Am. I Am the beauty, the innocence, the purity, and the wisdom that I Am. I Am the beauty, the innocence, the purity, and the wisdom that I Am. All else is just mistaken identity, in the process of dissolving." Let it be that simple, free of resistance.

Take full-body breaths. Feel the place in your heart that is determined to never feel shame again. Feel the place in your heart that is determined to never feel self-doubt again. Feel that place in your heart that is absolutely determined to be diligent in your awakening until every tiny speck of your consciousness and your identity have returned to the Light of Truth. Breathe into that place, and let the determination grow bigger. Let it fill your heart and overflow into your whole body. And be determined to always remember your own divinity, and to stay aware that any energy block within you that is less than Light is just mistaken identity awaiting your reclamation.

12

Trust and Discernment

A Teaching Given on Easter 1999

This is a transcript of the group teaching I gave in my home on Easter Sunday 1999, and the ensuing discussion. The channelings in chapters 25 and 26, from Mother Mary and Jesus, were from this same gathering.

> *Amorah:* At the Spring Equinox Gathering I led this year in Mt. Shasta, we did a process that I do with groups from time to time. We created a Pillar of Light to the Great Central Sun. [This meditation process is included in chapter 10.] While we were bilocated* in the Great Central Sun, a representative of the Elohim greeted us. The Elohim of Divine Grace spoke to us as a group, through me, to say that every equinox and solstice is a time to align ourselves with the next aspect of the Divine Plan. Earth and her human inhabitants, as well as beings in other star systems, are constantly being impulsed to realign with the macrocosm. This is especially true during solstices and equinoxes, which are like cosmically synchronized time clocks. These are wonderful times for meditation, ceremony, and renewal,

*Bilocation is the experience of being lucidly in two places at once.

because on these days special dispensations are given, all the way from the Great Central Sun through our local Sun. These dispensations release a time-encoded plan within our Sun regarding the next karmic pattern to be healed in human consciousness. Sometimes it is an impulse to release very old karmic patterns that have been withheld from Earth for a long time. Sometimes it is a healing dispensation sent like encoded waves of Light, or a teaching impulsed into our psyches in a similar manner.

The Elohim of Divine Grace said that at this particular Spring Equinox, the dispensation was a combination of those types of impulses, because in order for us to move to the next level and be in alignment with Earth's higher purpose, the pattern most in need of release involved all aspects of distrust and lack of self-trust. The teachings brought in that day have been expanding since that time as I work with more groups. They have shed more light on this subject, which I think is clouded for a lot of us. Some of the cloudiness in our thinking occurs because we know that people do things that are not trustworthy, and we assume that distrust is the only way to respond. Sometimes people deliberately lie or steal or harm or act in other ways that are not in alignment with higher purpose. People sometimes behave malevolently, and we need to be aware of that in order to make discerning choices. However, according to the Elohim, there is never a moment when distrust is appropriate, because distrust is an inverted energy that creates chaos. It blocks the flow of light. In healing trust issues, we must first heal self-trust. Why? Because we have to learn to trust ourselves to use discernment and make proper choices before we can feel safe to release distrust of others. But most people do not trust themselves to know whom to trust, and therefore they choose to embrace the stance of justified distrust and to remain on guard, based on people's actions.

Close your eyes for a moment. Think of what it feels like to be in a state of distrust and on guard. Maybe someone has done something harmful or dishonest to you. Feel what it is like when you start to close yourself down in that state of distrust. Monitor your body, observing where you contract. Notice that your heart chakra closes a little—or a lot. Some people tend to stop breathing when they are in distrust. Think about how it felt the last time you actively distrusted someone. Continue monitoring your contractions, breathing, emotions, and heart while remembering this experience. Take a couple of minutes for this feeling and observation.

Continue focusing on the same person and the same reasons for distrust. But begin to shift your attitude to this: "I have an ability to keep my heart open. I have an ability to keep radiating my Light. I even have an ability to see that this person has a Divine Essence right now. I can choose to use my discernment to not place *absolute trust* in his actions, because I can see that part of his consciousness is still identified with the ego's need to be dishonest" (or whatever the situation was that evoked feelings of distrust and betrayal). Perhaps someone gossiped about you, and you felt really hurt. You began to lose your trust in that person. Maybe you were accused of something you did not do, or your lover was unfaithful. Whatever the situation, bring yourself to a place of saying, "Now I have learned not to place absolute trust in this person at a personality level on this issue. It will help me make my choices on how I relate to him, and yet, I can keep my heart open and love him. I do not have to contract." See if you can breathe through the memories of the experience again while letting go of the contraction. Shift your perspective to one of using discernment in your connection to the individual, *while still trusting that his Divine Essence will eventually rule his consciousness again.* This is called trust in the Divine Plan. It happens when you know that eventually the individual will work through all of his or her karmic challenges, pass all initiations, and become fully trustworthy again. It is only because you are looking at this person in time that there is a problem. In the framework of time, this person appears untrustworthy in the moment. You could still choose to simply trust that the person is doing what is needed in order to learn and grow and eventually transcend malevolence. At this time the individual has a need to explore malevolence before finally letting these behaviors go, and before he or she can learn the value of the intimacy that comes with benevolence.

You can even take this corrective way of thinking and responding a step further: You can choose to have compassion because you realize that this person is so cut off from his or her own spirit as to be able to indulge in harmful behavior. Then you do not have to take what has happened personally. You realize that the individual is simply exploring realms of consciousness and behavior, and that he or she has not fully evolved in the area in which you have been harmed. Can you come to the place inside in which you can think about the person and situation with your heart open, and remain devoid of judgment and contraction? One of the basic rules of thumb is this: *No one can ever behave in a way that is more evolved than his or her current state of evolution at any given moment.* People may have glimpses of higher awareness from time to time, but you cannot expect them to behave in a way that they have not learned, internalized, and chosen to make a priority. Open your eyes now.

This approach to trust is one about which I had never thought until the Elohim began the teaching. I knew that I was responsible for discerning and for not being a victim, but to actually think of eliminating the energy of distrust was a bit unnerving at first. Most human beings have learned how to survive in the world by creating walls, and many of those walls are walls of distrust. We have learned to be on guard and to treat people as if they are untrustworthy until they prove themselves innocent. In that way of thinking, we keep certain barriers up and create separation.

Some people handle this in another way that seems to be more spiritual, but I question it. A few years ago, I had a housemate who was working on trust. I would start talking about trust, and he would literally start panting in fear. He would almost go into anxiety attacks when I started to talk about opening his heart and trusting people. Then he chose to become involved with someone whom he knew to be an extremely controlling person. So I said to him one day, "If you really want to heal trust, then you have to take responsibility for not projecting onto anyone, especially your new lover, that she is going to fulfill your expectations. Because you know that this is a really controlling woman, you could be choosing, from a subconscious ego place, to get involved with her because you know that she is really going to hurt you and try to control you. You could be choosing this scenario to prove to yourself, once and for all, that no one is trustworthy. Then you could justify shutting down because you opened your heart to this person and trusted her. She was even on a spiritual path—and look at how badly she treated you."

Unless you are out to justify putting up walls of distrust and being on guard, this is what you need to do:

1. Be responsible for using discernment. Give yourself time to observe the individual before placing intimate trust in his or her hands.

2. Trust in the Divine Plan, and know that everyone will eventually be worthy of deep trust.

3. Do not personalize the behavior of others, even if it is directed at you. Whatever happens, everyone is just being themselves at their present level of growth. What else can they be but who they are right now?

4. Do not expect others to behave as you want them to unless you have enough life experience with them to know what is safe to expect.

5. Before taking an individual into a deeply intimate role in your life, talk to that person about personal values and what you want and need in the relationship. Then ask the person to share his or her wants and needs and values with you. Are your values, wants, and needs compatible? Make a decision about deepening the connection and placing trust based on experience and on this sharing. Then, if you are lied to or hurt in some way, know that you did your best to be discerning, and that the person did not have the ability to live up to his or her promise. Forgive, and move on.

Do not be stupid by going out there and placing your absolute trust in someone who, as you already know, is spiritually and ethically immature, unless you want to take responsibility for creating a bigger barrier of distrust than you already have. A lot of people say, "But I trusted and loved him unconditionally. I did this, and he did that." And on and on. Just because you trusted and loved someone does not guarantee that the person is going to live up to your expectations. It may mean that you are setting your ego up to have more reason to stay in control, more reason to shut down and distrust—to prove to yourself that it does not work to release distrust.

One necessary ingredient to healing and releasing distrust is to choose a genuinely trustworthy person and to trust that person. In order to do so, you have to let go of the barriers and the ego controls. One way to finally heal trust comes when you have used your discernment enough with someone to know that the person is a really good-intentioned person. Maybe you still notice that in the area of sexuality in relationship, the individual still has confusion or fear. This observation helps you know that in the area of sexuality you might not be able to put total trust in the person's judgment or behavior. And even in that area, he or she is a good person with unhealed karma, not deliberately malevolent. But in every other area, you know that the person is mature and trustworthy, so you choose to let go of control and be really vulnerable with, and trust, that person. That is how you can heal self-trust: by using discernment. And that is how you heal trust of others and of the Divine Plan: by using discernment. Even if you select someone to trust who is not spiritually mature enough to be ethical, you can still trust that he or she will eventually get there. You can still love the person and choose not to have to contract, brace yourself, or be paranoid. You can just choose to use what you have observed, with discernment, to take care of yourself, to have healthy boundaries, and to keep honoring that the other person is on the path, moving at his or her own pace.

I have never worked with anyone who did not have to deal with trust issues at some level. But I also know that we are all mature enough beings to take responsibility for maintaining healthy boundaries. None of us need ever be the victim of other people's energies and actions. Carlos Castaneda talked about our "petty tyrants" as our greatest teachers, and there is truth in that. They are not always the most fun teachers, especially when we take ourselves too seriously. The time comes when you have to accept that others are a real challenge to you, and this means that you need a little more work on issues of discernment, trust, speaking your truth, or whatever. Having Pisces rising, I have always had the tendency to try to intimately include everyone. There is a lot of naïveté in that attitude. Unless we choose our intimate others from those who are at compatible stages of growth and spiritual development, we can be extremely naive. We can be so caught up in our own dream that we cease to realize that not everyone is dreaming the same dream.

Many years ago, a Virgo teacher of mine said that one of my problems was that I wanted everyone to be in my inner circle. She said that the inner circle is just for the people with whom you can share everything—the people whom you can safely trust on every level, with whom you can share your deepest secrets and know that they will not be used against you. In the next ring out from this inner circle is a group of close friends. In this group, you really love each other and share a lot, but it is not that absolute sharing of everything that occurs in the inner circle. The next ring contains the people you go on nature walks with, share music, or go to movies with. You have fun and share less intimate life information with one another. Then there are the people further out whom you see only if you are going to a certain kind of concert. Next out are those you see only in gatherings with specific groups of people. Following those rings out, you reach the rest of humanity—people you do not even know or do not choose to know better than in passing. You still can choose to love all these people, but use discernment about where they belong on this circle. By appropriately choosing where you put people in your circles, you are not creating separation, or judging.

As humans, we are still learning how to remember that we are something other than what we experience in the moment. If we are in pain, our consciousness still has a tendency to identify with that pain and forget about love, self-compassion, and peace. One of the greatest spiritual teachings is how we can remove our identity from, and release the narrow perspective of, current experience while still being fully present in our lives, in the now. It seems like a paradox; but this helps us learn how to remain in our centers so that our self-identity has constancy of presence, spirit, awareness, love, and goodness.

If you feel illness in your body, you can be aware of it, feel it, and take care of it, but you do not have to be sick. Think of the power in the words "I am sick" versus "My body has the flu." The first identifies you as sickness. The second says that your body is having an experience of sickness. The challenge is to maintain your true identity while experiencing physical problems. One thing I have learned through health challenges is that certain types of depression can be solely related to a lack of physical vitality. Even when your body is not feeling well, if you can witness it with love and compassion, and communicate with the Elohim of Divine Grace and the Angels of Grace asking that your body heal with as much grace as possible, the illness will not take over your consciousness.

As long as you are still identified with the circumstances of life as your reality, you will still tend to judge others and yourself. When you remain spirit centered and identified, it is easier to remember that you and everyone else are simply learning and growing. And sometimes, beings who are still in the process of awakening misplace their conscious identities and get caught up in the moment. Forgiveness and tolerance come in quite handy at those times. How you identify yourself is really important, because what you identify with is what you become. Choose your identity well. Remember that the way you think of others either engages you in the astral world of karma with them or allows you to be even more in your spiritual identity and hold the space for them to go beyond their false identities more easily. How you view others can pull you out of spiritual identity as much as the way you view yourself. If you are identified with judging others for anything, then that part of you that is the judge has no place for spirit. It is totally absorbed in ego identity in that moment. There are things that are hard not to judge. The alternative to judgment is right use of discernment with compassion. People seem to need to play out their karmic dramas either until they get bored or until they have an awakening, when their hearts open and they see what they are really doing. It is not anyone's place to judge how long that takes. Probably the biggest challenge is to see others, or yourself, get hurt but to remain compassionate and free of judgment. You can always find someone to agree with righteously justifiable judgments. It is simply true, however, that you lose spiritually in that situation, and your negative ego gets stronger. Pray for those who are still behaving malevolently that they will learn their lessons in a gracious way. Send them love without attachment to outcome. And let it go.

A question is asked: "What can we do if we use judgment as protection?"

Amorah: Judgment is often used as a protection from other persons having a judgment of you. If you judge others as being bad in some way, then their judgment does not seem to matter because you have eliminated their importance by judging them as unworthy.

What if you were to just choose to have healthy discernment and boundaries instead of erroneous protection? In your day-to-day life, choices move you either into happiness and spiritual peace or into

negative ego identity. There are always challenges. It was hard
for me to stop judgments. My self-esteem was one of my biggest
problems, and I used judgment of others to dismiss their attitudes
toward me—because I could not rely on my self-esteem. Until self-
esteem became more natural, other people's opinions of me were a
constant threat. Now I choose to trust that when others judge me
harshly, they are on their path doing what they need to do. It has
nothing to do with me, even if it is about me. I need not take it personally. If it still pushes my personal buttons, then I know I have an
issue to clear within myself—not with the other person. The expression, "other people's opinions of me are none of my business," is a
good one to remember.

Another dilemma comes from thinking that you should be able to
fully love everyone intimately. Then you put yourself into a situation in
which inappropriate and unhealthy energies are exchanged. Sometimes,
in holding healthy boundaries, we need to love certain people from a
distance. Loving everyone is great. How you express or share that love
requires good discernment. How do you trust yourself until you learn
to use healthy discernment? How do you learn to make your choices
based on healthy discernment, rather than on distrust, judgment, or
fear-based protection? Some people would say that tools for protecting
our boundaries are inappropriate because they reinforce fear. This can
be true if you put up walls and call them boundaries, or if you create
psychic barriers and live in fear of other people's energy, or even live in
paranoia. Many people who use tools for protecting their boundaries
have become obsessed with psychic and astral phenomena; as a result,
they become more deeply enmeshed in the lower astral planes through
their own constant investment of thoughts and emotions.

With a healthy perspective about boundaries, you can just practice
using boundary tools, knowing they will be obsolete once you have
cleared your own karmic magnetism. No one can plug into you psychically unless you have a magnetism that holds the same frequency
as the invading energy. Therefore, a healthy perspective about psychic
invasion means learning from it about your own magnetic attraction,
and then clearing it. Meanwhile, healthy boundaries can help elimi-
nate the invading energies with which you do not have direct karma.
Effective boundary tools are available in chapters 5 and 6 of my book
The Pleiadian Workbook: Awakening Your Divine Ka. There are many ways

of holding awareness that can assist you in never being the victim of anything, and you do not have to shut down. I noticed that many people were going through issues around trust, and the guides said you are all being impulsed now.

The photon band that Earth is now in all the time impulses us with the Divine Plan. It does so by sending higher frequencies that clear mutations and remedy karmic issues—if you work with it. The chief mutation that was being impulsed for healing at the time of this teaching [April 1999] was distrust. Distrust blocks awareness of your soul and of your soul's ability to shine its light through your cellular structure—just as the Central Sun shines through the universe. Earth is in a process, within this photon band, of realigning this microcosmic planet, and all humans, with the rhythm of the planets and stars. When this realignment is complete, your soul will once again illuminate the cells of your body and keep them spinning with the rhythm of the universe, also called the Divine Flow.

Amorah: Observe, in your daily life, what choices you make around issues of trust, discernment, distrust, judgment, and so on. When distrust, which is contracted, arises, breathe deeply until you can feel yourself out of contraction and radiating again. Then choose to stay loving and flowing while using appropriate discernment.

It is sometimes easier to judge people who are on a spiritual path than those who are not, because we expect less of those who have not awakened to spirit. But those on the spiritual path sometimes experience that their karmas are more on the surface and "lit up" than they were before they began to awaken. That is because old repressed energies are continually coming to the surface for clearing. Just because someone is on a spiritual path does not mean he or she is perfect all the time. Sometimes we all stumble before we learn to walk our paths gracefully. I just had a flash of a comment I made earlier about someone who has been doing the same thing ever since I have known him, for many years. I could have said that the particular issue must really have a big hold on him for it to have lasted so long, This attitude could actually help me have more compassion, instead of any minor judgment or observation that he is not "getting it." My compassionate self could observe that the issue has such a strong hold on him that even with all the spiritual teachings and all the meditations he has done, he still gets stuck in the pattern. So it must really be a core karmic issue for him. Therefore, I will pray for him to receive even more assistance from his guides.

When we hold on, over time, to attitudes that diminish others in any way, those same problems will manifest themselves in our own lives, because you cannot hold a negative frequency without eventually having it manifest in your life. We need to choose our attitudes toward others from love, compassion, understanding, and trust that at some point everyone will heal everything and return to divine alignment. Otherwise, our attitudes are like weights pulling us in a downward spiral on our spiritual paths. When we reach the point where enough of us are acting from love, compassion, understanding, and trust, we will create a "hundredth monkey" effect. It is another opportunity to "think globally and act locally"—and in this case, "locally" is inside yourself.

I am becoming aware that it is absolutely vital to meditate daily—and to make sure I am in that meditation long enough to enable me to always reach that place of sustained Divine Presence. If I do not do this, as I go through my day I do not have a recent reference point to fall back on, to show me a contrast when I am out of spiritual identity. Those spiritual reference points are indispensable as foundations in truth. And the more we build our spiritual energy, the more we sustain it outside of meditation as well.

Many people are caught up by the belief in an outside source of every problem. It is so sad, because you can always righteously justify such an attitude and find people who will agree with you.If you perceive someone as an enemy, you are on the battleground, ready with defensive comebacks. Yet it is impossible for spirit to be in a defensive mode; only negative ego can do that. It is absolutely impossible for spirit to perceive itself as a victim. It is absolutely impossible for spirit to perceive judgment in anything. So the moment you step into judgment, defensiveness, blame, and distrust, you are in negative ego identity. And there is no access to truth when you are in negative ego—except out of it. Even if you perceive yourself as being put down and criticized, defensiveness is a negative ego's way of warding off a counterattack—which is still an attack—whereas simply holding a sense of high regard for yourself, and taking responsibility for self-esteem, will afford you the ability to choose not to engage with a person who is genuinely hostile. Why should you argue with someone's ego? No one who is capable of truth and harmony is at home in his or her consciousness when attack and defensiveness are being expressed. To remain in spirit identity, you must simply choose not to engage unless the person is willing to reengage in a spiritually responsible manner. Sometimes you simply need to stop and ask yourself, "Does where I am in the moment feel the way I feel when I am in my spirit? Does this feel like what I feel like when I am in my Higher Self? Am I holding contraction, or am I open? If I were Jesus or Mother Mary, is this the attitude I would choose in response to this situation, or am I in ego-reactionary identity at this moment? Am I willing to drop ego-reactionary identity, give up the false sense of power and control that it gives me, step into the humility of spiritual identity and the power of right choice, and surrender to Divine Will?"

Some people believe that they have no choice but to move into ego protection mode. The truth is this: *There is never a moment in your life in which you cannot choose what attitudes you empower with your beliefs, and choose how you act upon them—never a single moment.* Another favorite expression of mine is: "There are no real problems—just the little ego in defense of itself." The moment you say you have no choice, you are identifying with your negative ego victim. And there is no place for spirit, and no place for reason, when you are in ego identity. You have blocked yourself from any possibility of truth until you choose another perspective.

For me, the key has been practice. When you realize that you have chosen ego in a daily life situation, reframe it. Remember the details vividly, and imagine yourself making a new choice to remain in spirit truth. Ask yourself the questions above, and imagine yourself reenacting the scene in surrender to Divine Will—or in a way Jesus or Mother Mary might do it. Practice reframing all recent incidents, or key life experiences, in which you became defensive, judgmental, revengeful, and out of integrity. When you have reframed enough past experiences to know what it feels like to choose correctly, you will find it becoming easier, faster, and more natural to respond to life experiences from spirit-identity. Then distrust, judgment, defensiveness, and blame will have become obsolete, setting you free to be the divine self you want to be and truly are.

13

Releasing and Transcending Attachment

A Channeling of St. Germaine as Spokesperson for the Collective Voice of the Dolphin Star Temple Higher Council of Light

St. Germaine: Dear ones, attachment is often misunderstood for dedication and commitment. Many believe that when one truly cares about a relationship, a creative project, or a planetary healing, one naturally is prone to worry about that situation or person. "How can you love someone and not worry about them?" this person might say. But I tell you that to worry about others is to invalidate their ability to heal and learn and grow. To worry is to presume the person to be incapable of handling what is happening. To worry adds your fear to their problems. It is like adding insult to injury. To worry about the planet "not making it" adds to its potential failure, because your worry adds fear of failure to the planet's future creation of possibilities. Attachment to outcome in relationships or in life situations always means that you are holding fear of loss or of not getting your way. Even when the person is still with you, you are already feeling what it would feel like to grieve over his or her leaving. You already believe you cannot live with the pain, and you therefore build fear of loss and attachment into

154

the life of the relationship. This will either help create the very loss that you fear or create a mediocre relationship because you do not relax enough to learn trust and surrender and unconditional love. Why? Because the fear of loss is in your way; it consumes creative loving space and replaces it with fear-based attachment.

How often have you heard people say, "Well of course I am attached; I love him" or "I just don't know what I'll do if I don't get this job" or "I could not bear to live if I thought the planetary ascension would not happen. I can't even think of another fall like Atlantis. It just has to happen." I am sure you are beginning to get the idea that attachment to outcome pollutes the creative energy toward even the worthiest cause. Humans tend to justify such statements as the ones above as being a sign of deeply caring. But fear is fear is fear, no matter what you may choose to call it.

So how do you care deeply and be dedicated to a cause or committed to a relationship and not be attached? It really is simple. You learn to care more about honoring free will and giving your best at all times than you do about getting your own way. Let me explain, using relationships as an example. Imagine the person in your life that you love the most and would most like to keep around. Feel your feelings toward that person. Feel deeply. Breathe into your heart, and notice what is there when you think of that person. Notice your solar plexus and your root chakra areas. Do these areas contract or relax and feel warm when you think of this loved one? Do you feel sadness or worry in your brow, or expansion? Observing yourself is a great way to understand more about your own nature.

Now imagine that loved one telling you that he or she has felt a powerful inner guidance that celibacy and seclusion are next on the path. See the light in this person's eyes as he or she tells you this. Feel how even though this person is telling you that your relationship is over, you can still feel his or her love coming to you. Now observe yourself again, and notice how you feel. Observe your heart, solar plexus, and root chakras and your brow area. What do you feel? Do you contract in fear? Can you feel yourself wanting to hold on tight or scream "No!"? Are you holding your breath? Are all the feelings you are having totally self-absorbed? Or have you been able to feel good that the person is following his or her highest path—maybe a little sad at the thought of the person's leaving but genuinely wanting him or her to have what is the highest good, because you love this person. If this last statement is true, then you may already be healthily detached.

Healthy detachment means that you still choose to give your best to people and causes about which you care. You do not hold back love and commitment out of fear of loss. You simply ensure the best possible chance of success by giving your best. Without your giving your best, the chances of success are greatly diminished. Of course, in relationships, you still must realize that success may or may not mean staying together for life. Success in relationship comes from staying together the right amount of time that is mutually beneficial. You may hope it is for life—but always be willing to let go in love if it is not. Learning to love means learning to stop giving time and power to fear.

Unconditional love demands no guarantees; it just flows.

Love never fears loss. Love just loves.

Love does not try to change people. Love just loves.

Love does not get hurt because someone fails to live up to your expectations. Love just keeps loving.

Love has no need of validation or reward. Love just loves.

Simple, yes? Do not misunderstand our teaching as lacking in compassion for human nature. It is clear that when you have been neglected by parents or abused by former loved ones, you seek consolation in another, in the hope of making the old pain go away. And it seems to work for a time. But eventually the old pain will surface again, unless it has been completely released and the attitudes causing the pain transcended. The deeper new love reaches into your heart, the deeper the potential for release of old hurts and pain. And when you truly understand this, you will be able to stop projecting that pain onto your new partner and love him or her no matter what. Until then, learning to care about the well-being of your partner without worry and fear of loss is a good goal to set for yourself. How do you accomplish this goal? With practice. When you find yourself in fear, hurt, blame, or worry—stop! Take a deep breath, and remind yourself that you are feeling an emotion and that it is not your higher Truth. It is just a feeling. Be compassionate with yourself, not self-pitying. Compassion has a warm and loving quality. Compassion cares, but it does not suffer over the suffering. Self-pity suffers over the suffering, like a vicious circle. Compassion radiates. Pity contracts and implodes. Be tender with yourself, but not self-indulgent.

Now imagine yourself standing in a crowd when suddenly a thunderous noise is heard. The ground is trembling, and people begin to panic. It is the "big earthquake"—just like Atlantis. There is no hope for physical survival. Do you die in panic and horror? Or do you die in surrender and love? Believe it or not, it is a choice. Attachment to outcome in this situation might trigger a deep sense of failure and hopelessness: "Oh no! It is Atlantis all over again!" Your dying thought would be filled with this fear and horror. Is that what you want to take with you to the other side? I don't think so. It is a great way to get stuck in the astral planes with others who are also in panic identity.

What if the realization that you could not ward off this seeming disaster, no matter what you did, triggered you to go into a deep peaceful place? What if you chose in that moment to consciously focus on your breath and on affirming, "I surrender in love and gratitude for the life I have lived." These dying words would help you move painlessly into the Light. And what's more, it could set the path for others who are less conscious to let go and follow—if they are willing. Which scenario would you choose? We are not predicting this in your future, so please do not misinterpret our intention. But if you have attachment to saving the Earth, it is a good idea to practice conscious surrender and love no matter what happens. This will assist you in releasing attachment to outcome and eventually to transcend attachment altogether.

Healthy detachment requires practice and conscious choice on the part of those who have been attached. It requires willingness to feel deep emotions without allowing them to rule your choices. Healthy detachment requires being determined to always love, and to always give your self totally in love to people and causes, without guarantees. Attachment creates psychic hooks in people or in the future creative process. When you release and transcend attachment, you remove these hooks that hold back others and your own process. You create a greater possibility of getting what you want. And yet, you cannot do it only for that reason, or it will not work. Aye, there's the rub. Genuine caring and willingness to let go must go hand in hand. And caring and loving will eventually become so powerful that you will spontaneously care more about honoring free will in your relationships than you do about getting your own way.

You are master creators—all of you. You just may not realize it yet because of the pollution of attachment in your creativity, clouding and blocking the outcome. To "want something so bad" defeats. To want something "with all your heart" is very different. When your love and surrender become major parts of your creative process, you will realize that you are a master of creation. In every creative and manifestation process, be clear that you are not limiting the free will of others by imagining scenarios that include them. Visualize what you want with no other specific people involved. And always ask that everything you ask for and create be in alignment with the Law of the Harmonics of Co-creation, in which everyone experiences "win/win." In other words, no one loses in order for you to win, and no one's free will is limited in any way. Your pleasure will actually be greater when you create in this way because there will be no undercurrents of guilt, fear, control, contraction, or attachment. And self-respect will grow instead of diminish.

Several years ago, when I was learning about attachment and detachment, I was given a process for clearing attachment psychically. It does not replace the changes in attitude of which St. Germaine spoke, but it does help clear the astral accumulation, and it frees your energy and the people and situations to which you are attached. It is important to realize that healthy boundaries are impossible to maintain as long as you are attached to anyone or anything. And in order to love others and not psychically and psychologically control them through your attachments to their behaviors, or fear of loss, you must let go of your attachments to them or to what they do. If a healthy loving relationship is possible between you, it will have a better chance of surviving and growing once all attachments are cleared. You may use the following guided process for that release.

A Clearing Process for Releasing Attachment Hooks

1. Close your eyes and take two or three full-body breaths. Breathe all the way in to your fingers and toes, and all the way into your whole body, exhaling through your skin. Take as long as you need to accomplish this before you move on.

2. Pull your aura in to two to three feet around you. Visualize an egg-shaped bubble around you, two to three feet in every direction. Pull your entire aura into that bubble, and fill it with your energy.

3. Call in Ascended Master St. Germaine to be with you and to hold the violet flame.

4. Invite the Dolphin Star Temple Higher Council of Light, including the Pleiadian, Sirian, and Andromedan Emissaries of Light, to come and to place you in an Attachment Clearing Chamber of Light.

5. Ask that the Interdimensional, Evolutionary, and Intergalactic Cones of Light be placed at the top of your aura. Ask for the Earth Cone of Light to be placed at the bottom of your aura.

6. Ask your Higher Self of Light to be with you for the session.

7. If you know what you are attached to, and want to clear, ask the guides to impulse you to feel where the attachment hooks are in your body. If you are unsure of what you are attached to, ask the guides to begin to impulse you to feel where in your body you have attachment hooks with other people or situations, so you can identify them.

8. Once you have identified one or more locations in which you are attached to someone or some agenda, visualize a liquid golden light flowing around the entire hook in your body. Then gently and slowly remove it, breathing deeply to assist in the release. Hold the hook in one hand until you have removed the hook at the other end from a person or a bubble with a scene in it that depicts the agenda to which you are attached. The two hooks are connected with a ropelike psychic cord.

9. When both hooks are removed, ask St. Germaine to dissolve them in the violet flames. Watch them burn.

10. Send liquid golden sunlight to fill the hole in the other person's aura or the bubble, and fill in the hole left in your aura and body with golden sunlight as well.

11. If you still feel resistance, pain, contraction, or emotion about this attachment, breathe deeply into the area of your body in which you feel it. Ask St. Germaine to send violet flame into that part of your body, breathing deeply and affirming your intention to release attachment and honor free will. Continue until you feel complete.

12. If you have more than one attachment to clear, repeat steps 8 through 11 for each one.

13. When you have completed this process, affirm, "I align with the Law of the Harmonics of Co-creation in which free will is honored and win/win is the outcome. So be it."

14. Open your eyes, and continue with your day.

I highly recommend repeating this process any time you become aware of attachment and fear of loss. It will greatly assist you in removing certain astral plane connections that are not conducive to spirit.

14

Living in Beingness

A Blending with the Goddess Antares,
February 1999

This chapter is a transcript of a process and teaching that came through during a Pleiadian Lightwork Intensive in February 1999. During the morning meditation, the Goddess Antares came into the group to blend with us and give an activation. She is a member of the Dolphin Star Temple Higher Council. Bringing her energy through for the group was unusual in that she does not channel messages. She anchors the room in an energy state of feminine surrender to Divine Flow—a very exquisite state of pure beingness devoid of agendas and mental interpretation. Her energy is exquisite, to say the least. When her half-hour blending with the group was complete, I was in a deep state of my own Divine Goddess consciousness and delivered a teaching and energy transmission for the group from that state. I hope that by reading the transcript in a state as near to its original form as possible, you will be able to experience the energy transmission as well. I will include the minimal guidance for connecting to Goddess Antares that was given on that day. Once you have blended with her, take as long as you like to be in that state before continuing with the teaching and transmission that I gave afterward. As you read the beginning part of this morning invocation and meditation, simply add your intention to call in the same beings and grids into your home and aura that I brought in for the group on that day.

Guided Meditation and
Goddess Antares Connection ⌨

Amorah: Let us welcome the Dolphin Star Temple Higher Council of Light, all those beloved ones, to come and encircle us and impulse us with their love. Help us, beloved ones, to feel your love and your encouragement. I invite you to bring in the Interdimensional, Evolutionary, and Intergalactic Cones of Light above this room and property, and above each of us individually. Also place the Earth Cones of Light beneath the building and beneath our auras, connecting our grounding to the highest Christ consciousness and Divine Plan for Earth, bypassing all of the astral and elemental regions and Earth karmas, connecting only to the Divine Source of Earth.

I am going to invite a member of the Dolphin Star Temple Higher Council with whom I would like you to become acquainted. She has never actually talked to me. She just holds an incredibly sweet, loving, feminine presence and seems to lend her assistance in times of surrender and letting go. She calls herself the Goddess Antares. She is from the Antares star system, and I acknowledge I know absolutely nothing about that system other than my acquaintance with this one being, who is part of our council. She holds an incredible presence of just being. How can I explain it? What is funny is that even now, she is not saying words but is impulsing me with energy. So the words I would put to the energy she is sending right now are that she holds the energy of loving surrender to Divine Flow. Let us together ask her to come and hold us within her field of consciousness. She is a very large being and can certainly hold this room within her lightbody easily. Let us ask her to come all the way through now and to just hold us in her loving presence and impulse us with her love. Breathe deeply as you welcome her to blend with the room and with your own auric field. Relax into feeling that quality of total feminine beingness in surrender and flow.

Just breathe, and let the transmission move through you. When she communicates, it is through transmitting energy states. Right now my Higher Self is beginning to interpret her energy transmissions into words. She says, "I am here to assist you into coming home to yourself, to help you learn to be at home with yourself, to just relax. Just simply become aware of the agendas that keep you from ever feeling deeply that relaxed state of at-homeness. My energy is that of simplicity, of letting go of the complexities of the mind that interfere with the simple naturalness of being. Returning to flow is very simple. It is simply being at home with yourself by letting it be simple."

Goddess Antares is inviting you to feel something that some people never feel in their entire lives. It has to do with being in a state of pure presence and feeling without any words in your mind defining that state. What does it mean to just be, with no mental interpretation? She is asking you to just let go of any need to have an interpretation of her energy, and to just experience it. She says that for some of you, the closest you can come to that experience is the final letting go into sleep.

Breathe in through your heart, gently and deeply, as if you were breathing in the sunlight on a warm day. Allow the energy to come into you the way sunlight does. If there are places in your body or your mind that are still holding on, see if you can just welcome that loving, simple, divine energy to penetrate that part of you until you can move into the purity of experience free of mental agendas. Often I get a pressure in my forehead from having trouble with letting go of my mind. If that happens for you, breathe into your forehead, or into your jaw or your back—any place where you feel you are still having difficulty letting go into just being. Breathe, and ask the Goddess Antares to send her love and her simple Divine Flow into that part of your body in need of assistance in letting go.

Stay in that place and continue to breathe.

As you hear the words to this song, let them become part of your breathing in divine simplicity of the flow of love and presence. Just keep breathing.

What will it take for you to know
That you are perfect, that you are whole?
What will it take for you to feel
That you are beautiful, and the love is real?
You are the One. You are the Glory.
The angels sing your special story.
You are the One. You are the Love.
The angels watch you from up above.

Against all odds, you choose to love.
Against all odds, you live in Truth.
Against all odds, you live in Peace.
You are the victory. You are the One.

What will it take for you to trust
You're not forgotten, and all is well?
What will it take for you to see
That God is everywhere, in you and me?
We are the One. We are the Glory.
The angels sing our special story.
We are the One. We are the Love.
The angels watch us from up above.
Against all odds, we choose to love.
Against all odds, we live in Truth.
Against all odds, we live in Peace.
We are the Victory. We are the One.
We are the Victory. We are the One.
We are the Victory. We are the One.

Take a few nice deep breaths, letting them be gentle, just like the kind of breaths you would take while lying on a meadow hillside on a summer's day with a gentle breeze blowing over you—just simple, deep breaths of welcoming receptivity to the life force in the air, and to love. Continue with the kind of deep breath that is inspired by the joy and comfort of feeling your own breath.

As the Goddess Antares begins to lift from the room and from the blending, continue feeling your own energy. Breathe in a manner that allows you to be in a more intimate connection to whatever you are doing in your life. Few people experience life in an intimate, present way. Choose to affirm your intention to bring that quality of intimate presence to yourself, to your activities, and to other people.

See if you can just take a full deep breath through the length of your body and simply feel it without any thoughts of doing it. See if you can be present and empty, and then breathe through your body from the standpoint of experiencing what this feels like.

I would like to thank the Goddess Antares for this loving gift of her presence and for the gentle reminders she has brought, helping us to remember what it really means to nurture ourselves.

Become aware that you are sitting on a chair or couch, and feel your body's contact points. With your feet on the floor, become aware of the room around you, gently opening your eyes and coming back to the room. Do not adjust yourself to the facade you normally show to others. Take a moment to allow yourself to remain in this state of beingness with your eyes open. Very slowly, look around the room without interpreting what you see. You are so beautiful right now. What would it feel like to let people see you in this simple deeper place? Maintaining this simple presence, close your eyes for just a moment and tune in inside. Without brainstorming about it, breathe into your heart, and feel what you want for yourself. From the deepest place in your heart of hearts, what do you want to give to yourself right now? What qualities do you want to become a part of your life? Just feel it without mental analysis. Make a pact with yourself, your Higher Self, and your guides to give this to yourself. Open your eyes.

I am feeling such a deep alignment with my own Goddess presence that I would like to speak to you from this state.

When the Goddess Antares began to cradle us in her energy, it was such a divine reminder that the greatest gift we can ever give is the gift of just being in the simplicity, in the flow, of our own beingness. When she was here in that capacity, she did not speak. She did not *try* to do anything at all. All she did was enfold the room in her energy and simply be herself.

In our lives as human beings we have succumbed to a planetary thought-form that we have to show our "okay-ness" through what we do. It is another of the symptoms of the repression and oppression of the divine feminine. More often than not, even in our giving, there is effort behind it. We try to be good people, doing what we think good people do. And it is not that we do not have love for others, within our giving. The love is there, but there is an extra little push. There is extra effort behind it so much of the time that we rarely—except in those exceptional relationships—get to experience just being our loving and beautiful selves, simply flowing in love and beauty. Rarely do we allow others to share love with us fully and simply by just being it. The push to do, the push to accomplish, the push to give, the push to say the right thing, the push to prove that we are okay, the push to prove that we know, the push to show that we are intelligent, gets in the way and diminishes our availability for giving and receiving in a fully satisfying way. Seldom do many individuals have that experience of simplicity, free of agendas, that brings deep peace. That peace is like a deep well that is never dry, and it can be experienced only when our doing flows in simplicity from our beingness.

The divine feminine aspect of men and women alike was told several thousand years ago on this Earth: "You are not wanted any more." So humans gradually lost their connection to their divine feminine selves and to the Mother Goddess. Men need that feminine aspect within themselves, as well as women. And it does not mean that females need to be receptive and passive all the time to be real women.

In accepting the task of finding peace and finding home, how can we accept the task without trying to achieve it? This is the challenge of spirit at this time. How can I accept the task without attempting it effortfully? How can I accept any task without trying and efforting and struggling? How can I accept it from an attitude of giving myself gentle reminders, when the flow is not there, to let go and return to flow? How can I feel safe to remind myself without undue concern about what others will think? Will others think I am thinking I am better than they are? Will they think that I am being airy-fairy? What would it take to let go of caring what they think, and to know that being yourself is the greatest gift—not only to you but to existence in general?

There are times on the path when no one can really give you an answer. All anyone can do is ask the right questions and let you find the answers for yourself. Years ago, while I was receiving a healing, one of my guides came through and said, "This man [meaning the man doing the healing session on me] is a real Jesus man." And I asked, "What is a real Jesus man?" She replied, "A real Jesus man is one who digs deep inside to find the best parts of himself and bring them out to share with others. He doesn't go digging around, wallowing in the dirt trying to find the crap." I believe there is a message in that for us at this time. If we could devote our spiritual paths to the gentle search for the discovery of our beauty and our goodness, then all the pain and emotions that need to be cleared would naturally come out for clearing as we move deeper into that place of being at home with ourselves. We do not have to meticulously search out the sources of our pain and shut down. Some of you have become obsessive about looking for what is wrong in yourself and others. All you need to do is to be the best that you can be, regularly bring Higher Self into your body, and have the courage to show your beauty and Divine Truth to others. Either the rest will simply dissolve in that love and that Divine Presence, or it will come out for healing and transformation. You will not have to look for it. You will not have to push and try so hard. It will just be a natural part of the process. What would it mean to trust your own process that much? What would it mean for all of us to trust our own process that much? Are we ready to let go of being in process and just be? How have we used being in process for some erroneous payoff that is not really a payoff at all? Let us not analyze to find the answers to these questions. Let us just observe ourselves and allow the answers to surface through our life experience and through our willingness to just be present and witness ourselves.

How can we find the answers by allowing instead of actively doing? Let us just allow those questions to be a gentle undercurrent in the background that we do not have to work to answer. Trust that the questions will be there in the right moments when we need to remember to ask ourselves, "How can I be more real right now?" Let it be step-by-step. And when the question arises, just take a deep sighing breath, and without trying to figure out the answer, just feel it and affirm a new choice. If it will not shift through your breath and consciousness, then there are plenty of processes or healers to assist when they are really needed.

You might wonder, "How can I find what I really am and just let that be in this moment without making it another project to process through?" I know that someplace inside you, you understand how, because understanding is in the feeling that is there now. The understanding is in the feeling, in the wisdom of your heart. And it is not that the wisdom of the mind does not have value. Indeed it does; and yet, it must be balanced with the wisdom of your heart.

The end of the Lemurian era was brought about by humans becoming addicted to physical sensation removed from the heart. The Lemurians were very loving, very sensual, very sexual, and very connected to the spiritual and Earth kingdoms. But there was a tainting of energy that transpired over time through the substitution of addiction to sensation for presence and sacredness. Magnetized by that disruption in the Divine Flow, an invasion of controlling beings occurred. These invaders convinced the Lemurians that they were inferior because they were so feeling natured and not mental enough. Of course, this was a distortion of the real problem. At that point, an imprint came into our planet's collective consciousness. This imprint convinced the Lemurians that they/we had to learn more technologically and to control our feminine side, our feeling nature. Therefore, the transition from Lemuria to Atlantis was corrupted by the belief that the mind is superior to the heart, male polarity superior to female polarity. The truth is that neither is superior to the other, and healthy polarity is needed for Divine Flow. Both male and female aspects of self and of our world need to be functioning fully and in balance for the whole being, and for a healthy culture, to exist. When we believe that an individual who displays intelligence and technological understanding is superior to the person who can sit in a field and gaze at single flower for an hour, we are badly mistaken.

The fall of Lemuria and the beginning of Atlantis, therefore, came from that patriarchal, mentally polarized standard of excellence. And the subsequent fall of Atlantis came from the extreme exaggeration of that patriarchal ego hunger for power and control. Please do not misconstrue that I am saying the matriarchy is superior to the patriarchy. At the point of the invasion, the feminine side had become addiction motivated and was quickly losing the heart and spirit connection that had formerly been so key to the sacred tantric practice. The male and female initiates who had previously learned the balance of the mental and the intuitive feeling natures, the balance of sacred maleness and sacred femaleness, had become nearly extinct. Addictive patterns were destroying the spiritual nature of both men and women before the invasion.

Now we are in the time in which we need to find the balance and healing of our Lemurian and Atlantean past lives and planetary heritage. Within ourselves there is a great yearning to find home: that inner sanctuary in which our intelligence and capability flow from being present and empty. Our feminine being nature can exist only in the safety of surrender when it is balanced by benevolent masculine Divine Will in action. Even in this understanding, we need not figure it out. We just need to recognize that there is an imprint in our Earth civilizations that has to do with the belief in the superiority of the mind over the heart and emotional body. The planetary mind still wants to override the heart and the purity and innocence of the being nature. So let us simply hold, in the background of our intention, the willingness and desire to allow ourselves to be like children who explore all the possibilities without harm to ourselves or others. Children look at everything in life with awe and wonder. They still have the presence of beingness to watch a bee flit from flower to flower for hours. And from that innocent presence, "Ah-ha!" happens, and they can create elaborate stories or creative projects with their inspiration of heart combined with mental understanding and intelligence. Perhaps we could simply choose to rebirth that childlike part of ourselves and remember how to be innocent, unselfconscious, and spontaneous with nothing to prove or solve. Okay?

15

The Nature of Divine Love
A Channeling from the Elohim of Divine Love, February 2000

When this channeling took place, during an intensive training in February 2000, several members of the Dolphin Star Temple Higher Council had made their presence known and were anchoring a specific etheric temple space for connection to the Great Central Sun. They then put the group into a Divine Love Chamber of Light within this temple matrix. In order for you to receive the maximum effect of this channeling, I will guide you through a similar process at this time.

1. Ground and adjust your aura to two to three feet around your body in every direction.

2. Call in your Higher Self to fill your Tube of Light with your own Higher Self energy.

3. Invoke the Dolphin Star Temple Higher Council of Light, especially the Goddess Hathor, the Elohim of Divine Love, and the guardians of the Great Central Sun Temple of Divine Love.

4. Ask these Light Beings, "Anchor around and through this room the crystalline Pillars of Light, and the sacred geometry, of the Great Central Sun Temple of Divine Love. I want to experience the Source and fullness of Divine Love now."

5. Ask the Pleiadian, Sirian, and Andromedan Emissaries of Light to anchor above your aura, and above the temple space, the Interdimensional, the Evolutionary, and the Intergalactic Cones of Light. Below the temple space and below your aura, ask for the Earth Cone of Light, anchoring your grounding to the Christ consciousness at the Earth Star Crystal at Earth's core.

Elohim of Divine Love: Divine Sources of Light upon this Earth, the longing for love is probably the greatest longing of all beings—until that longing is satisfied, of course. Especially for those who are existing in the fifth dimension and below, it is especially important to be aware that to satisfy your longing for Divine Love—which is in the long run the only love that can ever satisfy, the only love that can ever bring lasting peace—you must be ready in every moment, and in every situation, to release attachment to outcome for yourself and others. Even in spiritual beings who are learning to shift negative behaviors and attitudes and become morally, and behaviorally, in integrity and divine alignment again, and even in those who are meditating and doing their spiritual work, the attachment to how things are appears still to be the greatest source of blockage to the sustaining of love. When you are attached to a person treating you a certain way, when you are attached to people seeing you in a certain way, and when you are attached to getting your way, the nature of attachment itself hooks you into a lower reality [as explained in the previous channeling by St. Germaine], to which you are then bound until the time comes in which that attachment is released. Often the things you long for, the things to which you are attached, and the circumstances that bind your hearts and souls, all in the name of love, while you continually wait for a result, are the greatest obstacles to the sustaining of love.

Love by its very nature simply flows and attaches to nothing. Even in filling yourself up with Divine Love, the very quality of love itself is that when it has filled you it will naturally overflow, for it moves through everything and it does not stick. So, to find that lasting peace and comfort and renewal that one finds in Divine Love, you must first find the state of surrender. For surrender is a receptive state of being, and one that simply allows flow to happen. From that state of surrender action can occur; but it is not action based on personality and ego

willfulness. It is action that is simply a natural overflowing from Divine
Love. Your presence and receptivity in surrender create the space for
your Divine Will to give birth to uncontrived action. When your actions are based on the desire to evoke a response or outcome from another person for your own benefit, you actually block your ability to
receive that which you hope to evoke.

To love for no reason, to give simply because you love, to be
present with your life and people because it is the nature of spirit—
these are the qualities that accompany Divine Love. We are not suggesting that you become passive and do not create your own reality.
We are not suggesting that you become so allowing that you do not
step up and act when it is appropriate. We are suggesting that in your
heart of hearts you accept responsibility for learning the difference
betwen loving and manipulating reality to obtain an outcome. And
no matter what logic you can apply to the manipulation, no matter
how beautiful or righteous it may seem, it will be the thing that stops
you from obtaining that which you seek. For true love honors the
freedom of all of its objects of affection and adoration. True love is
incapable of doing harm. True love is incapable of judging. True love
is incapable of even subtle manipulation. True love is given freely
with no expectation, with no manipulation of reality. It just flows because it exists to flow.

In your human need for survival, you have created many agendas
for yourselves and many thought patterns about the nature of reality.
You have created many limits for yourselves relative to how things
have to be before you will finally let go of the controls, and the holding back. We do not say these things to make you feel wrong. We say
these things to assist you in moving toward that goal of living in Divine Love all the time, unceasingly, for it is your destiny. To move toward that goal graciously, and in self-respect, you must let go of all of
the subtle manipulations of reality that you use to get attention, or
to mold circumstances into the way you think they should be. Let go
of your need to form opinions about other people's choices. It is a
waste of energy and a block to Divine Love.

As you observe people, observe in neutrality. Let your discerning
choices simply be a matter of compatibility of frequency. There is a
natural harmony between people that is determined by frequency of
consciousness and by level of availability to love. That compatibility of

love does not depend on agreeing with each other all the time. It does not depend on doing things in the same way. It is not concerned with one person being the manipulator and the other the yielder. True divine harmony is simply frequencies being drawn to one another that are compatible.

When you truly relinquish the need to believe that you know how someone has to be—when you truly relinquish all the walls you have created through your beliefs about what your life has to look like—when those walls come down, then the true Temple of Divine Love can be built, and it has no walls. When you are at rest in divine peace, self-respect, the knowing of your own beauty, and the fulfillment of your spirit's dreams, all these things will be a part of your natural flow. For you will have relinquished all the ways in which you manipulate reality and block yourselves from being in flow. Then the gifts of spirit can be given because you have simply knocked down the walls, allowed the ego to get out of the way, and simply said "Yes!" to love.

Become aware of those things to which you are attached, whether they be attitudes, ideas, people, situations, or outcomes. Even if it is a beautiful thing that you are moving toward, let go of the attachment and obsession with it. Let go of the need for someone to tell you how great you are. Let go of all of the subtle and gross manipulations to get your way. And take that empty-handed leap into the void that is spoken of in the spiritual cultures on Earth. That empty-handed leap into the void is the willingness to not have to know the outcome, to not know where you will land, to not know what will be there, to have no guarantees. Deep inside, you already know that holding on simply takes too much energy, too much consciousness, and too much time, and that it is time to let go. Fill that void with your own love, and all the rest that is meant to be yours will follow. Fill the empty spaces in you with love. Then those spaces that are overflowing with fear and attachment can be filled to overflowing with your own love. Then they will not be empty and scary places any more, and your neediness and desperation will disappear.

I know that you may not understand how to simply stop and do that now, 100 percent of the time. But we, the Elohim of Divine Love, bring the keys today, the keys for letting go of all attachment to outcome, all manipulation of reality to get what you want, or waiting for someone to make it up to you. As you release these old energies, the keys of the Divine Heart begin to turn and to open doors that have been closed for a long time. Then the Divine Flow of Love is the only true source of lasting healing, the only true source of lasting respect and peace.

As you return to your childlikeness, your inner child feels its beauty. It is in love with all of existence. It feels loved all the time. The child is in the Divine Flow unless it has been harmed. Many of you, in attempting to return to your Divine Child, at times become childish. Your identity becomes locked in being the damaged child instead of in loving it and healing it. It is only that blend that has been addressed to this group that creates the matrix of mastery: that blend of the mature spirit, living in impeccability and rightness, blended with the magic of the child. This matrix allows you the potential to return to Divine Love. So, in working with that child self, let go of the manipulations of the damaged child as well. Be willing to simply let go.

I would like to share just a couple of more minutes of love with you. So I ask you to open to the flow of Divine Love, like beautiful rarefied rays of light, moving through every cell of your body, every part of your consciousness. Allow yourself to let this love flow through you. Know, dear ones, that you are most loved and cherished. Within the words that are shared, the intention is to assist you in understanding that as you let go of the need to have your own way, the rewards are much greater than you could ever create for yourself through manipulation and through the strength of your opinions of how it should be. As you fulfill your destinies of returning to Divine Love, know that the source of love within yourself, within one another, from Divine Source, and from all of us who love you, is eternal. Just as you are asked to take the empty-handed leap into the void, know that beyond the void is infinite supply. *Know that beyond the void is infinite supply. Know that beyond the void is infinite supply.* Thank you for hearing us. We end this communication in deep gratitude, respect, and endless Divine Love.

16

The Nature of Victory
A Channeling from Ra, August 1999

*R**a:** Victory is in your hearts, dear ones. It is not in any single lifetime or brief experience; and yet each lifetime and each experience is perfect in its own way. And all your lifetimes put together are a great victory. They are a great Victory in that your learning is complete when viewed from the broader perspective of all of your lives. In your future, within the time/space continuum, you will see that you have completed everything. You have returned to Source, and nothing can stop that. But failure, in your consciousness, is when you believe that your faith must prove itself within a given period of time. We understand that when you are in a body, what happens in your lifetime seems like a full cycle. Whereas, when you are not in your body, as we are not, your lifetime is more like the movement of a clock, as the minutes move from five after five to ten after five. And another lifetime may be the equivalent of half a minute as the clock turns. It is only when your lifetimes are all put together that the real story is told. We understand that in your human perspective, your lifetime feels like all there is. But it is this belief that causes you unnecessary pain and attachment. Because there have been falls of great civilizations, most of you believe that this will continue to happen. The belief is that somehow, all your faith, and all your service, and all your hope, were to no avail. This is a misunderstanding that is deeply embedded in the psyche of human culture. For many, this belief is why you often stop short of completing goals or refuse to really "go for it," lest you fail.

There have been many, many cycles and karmic patterns acted out on this Earth. You are given periods on Earth to gain strength and experience peace, greater love, and security. But you worry most of your lifetime that it will be taken away. And when your culture has been overcome by those in darkness in past times, you believed that you failed. And you believed that the Light and all the Light Beings had failed you. You believed that your ancestors, who came from the stars to establish this great system, led you on a path of false hope. And yet the total story is still to be revealed. You see, these periods in which sacred law was the law, and most of Earth was living in harmony, were times when certain karmic patterns were withheld. It is as if these painful and challenging karmas slept. When enough Light and strength were built, so that you would have the potential to break through these karmic challenges to the other side, and you built, in that lifetime, the strength that it would take for you to awaken in your next life, then you awakened at the right time and developed great strength and spiritual experience. Then the withheld karmic patterns were slowly released into your psyche and into your world at large, to be experienced and, hopefully, transcended. And even though it may have appeared during the times of challenge, struggle, corruption, and overthrow that all was lost, the strengths and spiritual attainments you achieved during those times have never been lost.

It is time for you to lift the veils from your own psyches—the veils of disillusionment, the veils that see life as a failure—and recognize the victory of spirit. We are not uncaring when something that seems to be in the Divine Plan falls through. We understand that, for those of you who have been working on the human side of this Plan, it has left a great hole inside your soul. And yet it need not. *It is your attachment to outcome, within a visible time frame, that limits your ability to see the overall Divine Plan.* For is it not a miracle that in the most technological age that has existed on this planet in a great long time—a time when your human family is most robotic—is it not a miracle that billions of people around the world are awakening anyway? Is it not a miracle of the Light that in this environment in which there is literally not a place on Earth to be found without some pollution in the planet, the air, the water—is it not a miracle that there are those, like you, around this Earth who are gathering, still determined to find Truth, still determined to be the best they can be? This is the Victory! It is the Victory of the determined soul. It is the Victory of the human spirit who refuses to accept limitations even after many lifetimes when it has seemed imminent. You are refusing to settle for less.

If your world were to end in this moment, that Victory would remain untainted. This is how it is seen from another level. From your perspective, if Earth were to be blown up at this moment, some of you would be devastated. You might feel as though you had failed and all was hopeless. But you could choose to see it as a Victory of the human spirits who chose to hold to the Light and to the search for Truth and Love, even in the face of total chaos. And by holding to the Light in that time, you would be able to assist thousands of others in not anchoring the lower astral, fear-based, and hopelessness-based reality, because you refused to do so, because you chose wisely. This is the Victory. Do you not see that even in the face of what humans see as disaster, you hold fast to Truth and Love? Do you not see that when you come into a body after a lifetime or many lifetimes of persecution and pain, or even your own corruption—and you still have the courage, even with the genetics you have anchored, to seek the Light against all odds, to seek Truth, to Love (even when it is not popular with your families, your neighbors, your bosses, and your teachers)—this is the Victory of human spirit? Each moment you show that kind of determination, each moment you refuse to give up against all odds—that is the Victory, regardless of the outcome. And it is your own attachment to the outcome that blocks you from feeling and seeing this miraculous Victory.

So we now invite you to take a different view: to see with the eyes of the Holy Spirit and to recognize the Truth and the Divine Power that you anchor on Earth, regardless of whether you change the world and live to see an Age of Light, or total destruction occurs. We also know that you won't stop giving it your best until All That Is is returned to Truth and harmony of Oneness—and that has a different feeling, and way of manifesting, in every aspect of existence. And that is the Victory. We invite you to free yourselves by letting go of your attachments and your ego-identification with past results. Choose to see the Victory within your own heart, within your own life: that against all odds, you have chosen Mastery, Truth, and Love.

We celebrate you constantly. We celebrate your lives constantly. We have so much admiration for you. Because, as you know, some of us occasionally choose to create our own lives, we know the challenges you face. And we also know the Victory of not forgetting in a world that forgot. If you were the only person left on Earth who believed that there is a greater Truth, that would still be a Victory of your spirit—that against great odds you still awoke to that understanding. It is all a matter of perspective, is it not?

We are so happy to commune with you. It gives us such great pleasure, because we fully understand that you are the courageous ones. Our job is easy compared with yours, and we know that. Yet, we invite you to remember how to make yours a little easier, simply by being willing to shift your perspective a little. God bless you and keep you always in the Light of Love. So-la-re-en-lo, Ra, of the Pleiadian Archangelic Tribes of Light.

17

Victory of Living in Divine Truth

A Channeling from Ptah, August 1999

This channeling came in August 1999, immediately after the Ra channeling on Victory, as a continuation of Ra's teachings.

Ptah: Picture a pyramid in the center of the room. It may look different for each of you. Focus on that pyramid, and ask that the pyramid reflect your current perspective on the issue of spiritual failure and success. You will know that if the pyramid is glowing, it is a symbol that you hold great belief in spiritual Victory and success. If the pyramid is missing some blocks, or looks damaged in any way, then you know you are in need of healing your perspective in order to release old illusions of failure and/or hopelessness, and lost faith. We ask you to use this symbol to represent this issue of success and failure, of which Ra has spoken. You are going to do a healing on this pyramid to remove all the stains of your limiting beliefs in failure. Then you can build your pyramid of Light again. Even though it is a symbol, if you hold clear intention of releasing all of your pain and limitation associated with your belief in failure and hopelessness, healing the symbol will help you begin healing the issue.

At this point, Ptah had the group for whom this channeling was done silently do a healing on this issue. I will include a brief instruction to assist you in doing the same:

Guided Process for Healing
Your Relationship to Victory 🔲

1. Close your eyes and imagine a movie screen just in front of you with a grounding cord going just into Earth like roots.

2. Place the image of a pyramid on your screen.

3. Ask your Higher Self of the Light and the Pleiadian Archangel Ptah to assist in this process. Ask them to alter the image on your screen to reflect your current belief structure and karma relative to success and failure.

4. Envision golden sunlight streaming into your crown chakra, down your arms, and out through your hands. Place your hands on the screen, and fill and surround the pyramid with as much golden light as it will hold.

5. Then stop and look at your pyramid. If there are areas or spots that appear black with pain, place your hands on each side of the image and ask the Pleiadian Emissaries of Light to place an Erasure Chamber in your hands around the entire pyramid and erase this black pain. When it is done, the black will be gone and the Erasure Chamber will be taken away.

6. Next, notice whether any stones are missing, chipped, or cracked anywhere on your pyramid. If so, you may repair and replace these blocks in a couple of ways. The first way is to place your hands around the image and ask the Pleiadian and Sirian Emissaries to create a Ki-Quantum Transfiguration Grid in your hands, around and through the pyramid. Visualize or imagine this grid in the form of a cube.* Hold the grid in place until the pyramid looks whole again and the grid is removed. The optional method is to imagine yourself actually climbing up to the damaged or missing areas. Use mortar to fill in the cracks and to restructure missing fragments.

---

*For more information on the Ki-Quantum Transfiguration Grid see chapter 9 of *The Pleiadian Workbook: Awakening Your Divine Ka.*

Carry replacement stones, with your helpers, or use a crane to lift the stones and put them back into the empty spots and mortar them into place.

7. If there are still areas that look stained and discolored, use your own intuition or ask for guidance on what colors you need to run to transmute these stains and clean these areas. You might, for instance, run violet, green, or any other color of light or flame into the stained spots until they look bright and clear again.

8. If you still perceive any other problems, use your imagination and ask for help on how to correct it, all the while holding the intention to embrace your own sense of spiritual Victory.

9. When this work is complete, place your pyramid in a radiant golden Sun. Then imagine placing this golden Sun, with the pyramid inside, about a foot above your head. Ask that it work its way through your chakra system, stimulating any further clearing needed on this issue and giving you new reference points in the higher perspective of spiritual Victory of which Ra spoke. Then open your eyes and continue.

Ptah continues: Another source of pain for some of you is that when you go through hardship, you believe it is a sign that you have failed. Or perhaps you believe that you have been abandoned by your guides, or by God. I tell you now that it is you who have tested yourself through hardship. In your Bible is the story of Job. This story has been somewhat distorted, because the part was removed that explained that Job was so afraid of losing his faith in God, he chose that lifetime to test himself with every imaginable peril: loss of home, loss of health, agonizing physical pain. He chose to put himself through these challenges to see if he would come through it all believing in the Light of Truth. And he did. He had, in his own mind, failed to remain steadfast in other lives. And his guilt, shame, and distrust of himself were so great that he felt he could never trust himself again until he faced extremes of pain and held true to his faith. But you need not test yourself so vigorously. When you perceive yourself in any lifetime as having failed, whether it is because of an attitude or an actual action, you tend to give yourself another lifetime to face that problem even more vigorously, to challenge yourself to succeed by transcending the karmic pattern this time. And this is allowable within the laws of karma. But you need not test yourselves with so much pain. Once you know that nothing can stop you from returning to, or remaining in, the Light of your own presence and of Divine Source, the need for these tests will be done. Once you know that you can trust yourself fully not to give up faith and give up acting from integrity because of illness, then you can stop testing yourself in that way. When you realize that you will not give up on Love and Light because of disappointment, you will not have to create situations that bring about disappointment.

On a very deep level, how much—and even whether or not—you test yourself is your choice. It is a choice made at times by a part of you that feels that you are a disappointment to God. This is what I will be working with you to release now. I am Ptah: the one who anchors, cherishes, and protects the essence and the Source of all life. And I tell you it is only your belief in failure and disappointment that has made you test yourselves to the extremes that you have done. Once you have transcended the potential to repeat a negative pattern through a couple of successful attempts, it is enough. Choose to accept your Victory of transcendence. And it is not a failure that you have tested yourselves in this excessive way, for if you needed to explore all those realms of possibility to find out if there was any place where Truth could hide, then you needed to explore in order to know. And it is time now for you to simply remember that it is a choice. It is your choice. It is not virtuous to needlessly suffer or to be a martyr by withholding from yourself that which you need and want. In fact, even subtle self-abuse and martyrdom are karmic patterns that must eventually be transcended before you move to higher levels of initiation and mastery. Keep focusing on Light. Find the best in yourself, and share it with others. You will accomplish much more this way than through overtesting yourself and searching for what is wrong with yourself continually. *Overprocessing can be just as great a deterrent on the spiritual path as laziness.*

There was a pause at this time before we moved on to the next phase of the channeling. A little of the original channeling was lost, but I asked Ptah to assist in restructuring it. The first couple of sentences are the new version of the original few sentences that were lost.

Ptah continues: When you realize that something you did or did not do in the past was out of integrity, or at the least not your highest option, then do not misuse your energy by feeling guilty and ashamed. The fact that you now have a higher understanding, and would not make that choice again, is the Victory of transcending your own karmic pattern. And when you know that you will never repeat the old karmic pattern, whether it is as simple as being insensitive to someone or extends to killing someone, the karma is done unless you impose penance on yourself. When it is done, then you know you can deal with it with integrity, and you can use that knowing to heal the past. When you heal the past, you simply apply present higher understanding to past situations. You can go into a meditation or a quiet, centered space and imagine redoing, or reframing, the past situation, applying your present transcendental understanding and integrity. And every time you have a moment of Truth, you can send it back through time to the first time you misunderstood and/or behaved out of integrity. You can send this message to yourself in the past: "Hey, guess what? God isn't disappointed in you at all. It was just you that was disappointed in, and judged, yourself. And that was a misunderstanding, so you can relax now. All is forgivable and forgiven by God, and by me. So let it go." And because it was you in the past, and you now, you release certain dense energy ties that bind when you release the past in these ways. It is as if you give yourself a new past-life or current-life reference point in your psyche of the newly healed, forgiven, and changed version of the past you created with your reframing and communication.

Question from a student: This is a powerful lesson about the existence of evil in the world. But about learning to forgive—how can we learn to forgive unless someone does something to us that is harmful?

Ptah replies: It is true that someone, or you yourself, has to abuse you or victimize you for you to anchor the spiritual power and understanding of forgiveness. But we are not suggesting that you need to go out and be victimized in order to forgive. These seemingly abusive events have naturally occurred in your lifetimes as part of your learning and growing. And there is a deeper level on which you might realize that the person who appears to harm you is serving the Light by being willing to play that role that you have magnetized to you for whatever reason. Remember what was said in class yesterday about

Gandhi loving the man who was beating him. He had gained spiritual Victory. He had attained it in that moment.

Student: I want to liberate myself from the concept that I must suffer in order to grow.

Ptah replies: This is good. We also want you to transcend this need. If you need to repeat something to make sure that the law of magnetism does not draw you into an old pattern that is less than your Truth, then it is a gift to give yourself that challenge. Because when you have totally defused the law of magnetism by seeing a new result in your life, then you can truly transcend any remaining insecurity and doubt about the issue by knowing you have left nothing behind unfinished. You will know that you left nothing behind to dread, because you went through that situation and did so in truth this time. But some people seem to need to challenge themselves many times on the same situation. And that is when it goes amok, because some people will put themselves in this predicament and then say, " I have always succumbed to this addiction" or "I have always succumbed to this fear, and I did it again." Then this individual finally receives an opportunity to try again, and the person has gained enough strength so that he or she doesn't do it this time. But maybe the human mind tricks itself into thinking, "That could have been a fluke. I had better do it again, just to make sure." So you create the right circumstances again. You break through it and don't make the mistake. You say, "Ah, it's so much better now! But I messed up so many times, how do I know that two times is enough?" So you do it to yourself again and again and again.

By the time you are finally ready to stop testing yourself, you are weary and do not experience the full weight of your Victory. It is more like tired relief, and even dregs of distrust in yourself. Why? Because you know, on some level, that the excessive testing and pain you have put yourself through in order to learn and grow was unnecessary. You know it was motivated by guilt, shame, lack of self-trust, and unwillingness to let go of the past. The dregs of self-distrust that remain, even when the karmic pattern has been healed, are a direct product of these reasons you overtested yourself and insisted on growing through more and more challenging and painful situations. This is unnecessary, because when you have transcended the pattern, and you know that, it is your responsibility not to believe in doubt anymore. When you know that the experience of transcending the lower pull has anchored something in you that will not allow you to lie to yourself and repeat that mistake, it is a spiritual responsibility to stop punishing yourself with repetition.

So, to give yourself a challenge can be a gift, if you need it for karmic completion. To give it many times is a dysfunction. We are glad that you pointed this out, because this is an important fine line.

While I am here, does anyone else have questions about this? I am glad to talk with you.

Question from a student: Sometimes life is really, really unfair. I mean all the evidence mounts up so it seems unfair. And I try to believe that it is all in the Divine Plan. But there has been so much suffering that it seems unfair, and I haven't been able to get over that.

Ptah replies: There was a time when a turning point was offered to the human race. What it would have taken at that time was for the people, a multitude of people, and for those of you who were priests and priestesses in the temples that were still holding the Light, to stand up and have the courage to reclaim your sovereignty from those corrupt leaders who seemed all-powerful. What happened on Atlantis, at that time, was this: The planetary human collective consciousness aligned in the belief that these leaders who were holding devastation and destruction in the palms of their hands were unapproachable. And the collective consciousness agreed that they would not do any good anyway; that those who rebelled would just be killed for nothing. Even the priests and priestess who carried the Light and teachings to other countries before the fall helped support the fall by yielding to this collective belief and supporting the decision to remain silent. They aligned with the collective consciousness and agreed that it would do no good—that the dark powers could not be stopped once they had gained momentum. They neglected to see that multitudes standing up for Truth and fairness would have brought about a spiritual Victory by refusing to succumb to dark power and intimidation, regardless of the outcome.

If you imagine the biggest tank in the world representing dark power and corruption, and many extremely small tanks representing all the "small, powerless citizens of Earth," and you put a thousand small tanks together in front of this one giant one, you would create a roadblock. You would say "No!" And though this giant tank would be many times over the size of any of the individual small ones, when you put them together collectively, they have power. There has yet to be a time, in the face of this kind of turning point you faced in Atlantis, in which we have learned how to impulse human consciousness to feel its power. This is because of the collective belief that "the dark is more powerful than the Light." We cannot, and will not, force your race to choose differently or to feel something you do not choose to feel. We can only offer it, and leave it up to you to receive our offering or decline it. The collective belief that "once the dark has momentum it is impossible to stop it" blocks many of you from receiving the Divine Grace that is offered. That belief is so great that it has stopped even high initiates from taking action, thinking that it is better to practice in secret than risk challenging dark authorities in power. We don't see this as a failing, but you do.

We see this long-standing pattern as a mystery yet to be solved: why those who are embodied in human flesh continue to believe the same thing over and over again when it keeps leading to an end that you would not choose and that brings so much pain and devastation. The human population has become quite ashamed of itself for not having enough faith and courage to join together and say "No!"

This karmic turning point is coming again, quicker than you might like to think. But we invite you to think—to really think—about your options. We are not talking about ego gibberish in the mind. We invite you to think. We are not talking about getting a bigger tank or more guns. There is a slogan that says "Think globally; act locally." There was a great celebration in the higher dimensions when this phrase was first coined. This is the first phrase that has the potential of getting the message across. "Think globally; act locally." What you can do together is great. Yet even your trust in one another is at times so slim that it is hard for you to put your energies together for a single purpose for more than a very short time. There is a point at which you must be willing to accept that a person truly wanting what is in the highest good is going to have to be enough for now. Even if you don't agree with each other on how to get there, you must stop judging one another's paths if you want to have hope of co-creating a better world. Stop comparing whether this Light system is better than that one. Look at the dedication and purpose behind that group or individual's life.

The other phrase that brings hope of healing this human dilemma is "unity in diversity." But "unity in diversity" can be achieved only when "Think globally; act locally" has been acted on in enough spots on the planet to create a matrix. Then that matrix will create an "ah-ha," and that "ah-ha" can trigger a whole new level of the people saying no to false power. No to pollution. No to the propaganda. No to governmental subliminal programming and mind control. What if thirteen major communities around this world, in different countries, all chose to disconnect their cable televisions and throw away their microwaves and computers, all at the same time? What impact could that have on Earth? What could happen if thirteen areas around this planet said no to being on the grid that is supporting subliminal programming and holding the human frequency at that level of subliminal fear? What do you think?

There are things that have gone too far on this planet. Things happened in World War II, for example, that went further than was part of the plan of the human collective consciousness. But what happens sometimes, when human consciousness gets on a roll, is that it makes a bigger avalanche than was expected. There was a false sense of power that German soldiers experienced when murdering innocent ones—even those soldiers who were terrified and ashamed at contributing to the deaths of all those Jewish people in World War II. There were times when those men, even through their tears, felt a rush of power as those souls left their bodies in fear. And they instantly learned how to use other people's fear and pain to create more dark power in themselves. Events snowball sometimes. Unfair and unpredictable? Sometimes, yes. The map of your life is created in the blueprint that you embody in your soul. But what you do when you travel the roads of that map is up to you. When collective consciousness takes on an energy, it can snowball for the greater good or for the greater devastation. And in the end, it is all part of the learning. The end product is learning that there is nothing in existence that can trap your consciousness beyond your ability to find yourself. And that is the actual goal. How it looks on the outside at times appears unfair. And yet the words that we spoke earlier, of Victory, transcend the belief in unfairness.

That is all we can say at this time, except that we invite you to think. And when you think, we invite you to welcome new thoughts that are beyond the limitations of your own beliefs of right or wrong. We are not talking about the ethics around whether you steal or lie or cheat or murder. These are obvious breaches of Divine Law. We are talking about right or wrong in the bigger picture. Many of you have labeled things in this world as right and wrong. It is time to remove those labels and see through unclouded eyes that there are billions of individuals who in every single moment of their lives are choosing. A roomful of you cannot change the destiny of billions of people, but enough roomfuls can. That is what we ask you to believe in. And remember not to measure success or failure by an outcome. This is an ancient issue, and it is not going to be resolved overnight. But we have invited you to think. This is what is needed: people who remember how to think. For you can righteously argue the same side of a point through eternity, but if it does not allow for higher understanding and change, what has holding that stance accomplished? If holding on keeps you in judgment, separation, and fear, what have you accomplished? Think about all sides of every issue, and then choose. It is a greater world you live in than you know.

Before I leave you, for now, let me propose a few questions worth giving thought to. When was the last time you spent twenty-four hours living 100 percent of your Truth? When was the last time each and every one of you spent twenty-four hours living 100 percent of your Truth?

What it will take to change what you call unfairness in this world is 144,000 people on this planet having the courage to do just that. That alone will create a quantum leap that will start the change in political systems, and in general. There is no unfairness on this Earth. There is only human consciousness choosing. The answer to your question is this: When you have at last chosen to live twenty-four hours in 100 percent Divine Truth, and the twenty-four hours after that, and the twenty-four hours after that, you will find yourself living in a benevolent world. Please do not hear this as a scolding. It is an invitation. There is a joy in finding a way to express these Truths to you that we know you can hear. Thank you for hearing. We invite you to think about that, also. In gratitude and respect, Ptah, an archangel of the Pleiadian Archangelic Tribes of Light.

Part 5

Divinity of Birth
and Reparenting

Your inner infant and inner child will always be a part of the matrix of your mastery. Restoring these aspects of self to their Divine Essence requires you, as a mature adult, to love those unhealed parts into the Light. In this section you will receive great understanding of how this works and loving assistance for achieving this goal. Remember to let it be real and loving. If you make it just a mental process, it will never go deep enough to work. Loving your inner child means loving every emotion and every reaction in life into healing through acceptance, love, and compassion. It is the stuff of which self-love is made.

18

Reclaiming Innocence

A Channeling of the Dolphins, Whales, and Intergalactic Federation of Light, Lake Titicaca, June 1997

olphin: We are very happy when we get a chance to speak to human beings, because not many of you listen very often. We are always here. We are always here making our sounds, saying, "Remember. Remember." We love to play with you, together again in the Light, as we have done before you were born into your bodies. There is not a person here, nor a person who will ever receive this message, who has not moved through our consciousness before coming to Earth. You see, before we became physical on your Earth, we were—and many of us still are—etheric spirits, your guides. Many of us exist etherically here in Lake Titicaca, as some of you witnessed today out on the lake. We jump and we try to get your attention. Sometimes you see us as a little sparkle of Light. Your head turns, and you ask whether something jumped out of the water. But you did not actually see anything jumping out of the water—it was us. At least we made some connection with some of you. Some of you did not realize what it was, but we are here.

We want you to remember, because before your souls entered your physical bodies, you played with us in the sacred etheric waters in Sirius. As you swam with us you purified your soul of everything from your past lives. You see, when you were born you came in with a blueprint of what is going to happen throughout this life, in terms of what you want to learn while you are here. But, you see, whether or not that blueprint unfolds depends totally on your choices, your consciousness, your free will, every step of the way. I tell you there is not a being born on this Earth who does not have the opportunity to become a Christed One in a single lifetime. Even though that blueprint includes the encodings of the karma that you have not yet completed, it also includes the map of consciousness that will allow you to transcend that karma in a single moment of willingness. It is that fast! We want you to think of how fast the snap of two fingers is. Did you know that every karma can be erased that quickly if you truly transcend the potential of repeating the negative karma? If you have been a rapist and murderer in another lifetime, and you have an "ah-ha!" experience during which your heart opens so wide that you could never harm another in any way, or if you choose to suddenly see that your sexual energy could assist another in awakening spiritually, and you choose in that moment never to use your sexuality in any other way again, all that karma would be erased. Most of you have transcended murder and rape and such intense karmas. Yet you still carry some smaller karmas.

Your life need not be so much struggle. We would like you to come and swim with us. When you know how to link through the dimensions, you can simply project yourself anywhere, anytime. You can bilocate and come and swim with us in Lake Titicaca. When you do it that way, you won't freeze to death. We know how shy you are of strong sensations. Though we think it is a little funny, because when you are Christed Ones, you will be able to swim with us physically in Lake Titicaca or in any waters on Earth. Extreme sensation of cold, or any other, will only assist you in bringing your spirit more deeply into your body. For when you cease to resist anything, you are the master of your creation. You are in dominion wherever you are. I tell you this is within reach now.

Just for a short time, because we know there are others who want to speak to you tonight, we ask you to imagine that your body is as limber, is as gentle, is as playful, is as erotic as ours. We are in a state of tantric ecstasy all the time. We will now bring in something called the Dolphin Wave Effect. This will help you feel energy moving through your body in the way it moves through us. If you want to feel this, let us know, and we will bring the Dolphin Wave Effect through your body. It will come up through the floor. You may find yourself wanting to move. The most natural way to move if your body needs to open more is in figure eights, or infinity symbols. If your knees feel tense, let them undulate in little figure eights until they feel open. If your pelvis is tight, as in so many humans who think you have to hide your sensuality, then just imagine doing little figure eights right in your groin a few times. Then let the Dolphin Waves move through your body. Little figure eights in your neck and shoulders can help you let go, because figure eights are the nature of your natural, unrestrained body flow. Breathe, and let the Dolphin Wave Effect move through your body. You do not need to be shy. You can make a sound if you want. You can even imitate us, and if you do a bad job, we won't have our feelings hurt. We'll just laugh.

As you feel the wave effect come up and through your body, imagine that you are deep beneath the waters of Lake Titicaca and that we are swimming all around you. Unlike the physical dolphins, we are white: white with golden and silver sparkles. We are like the ascended realm of the dolphins, just as Jesus and other Ascended Masters are of the ascended realms of the humans.

We like it when you get playful. You can tickle us if you want. We are going to take you right to the center of Lake Titicaca now. We want you to swim through a beam of light with us. Feel and imagine what it would be like if every moment of your life you had that kind of ecstasy flowing through your body. When you have lost all of your sexual inhibitions and shyness, and when your heart has become so pure that you cannot imagine making love in a way other than giving and playing, discovering and revealing, then you can have this feeling most of the time. We understand that you humans still display erratic patterns of behavior and moods, even in the highest of you. But it will rarely cease to be ecstatic when you have reached that level of surrender and awakening.

Now the others who wish to speak are telling us that we have to move along. We ask you now to feel your human feet upon the floor, your human spine limber and straight. We will stay around you. We will just recede a little.

Amorah: Invite the whale spirits to commune with you. You will feel as if you are inside the body of a whale. We ask that as the sounds come, you let them come out of you. Feel yourself in the heart and mind of the whale. There is a Temple of the Whales beneath Lake Titicaca.

Whale: I speak to you from the voice of the Father Whale. There is actually a trinity of us, for I have a partner and a child. We hold the sacred memories of how to link through the dimensions. We hold the sacred memories from every human on Earth who has ever been able to materialize and dematerialize his or her body at will. We hold the memories of your forgetting and your remembering, from your past and your future.

Our bloodstreams are like the Tree of Life. The DNA of the whales on Earth is like the smallest particle of consciousness of the Holy Mother and Holy Father. Our sounds impulse you to remember your connection to each other. Our sounds impulse you to remember your connection to Earth, to the other planets in this system, to the Sun, stars, Moon. Our child invites you to remember that you were created in sacredness, that you grow in the love of the Holy Mother and Holy Father, that you are the seeds of life, that your body is the Tree of Life. Every great potential is within you. We impulse you to remember not only your past but your future. It is time now on Earth to align with your highest potential destiny. We ask you in the next few weeks in your meditations, and in your life, that you sincerely contemplate what you want to be on this Earth. What is the highest accomplishment you want to make in this lifetime in your relationships to people, your relationships to the planet, your relationship with yourself, and your spiritual attainment? We ask you to pray. We ask you to call on us to help you remember.

As you contemplate your potential in each one of these aspects of life, we ask you to do one more thing. This is the thing that spiritual people on Earth most tend to bypass. If you have a vision of what you want to become spiritually in this lifetime, and it is a Christed One, then we ask you to sincerely and deeply contemplate how a Christed One would behave in every situation. How does a Christed One feel?

We ask you to begin living that way. If you have a tendency to project your anger and blame onto another, we ask you not to feel ashamed of that tendency. And we ask you not to act upon it—because a Christed One would not do so. A Christed One would remove himself or herself from the situation. As Christ went into the desert to purify himself and pray and understand, you may need to go to your bedroom, or on a walk, and move through that anger until you can understand it. Ask for help so you will not use it to harm another.

If you have a pornographic tendency, a Christed One would not indulge that tendency, or deny it. A Christed One would pray for help and act from a sacred place while bringing understanding and forgiveness to himself or herself.

If you have a goal of creating more intimacy in your friendships, then we ask you to take some time to look deeply at how you need to change in order to create that. Do not think about how to change the people in your life. Most humans still have a tendency to think, "I just cannot get closer to that person. She is just not available." Perhaps it is time to change your own limited thoughts. If you truly change your own behavior, and you begin to act in the way you would like to be in that relationship, and that person of his or her own free will does not meet your desire requirement, then your responsibility is to love and honor that person's free will. Pray for friends in your life who can share at your level, and never blame those who cannot.

We ask you to apply this principle in every area in which you want your life to change and be better in some way. The way to identify what you want is to imagine what it would feel like to be you in that situation. Then acknowledge how you need to change your own thoughts, your own use of your emotions, your own behaviors, in order to accomplish this. We declare that it will happen. It is only when you attach your expectations to a single person, only when you expect that person to change to meet your requirements, that you do what you perceive as failing. That is when your own tools of creation appear not to work. In reaction, you stop trying to use your creative ability and become lazy sometimes. We do not say this out of judgment. We say this so you can understand your nature. Some of you have gone further with this than others. We tell you: If you are in a situation in which you are dissatisfied, or you are still acting like a victim, begin to practice being in dominion in your life. Have the courage to speak and act in whatever way you need to in order to step into that dominion. No one can harm you if you are in your truth. If you are spending time with someone so as not to hurt the person's feelings, it is more honest and less harmful to that person for you to say, "This is not what I really want to do right now. Do not take it personally, but I am going somewhere else," or "No, I do not want you to be with me right now. I want to be alone, because that's what I need." If that person reacts, then you must simply see that the person's free-will choice is to react instead of understand. You can ask the person to have understanding and be at peace. But do not try to fix it for them or prove anything. Your responsibility is truthfulness, with benevolence, in every situation.

This is the way whales work together. When a whale clan comes together, you will sometimes see many of them swimming together. At other times only a couple swim together or one swims alone. The rest of the whale clan does not become upset when one separates itself and goes off for a while. We honor each other's free will. We honor each other's needs. We want our brothers and sisters to do what they need in each moment, because we care about each other. So if the person whom you choose to remove yourself from in a situation does not understand, then you must understand that this person has not come to a point at which his or her greatest desire is for you to be fulfilled. The person has not understood that and is still attached to what he or she wants. If someone leaves you, temporarily or permanently, your responsibility as a higher being of Light is to be grateful that the friend is living in his or her truth. You can heal the feeling of loss in yourself and choose to be glad that the person is meeting his or her needs honestly. *The greatest love is a love that wants for others what they want for themselves.*

We are happy to share this with you, and we feel that you have heard us well. We tell you: As you practice this simple process in your life your self-respect will blaze within you like the glowing light of the Sun on a clear day.

▣ Focus on the beam of light that moves through the center of your body, through what you call your Tube of Light, what we call your divine axis. Focus on that light flowing through the center of your soul. We speak to you now from the place of the collective voice of the Intergalactic Federation of Divine Light, Creation, Maintenance, and Nurturing of Life. That is our function. All of the Elohim, all of what you might call the Supreme Beings of every galaxy, every star system, and all the members of any higher council of any system are members of the Intergalactic Federation of Light. Our responsibilities are divided in this manner: We are the ones who hold the energy of the purity and innocence of original Creation. There are beings of the Intergalactic Federation who only hold that specific energy for all of the systems. We would like you to feel that part of the Intergalactic Federation at this time, because here, in Lake Titicaca, there is a direct link to all of us. We ask you now, within your hearts, within your minds, to welcome the members of the Intergalactic Federation of Light who hold the energy of purity and innocence of original Creation. We ask you to give us permission to come to you, to anchor in the room. We will begin to restore your memory. Some of you feel that you were created wrongly or in pain. There is nothing within Creation that was originally created outside innocence and purity.

Ask to go into your cellular and soul memory, and allow the impulsing from these sacred ones to reach you. Allow yourselves to remember first awakening to the understanding that you exist as an individuated consciousness within the heart and soul of the Holy Mother and Holy Father. It is a very loving experience to awaken feeling so warm and nurtured and wanted.

We wish to move the energy to the next level now. Have you remembered your first experience of confusion? Some of you are afraid to feel confusion. We want you to know that your very first experience of confusion was also born of purity and innocence. The first confusion in existence was when we asked, "How do we nurture the Creation?" It was natural to nurture it into existence in love. And yet, when each particle of Creation, each consciousness such as yourself, began to have your own responses to the Creators, the Creators had a momentary feeling of confusion. They had never nurtured Creation before. All was new. And it was a simple thought: "What do they need? How do we do it?" You know that confusion from your Creators, your Holy Mother and Holy Father. Allow yourselves to remember when your Holy Mother and Holy Father experienced this confusion. They looked at you and saw your beauty and loved you, and they knew that the way to nurture you was simply to love you and to learn from you. What a glorious moment it was—like a burst of Light in Creation, when the Creators thought, "We just have to watch and learn from them to know what they need." And joy spread. Allow that joy to be remembered, because everything that the Creators experienced, you have experienced. So feel the joy that came through the recognition that all they had to do was love you and learn from you.

Now allow yourself to remember the first moment when your Creators experienced overprotectiveness toward you. They saw you about to make a mistake. They saw you just about to experience something painful. It was so shocking to them to think about your being in pain that they overprotected you and rescued you. Within your consciousness was left a speck of curiosity about what would have happened if they had let you experience what you were about to experience on your own. You felt the sincerity of their love, a certain urgency in their protectiveness. Yet at the same time, you longed for the freedom to experience what you would have experienced. That was the first time a split occurred between you and Holy Mother and Holy Father. This split took place within your consciousness. Your desire to be in their warmth and nurturing, and your desire to have free will, created a paradox.

When the Holy Mother and Holy Father felt you and your confusion about whether to surrender to their nurturing and protection or whether to rebel and have your own experience, they felt confusion for the second time. All the Creators gathered together and held a council. They sincerely wanted to know what was the best way to care for the children: you. We came to the conclusion that we needed to allow you to make mistakes, as long as those mistakes did not go beyond a certain point. So we accepted the role of guardianship without interference. We made mistakes along the way. Sometimes we protected too quickly. Sometimes we held back too long. What we ask you to feel and know now is that every decision made was from innocence and purity, from a place of ignorance. We were learning for the first time how to care for Creation. We were novices, not the all-seeing, all-knowing ones that you thought us to be. Every decision was made out of love for you.

Open yourselves to feel where the feeling of betrayal by the Creators is trapped inside your body. We ask permission now to impulse you to feel within yourselves where you hold the energy of separation. Separation is created by the belief that your own Creators have harmed you, taken away your freedom, or in some way have done something that you perceived as wrong. We ask you now to give us permission to impulse you, so you know where you hold these feelings in your body, in your emotions. We believe that here, in Lake Titicaca, we can assist you in what could potentially be a final transformation of that energy into a memory that you were always loved and always cherished, and that the intent behind the decisions of the Creators was always made from innocence and purity—even when the decision might be perceived as incorrect. When experience is new, every consciousness learns through trial and error—even us.

Although you who are reading this are not at Lake Titicaca, your intention can call the same energy to you, wherever you are.

Whale: Open and feel your emotions and contraction regarding separation from the Creators, from God. Do not be afraid to feel it. With clear intention you can release it and free yourselves. Breathe. As you identify places in your body and emotions holding this old pain, anger, abandonment, betrayal, distrust, invite us to come and touch you in those places with the purity, innocence, and love of our intent. Ask us to touch you in those places, and as you feel our touch allow it to penetrate and dissolve your misunderstanding. Take as long as you need to do this.

Affirm now: "I am willing to be touched by this energy of the innocence and purity of Creation. I am willing to be healed and end all belief in, or attachment to, separation." Some of you have been afraid that if you let the touch of the Creators in, you will be betrayed again. Please, for your own sake, release the illusion of betrayal. We ask you simply to affirm, if you know that is your issue: "I am willing to release my belief now that I was betrayed. I am willing to forgive, and release the belief that I was betrayed." Say it from your heart and solar plexus now, in a different way: "Sacred Mother and Father, I am willing to forgive you and myself for the blame I have placed on you. I ask you to help me release the thought of betrayal and the contraction of distrust that has kept us separate." Be compassionate with the part of yourself that is afraid to let go, and feel our touch. Do not allow these emotions and thoughts to rule you. You are being given an opportunity to surrender these old energies in grace. Tell that fearful part of you that it is safe to let go and receive our touch. We are still here to nurture Creation in innocence and purity while honoring your freedom to explore your own potential. When you have tired of exploration and choose to surrender into Oneness again, we will honor that choice as well, and welcome you.

Beloved ones, some of you are a breath away. You can feel yourselves stepping through the portals of Light now. We are going to open the Great Portal of Light. You will experience it as a doorway. On the other side of the doorway, you will see a great Light. Walk up the crystal steps to the doorway, but do not enter yet. This is the doorway of the separation from the Creators, from God/Goddess, from Oneness. Before you go through the doorway, look back as if you were looking back through your entire lifetime, every lifetime you have ever experienced, to that time when you were still a spark of Light within our consciousness, within the consciousness of Oneness. We ask you to feel gratitude for everything that has ever happened. Even those things you have perceived as wrong have made you strong. They have given you the experiences you desired to have outside of us. Thank them all. Let your heart fill with as much gratitude and forgiveness as you can, and when that feeling permeates your consciousness, then turn and walk through the door. The Creators will be there to greet you. Take your time.

When you are through the door, allow us to hold you like an infant in our arms and love you with the innocence and purity of our beings. When you step through the door into the Light, it is your will closing the door to separation. If those patterns of separation begin to arise in your life, all you need to do is look to see whether you have gone backward through the other side of the door, or whether you are still in the Light of Oneness. If you have gone back through the door, all you need to enter into Oneness again is to release all blame and misunderstanding. Forgive and feel gratitude for whatever experience has created separation again. The moment you feel gratitude, you can pass through the door into Oneness once again. In our hearts we pray you will dwell here forevermore, and yet we will not interfere with your unique process of learning, discovery, and choice.

We ask to leave around you a light of love, a light of Oneness—like a golden gossamer cocoon around your aura. This will allow the healing, nurturing, and Oneness with us to continue for a few hours. Maybe some of you came here tonight expecting a great esoteric tale or a mystery teaching. But we tell you, the greatest teaching of all is surrender to Oneness, forgiving the past, and blessing it with your gratitude. For when you do so, all the dimensional veils are lifted, and whatever you are ready for next can be given. It is only when you live outside this consciousness that anything is perceived as being held back from you. The degree to which you are willing to understand, forgive, feel gratitude, and surrender is the degree to which you will receive your next level of awakening, initiation, and glory on Earth— and beyond. The truth is this: Whether intergalactic or galactic, whether guardians of your local Sun or the deva of a simple flower, we all hold the same goal of restoration of Divine Trust and Oneness within all of Creation. With that we leave you. We ask you to sleep in the arms of Divine Love tonight. We are always ready to hold you when you say "Yes." Spirit of the Holy Mother, Spirit of the Holy Father, and Spirit of the Holy Child, we are One.

19

Alignment with Your Spiritual Mother and Father

A Transcript of a Teaching Given During a Dolphin Star Temple Training Program

This chapter contains a guided process for clearing your etheric umbilical cord to your physical mother. After birth, it is natural for a child to maintain an etheric umbilical cord with the mother until five to seven years of age. At that time, ideally the child will have learned how to ground on its own, and the soul connection should be fully made in the body. And in an ideal situation, the child will have been given enough love and soul essence validation to give it a sense of who it is, and it does not need the umbilical cord with the mother anymore. In many ancient cultures, age five to seven was also a time of a rite of passage. For example, in the ancient Greek culture, the child would braid grasses to make a rope and then go off on a hillside journey overnight with the maternal grandmother. At some point along the journey to their destination, the grandmother would talk about how it is time for the Earth Mother, the Goddess, to be the child's mother now. Grandmother would explain what the physical umbilical cord was, then what the etheric umbilical cord was, and that the child no longer needed it. Then the grandmother would have the child get out the rope she had made and hold it to her navel. She would tell the child, "Imagine that this rope is like the umbilical cord that is still connected to mother's navel and womb. It is time to remove it now. Pull it free. Now throw it as hard as you can over the mountainside. As the rope dissolves into the earth, you will develop a new etheric bond with the Goddess of Earth, who is part of the Mother Goddess of us all." Imagine having that understanding at age seven.

What happens in our culture today is that very few individuals have been fully nurtured by the bonding with mother. Therefore, when you have not learned how to ground fully, and your soul essence does not have a full connection in your body through love and validation—or when the mother is overpossessive—you end up maintaining the etheric umbilical cord far beyond its healthy purpose. Sometimes this old umbilical cord is dried up and may have little roots attached to it. You may need to visualize a warm, melted, violet, salve-like energy going in and softening the roots as you pull it out graciously. Once the old etheric umbilical cord is removed, even if your mother is not still living, you will visualize removing the other end from her navel. Then you will give the umbilical cord to your Higher Self. Your Higher Self will dissolve the energy and return your connection with your mother to one that is purely on a Higher Self level.

By the time you reach the age of twenty-one, you are intended to be the parent of your own inner child. At that point you are intended to have a spiritual connection with Holy Mother and Holy Father. Ideally, you no longer behave as a child of your mother and father; you behave as a child of God/ Goddess. So what we are doing is like a rite of passage more than a meditation. Before coming into any lifetime, every soul makes a contract with its future parents to be their child. You actually contract with them and ensure that they will fulfill their role in a certain way. You agree to fulfill your role in a certain way as well. Because all souls come into new lives anchoring the unfinished karmas from other lifetimes, you choose parents who will help you reanchor these karmas through reenactment and eventual healing. Therefore, you are going to be burning the contracts with your mother first, then your father, ending your contracts with them to serve as parents. That frees you and your parents as well from your karmic roles and unhealthy psychic ties. This is done from respect rather than from an attitude of "You're fired!" The correct attitude is one of thanking them for fulfilling the job that you originally signed on for them to do. You let them know that you do not need them to serve that purpose anymore, and then you burn the contract.

When you have completed with birth mother and father, you will call in your spirit mother and, later, spirit father. You will create a new bonding with your spirit mother, who then begins to assist you in healing mother wounds without your birth mother's having any responsibility for this process. With the father you will be removing a third chakra cord, giving it to Higher Self, and then bringing in a new spirit father. Of course, this does not mean that you cannot still have this person in your life in a chosen role. But psychically the old connection is ended in a parent/child sense.

Meditation for Clearing Mother and Father and Aligning with Spirit Mother and Spirit Father

1. Close your eyes and go into a meditative space. Breathe deeply until you can fill your entire body with breath and presence.

2. Check your grounding and replace your grounding cord if necessary. Make sure your aura is two to three feet around you in every direction, including beneath your feet.

3. Ask the Lords of Light of the Rainbow Flames to surround your aura with Rainbow Flames, balancing all energy bodies and creating a filter around your aura as a boundary protection.

4. Ask the Dolphin Star Temple Higher Council of Light to assist you now as you tune in to your umbilical area. Ask them to assist you in the release of any remaining umbilical connection, or old energies, from your physical mother.

5. Bring one of your physical hands, or both, to your navel area. Before you remove this umbilical cord, ask that your mother's spirit and your mother's guardian angel come and stand in front of you about six to eight feet away. Take a moment to tune in to her presence there. Address your mother by telling her that it is time for you to be fully responsible for your own inner child. It is time to relieve her of any responsibility for your life, including any responsibility for healing what she might have done in the past.

   a. Anything she did not give you that you would have liked, let her know that it is done now, that there is nothing else that you will ever require of her, and that she is free to fulfill her own path in her own way.

   b. Tell her you know that before you were born, you made a contract with her for you to be the child and her to be the mother, and that you know that she fulfilled the role that she was intended to fulfill.

c. Tell her that she is not being punished in any way, or blamed, in the releasing of this contract. It is time for your relationship to move to a new level.

d. Even if you still feel anger or blame toward her, tell her that you take responsibility for coming to a place of forgiveness and gratitude, even if you cannot fully do it now.

e. If you have forgiven, tell her "I forgive you" for anything that seemed inappropriate or wrong in any way, that you release her from any karmic hold you might have on her.

f. Thank her for doing the job that you contracted for her to do.

Imagine your contract as if it were a legal document. It is the contract for her to be your mother and all the details of what that entails. Rip it into pieces. Then ask the Lords of Light of the Rainbow Flames to create a huge bonfire, and burn the contract in the bonfire.

6. Pull the umbilical cord out of your navel area. If there are any roots or dryness, run some salvelike violet light into the area as you pull the cord out. Then hold that end of the umbilical cord in one of your hands and pull out the other end from your mother's navel. When it is completely removed, hand both ends of that cord to your Higher Self. Ask your Higher Self to assist in releasing all of the past energies, so that your connection with your mother is now on a Higher Self level only and free of the karmic ties. Send golden light to fill the hole left in her aura, then fill in the hole in your own aura and navel area. Ask your mother's guardian angel to take her wherever she needs to go.

7. Now call in the Holy Mother of All That Is. Ask Her to send you one of her divine female guides or representatives, whether an angel or an Ascended Master. Ask Her to send your divine spirit mother. When that being comes, ask her to hold your left hand. It may be a being you recognize, or it may not. When you feel the spiritual mother connection, ask her three times whether she is of the Light. If she says no, ask her to leave, and then send out another request commanding that only your spirit mother who is of the Light come forth.

8. Ask this being if she has a name. Listen.

9. She is going to place one hand on your heart, to make a heart and soul connection with you now. At the same time, ask her to give you a new umbilical cord of light so that you can maintain this spirit mother connection, and she can assist you in beginning to transmute any remaining issues you may have with your mother. As you call on your spirit mother source to assist you—not only in healing your mother wounds but in helping your inner child align with Holy Mother in a sacred and loving way—let yourself fill with the new light. Take a nice deep breath through the umbilical area up into the soul area in the center of your chest. Spirit mother is going to stand nearby as you move on.

10. Ask for your physical father's spirit to be brought in, along with his guardian angel. Ask that he stand about six to eight feet in front of you.

11. Tune in to your solar plexus area and feel or imagine the psychic cord between you and your physical father. Before you remove that connection, speak to him in the way you did with your mother. Let him know that before you were born, and before conception, you agreed to be his child. Tell him you are aware that you made a contract for him to fulfill the role that he has fulfilled, and therefore you release all attachment to holding on to any blame, or judgment, knowing that he simply did the job he agreed to do.

    a. Let him know that you forgive him for all mistakes and damage. If you cannot fully feel the forgiveness now, tell him that you take responsibility for coming to full forgiveness. His responsibility toward you as a child is done, because as an adult it is time for you to take care of your inner child and to connect to the Holy Father.

    b. Let him know that you are releasing any and all attachment to his needing to suffer or repay you for anything he has done. His karmic debts are done as far as you are concerned. He is free to pursue his path in his own way now.

    c. Thank him for doing the best he could and for being willing to take on the role of father. Rip the contract with your father into many pieces. Burn it in the rainbow bonfire.

12. Now remove the cord from your solar plexus. When you have re-moved your end, hold it, and remove his end. Remember—if it has roots or is tight, run some warm violet light salve energy into the area to help loosen it. When both ends are removed, give it to your Higher Self, asking your Higher Self to help dissolve all the energies of the past so that you are connected to him only on a Higher Self level. Now send your father a little beam of golden light to fill up that hole where his cord was, and fill up the space in your own aura with golden light, all the way into your chakra. Ask your father's guardian angel to take him wherever he needs to go now.

13. Call upon the Holy Father of All That Is. Ask Him to send one of his guides or representatives, whether an angel or an Ascended Master, to send your spirit father. Ask that this new spirit father come forth now and take your right hand. When you feel the con-nection, ask this being three times if he is of the Light. If he says no, ask him to leave. Ask that only your divine spirit father of the Light come.

14. When that connection is made, ask his name. Tell this beloved one that you would like him to assist you in healing any and all father wounds that remain, and that you would like him to assist you in maintaining connection to the Holy Father of All That Is. Take a little time with him to feel this new connection.

15. Ask your spirit mother and spirit father to hold hands with you in a circle. Allow the energy to flow between the three of you. Make a pact with them to assist you in restoring your inner child self to the magical child, full of innocence and brightness, purity, joy, creativ-ity, awe, and wonder. Ask them to help restore this inner child to remembering that it is a divine child. Ask them to help you release the past fully, letting them know that you are willing to let go of the physical mother and physical father and any and all issues re-lated to them. Know that as an adult you can connect to the Holy Mother and Holy Father, and to your spirit mother and father, di-rectly now.

16. Take a couple of minutes now in this alignment. There is a matrix of the trinity that has to do with the relationship between Holy Mother, Holy Father, and Christ child (you). Ask these two to work with you and with your guides to restore your sacred trinity

connection. As the energy flows into your left hand and up your arm, allow the energy to flow into your heart.

17. Knowing that these two are there at your beck and call, just release the hand contact now. Thank them for being willing to be your spiritual parents and guides. Take a nice deep breath into your whole body, feeling the connection of your feet to Earth. Ask the guardian beings of the Earth Star Crystal to send a little of that loving Earth Mother energy into your feet. Calling on the Sun, ask the Sun to send some of its golden sunlight carrying the love of the Holy Father. Bring it in through your crown. Allow these energies of the Earth Mother and the Sun Father to meet in your heart and blend. Breathe these two energies into your heart until it is full and overflowing.

18. Bring yourself fully back into the here and now, opening your eyes and returning to the room.

When you are doing inner child work, you can always call on this new spirit mother and father to assist. Some people like to create an image of a home in which the inner child lives with the spirit parents. There is an outdoor playground, and the child has its own room. The adult you can go there in meditation to visit. Of course, it is really a place in your own energy field. You may prefer to envision the child growing up in your own body, calling on the spirit mother and father each time you imagine going to visit. Whatever approach you take to inner child work, creating times for you and your inner child to restore that matrix of trust can be very important. You, as the physical parent, help the child learn to trust adults by never breaking promises and by showing genuine love and caring. When you need nurturing, when you need assistance with healing, call in your spirit parents. They can place their etheric hands on the child within your body consciousness and assist in your healing process. They can come and talk to the child. Basically, from now on it is up to you how you develop your own relationship with them; it will be unique. Sometime you might like to call them in and just ask them, "What is the best way for me to connect with you? What is the best way for me to make the best use of this connection with you?" I am sure you will receive what you need.

20

Mastery—A Matrix of Inner Child and Mature Adult

A Channeling from the Goddess Hathor, February 2000

Hathor: Beloved ones, the innocence, the sweetness, the goodness, the purity have never been lost to you. They were simply hidden from you for a while, for it is impossible to destroy the very nature of your being. Yet, wrapped in the cloak of this human form, it is easy to forget that what you experience here is just a fleeting experience. When you are born into a physical body you are in many ways at the mercy of those around you. For most of you, those who were around you were not healed and awake enough to be accountable. Yet, at some level, that injured child has tried to hold them accountable and has sworn never to open again until that accountability exists. There is a mixture of wisdom and a certain curse in that decision. When you are an infant, it may seem necessary at the time to learn how to protect yourself and maintain whatever sense of self you can. But the curse of it is that it does not end with infancy. It does not end with the period in your life in which physical dependency is a human truth. I call it a human truth because every human experience is relative. Every truth within your life is relative, a fleeting experience. It is not an absolute truth.

The love we have for you—not just myself, Hathor, but the love that all of us have for you, all the way back to Source—has never wavered for even a moment. In the early stages of life your physical dependency, your adaptation to human form, your process of relearning how to use a physical body again—all these things—take precedence. Yet, in those times, your spirit is more present than most people ever experience again in a whole lifetime. You are courageous ones. You are the ones who have said, "That is not good enough." You are the ones who are now saying to your own inner child, "It is time to come out of hiding, beloved one." And you—the adult who was chosen for the path of Light, awakening and healing, wholeness and mastery—you are the one who can consciously now say to that inner child, "It's okay, sweetie. I am here. I am grown up now. I can take care of you. And I know whom to share my vulnerability with, because I am old enough and experienced enough to be able to tell who is accountable and who is not. And to those who are not evolved enough or healed enough to be accountable, I choose not to entrust my vulnerability." And, beloved ones, there is another promise you need to make to that child. Your child-self really needs to know that it can trust you. You need to know that you are ready to love your inner child through its temper tantrums, through its joy and play and silliness. Of course, this is really self-love, because your inner child is really you: an aspect of your being.

In direct proportion to your inner child's ability to experience the freedom to be itself and to be innocent and spontaneous, to feel its own beauty again, to know that its worth is not always reflected in the people around it, you, the adult, can experience the heights of your mature soul and spirit and can attain spiritual awakening and mastery. If there are still threads of resentment at having had the pain in the first place, make a pact with your child-self to go beyond it. Make a pact with your Higher Self, with us, with your guides, and with each other to go beyond resentment and resistance that have made you refuse to take that great risk of fully opening your heart in innocence and vulnerability again. Because, dear ones, you are not ultimately that anger, that pain, or that insecurity. It was only a short period in your life when you experienced those emotions in reaction to unaccountable adults. It is up to you now to love that child and to help it feel safe by making discerning choices, by taking risks, and by knowing that there are no guarantees on the outcome. But also know that if you are sincere about giving it your best, the amount of help available to you is beyond your ability to conceive with thought.

Every moment of your life, every emotion, every experience—even those you perceive as trauma—is cherished by your own Higher Self and by us. It is time to remember how to allow the parts of you that experienced trauma in such a way as to still feel damaged—it is time for you to re-member how to endear those parts, how to cherish them, how to wel-come them with loving, open arms. For you are now the parent you have always longed for. It is up to you now, in your maturity, in your spiritual awakening, to be the parent to that vulnerable child. Do not think that just because you are older and more mature, because you are so spiritually attuned, there is no inner child to take care of—be-cause there is. That child's emotions, feelings, and expressions do not always correspond to your higher understanding, because they are the feelings of a child. Yet, as that child awakens into its own magical self through your cherishing and loving in every way, and as your inner child experiences feelings of safety and trust, it will become the great-est blessing in your life that you can imagine. That deep sensitivity; that deep, innocent, loving nature; those eyes of your infant self that penetrate everything and see the whole picture—these are still part of you awaiting your healing and rediscovery.

As you open to healing your emotional body, releasing in grace, those gifts of the child are returned in fullness. In truth, they will be even greater because the maturity and the learning you have at-tained along the way will be added to that innocence, depth, purity, and sweetness—to that all-seeing infant and the child aspects of your total beingness. That is what makes it safe to open. There is a special divine balance of which we speak. We ask you to recognize that when we speak of the balance between innocence and wisdom, we speak of the balance between the infant and the mature soul in a healed state. When we speak of the balance between purity and power, we speak of that Master Being in balance and harmony with the healed child in its purity. When we speak of the balance between sovereignty and obedience, we speak of the balance between the sov-ereignty of the mature soul and the obedience of the divine child. When we speak of the balance between Divine Will and surrender, we speak of the balance between the Divine Will of your inner

Christ, or Master Presence, and the surrender of the child in trust. This is an important part of the Matrix of Mastery and the Matrix of Divine Flow. It is up to you to give it to yourself now.

You cannot wait for the accountability of those around you. You must be accountable now to your child-self. You have to give that child something to believe in, because you, in truth, are all it has; and yet it has all of us as well. If your inner child does not have you to count on, it cannot access the rest of us. If your inner, magical child does not have you to count on, no matter how much love we give, it cannot receive it. Until you are there for yourself in that way—until that child can fall asleep in your arms and feel safe, and dream the dream of what it wishes for its life, knowing that it can come true—there is not an opening for us to get in very deeply, or very often, if at all.

As you become accountable and the child learns to trust you, and you balance your mature soul with the innocence of that little being, the love of the Holy Mother and Holy Father, the angels, and myself, Hathor, and all the other Beings of Lights will be there all the time. We will be as accessible as the air you breathe, the water you drink, and the food you eat—for you are fed from the Source all the time. Until you trust yourself, until that child sleeps in your arms peacefully, you can never receive the full benefit of it, however. So we welcome you to take what we have to give and to remember how to give to yourself. *Know that to avoid any part of yourself is to lock the child in a dark closet.* And when the child screams to get out, you just put in bigger earplugs in the form of distractions, addictions, outside blame, or whatever else you use to avoid feeling and being responsible for your own well-being. It is time to remove those earplugs and to hear that great little being inside. It is time to stop judging your child by judging your emotions. It is time to stop resenting your own inner child's existence because you still resent your parents and the damage they brought about. If you resent a single emotion or experience in your own life, it is like telling your child that you resent its existence. And until you cease resenting that child within because of its pain and coping mechanisms, it cannot heal and give you the balance that you seek. When you completely accept your inner child self, learn from all your life experiences, and forgive, then the Love from All That Is will flow through every cell of your body and every part of your consciousness unceasingly. And that for which you have longed will cease to be a desire, because it will be tangibly present.

"Be ye as little children." This is the greatest of wise counsels to those who are wise enough to hear it. We cherish you. The true lesson from the Holy Mother is about remembering how to mother yourself whether you are men or women. Then remembering how to father the self is the source of true peace. In the human world, almost every other peace is fleeting at best. We are with you now and always. Be with yourselves. For in loving you, the true mother knows that the greatest gift she can impart to her child is to teach the child its own value and beauty. Then the child will naturally love itself always. It is up to you to teach yourself that now and to ask for assistance along the way.

These are the words to a song, channeled previously from Mother Mary and Mary Magdalene together, that I was asked to share with the group at the end of the channeling:

> *Angels, Children of the Light,*
> *Awaken and remember who you are.*
> *Angels, Children of the Light,*
> *Awaken and remember who you are.*
> *Let me touch you and wipe the worry from your brow.*
> *Let me touch you that you remember now*
> *You are loved always, divinely perfect in my sight;*
> *Innocent, beautiful, you are God's delight.*
> *Angels, Children of the Light,*
> *Awaken and remember who you are.*
> *Angels, Children of the Light,*
> *Awaken and remember who you are.*

21

Healing Through Deep Sleep

A Channeling from Ra,
February 2000

Ra: Beloved ones, relax with your attitudes about how things are supposed to be, and you will find that the Divine Flow is hidden in the patterns of your life in a way you may not have realized. When you have ego agendas about what is right and wrong, you block that flow. For instance, many years ago, Amorah realized that she had been programmed that to sleep beyond a certain number of hours a night was shameful. Then she realized that even at times in her life when she allowed more sleep, she did not like to tell people about it because she was ashamed. So she worked at changing the beliefs. And when she gave herself more sleep, instead of feeling ashamed of it she began to say, "Good for me, I slept longer today." For a while it did not feel quite real, but now it does. Now when a friend tells her, "I slept until noon today," she spontaneously and sincerely says, "Good for you."

We want to address this issue specifically, about sleep and tiredness, because there is a cultural shame that is implied when an individual has the need for "too much sleep" or feels tired without having a "good reason." As a child, many of you used sleep as your only escape. When you went to bed at night, it was finally a time when you could let go and not feel hassled or afraid or not feel as if you had to put on the face that mother and father would approve of, or that would keep you out of trouble. But sleep is intended to come from an inner space of natural surrender into peace, in which you simply allow your body to rest and your spirit to have a break from being in your body. So, even if you had a normal amount of sleep in childhood, if you did not feel a hundred percent safe, if you did not fall asleep feeling truly loved and at peace, your sleep did not satisfy you in the way it was meant to do.

Now you are adults. And as adults, you find yourselves feeling tired beyond what seems appropriate at times. You have thoughts such as "God, I don't know why I'm so tired!" or "What's wrong with me?" And these very thoughts and attitudes negate a simple, natural flow of the need for more rest, because some of you are just coming to the point in your life when going to sleep at night can genuinely be just a process of relaxing into a peaceful state with anticipation of nice dreams. Falling asleep tonight can be an experience in which you lie with yourself, feel your own love flowing from your heart, and are nurtured by that. And as a result of simply feeling your own energy, and letting go of responsibility, you can fall into a deep peaceful place. When this happens, there is sometimes a need for your body and psyche to make up for lost time, so to speak. You need to give yourself extra hours for that type of sleep if you did not get it when you were a child. You need to make it okay, that when you are tired and feel the need for more rest and relaxation, you guiltlessly give it to yourself. And do not give yourself relaxation just via time off; also do things you love, and simply be relaxed without worry about what awaits your doing.

For some people, the idea of relaxation is time to read a book, time to get caught up on a project, time to do the things you want to do. Very few people know what it means to truly sit and do nothing and just simply feel at peace. To stare out a window at a tree for a long time and be filled up with the awe and wonder at the beauty of the tree brings a deeper space of inner peace than reading about it. As a child, awe and wonder are a part of your natural state of being, unless those things are snuffed out by disapproving adults or peers. A child can sit outside and watch a honeybee around the flowers for hours at a time and experience what adults work at for many years to experience in meditation. Children have an ability to hold singular focus and presence in the here and now. Unfortunately, adults who have forgotten how to be comfortable with presence, awe, and wonder attempt to pull children out of singular focus. This is often done in the name of teaching children to be more responsible or not to "space out" so much: "Why are you wasting time just staring at a butterfly when you need to clean up your room?" The child is jerked out of its state of natural release, that state of natural relaxation and creative thinking, that spontaneous meditation or experience of adoration, awe, and wonder by adults who do not know how to deal with another person in the house who is simply being that real and that innocent. To ask a child to do a chore is fine, as long as you do not make the child's natural, innocent way of being seem wrong in the process. Because the parents have lost their relationship to their own innocence and often carry great amounts of shame, anger, or other emotions as a result, the child becomes a reflection of what the parent feels he or she has lost. And this is a reminder of the burdens the parents are carrying internally. When a child is in that deeply present energy state, it impulses the parent to feel the absence of that state. So they try to change the child, because they do not know how to change themselves, or are unwilling.

When most of you were growing up, your parents genuinely did not have a clue about how to deal with their own areas of discomfort and pain. Therefore they tried to make the circumstances around them change to what they were capable of experiencing as conditional comfort. Of course, this required that you, as their child, change and allow them to control you to make them feel comfortable. At the very least, making you wrong gave them an outlet for some of their excess emotions, or gave them something outside themselves to focus on as the source of the problem. This distracted your parents from the fact that they were not relaxed and comfortable inside themselves. They were not in self-affinity and, therefore, did not know how to allow you to be.

When your inner child begins to heal and feel safe, it is a normal process of healing and growth to learn how to have truly peaceful sleep—sometimes for the first time in a whole lifetime. You may think you have slept deeply and well. But if that sleep came from a space of escape or relief, it was not as rejuvenating and satisfying as it is intended to be. Even if you think you have slept well, you may not know what it means to sleep so well that you wake up feeling peaceful, somewhat sensual, and even eager to start the day. There is pleasure in that time of waking up and simply lying there and enjoying the transition from sleep to awake in a slow and gentle manner. The tiredness that you experience and the need for extra sleep are genuine needs of your inner child. And you will find the excess tiredness and chronic fatigue in your lives disappearing when your child feels nurtured, safe, and genuinely relaxed anywhere, not just in circumstances and places where safety is a known. As long as there is fear—in general, as long as there is something in life to avoid—there will be tiredness. Even if your life is going along okay, and even if there is a semblance of safety and things seem to be good, if you are experiencing comfort by avoiding normal life situations out of fear, there will always be a level of contraction inside your body that holds in emotion. And that contraction takes a lot of energy to maintain, and it results in tiredness, sleep disorders, and even chronic fatigue.

You are not intended to work hard at being happy or creating comfort in life. These states are a natural product of being in flow. How to return to natural or Divine Flow is very important to physical, emotional, mental, and spiritual health. Therefore, understanding the natural flow of sleep patterns, tiredness, and creative energies, and how these relate to the freedom of your child-self, is another piece of the puzzle that makes up the Matrix of Divine Flow.

Take a moment to ask yourself, "When was the last time I just felt so at peace that I dozed off? When was the last time I fell asleep smiling or in a deeply nurtured state of being?" When you are experiencing wholeness, that will be the way you fall asleep each and every night. Until then, some of the extra tiredness is just simply a natural phenomenon of the process of healing. So release your ideas of "I had my eight hours of sleep; I *should* be okay." Let the right amount be what is needed in the moment. Find a way to adjust your life to give yourself that.

There are so many facets to the process of healing and releasing the past, and so many areas in which your thoughts are taken for granted as being real, or the way it is. And yet these thoughts and behaviors are often just more societal or parental programming.

So when you are tired, instead of being embarrassed to share it with someone, just say, "Oh, I'm tired. That means I need more peace right now. What can I do that makes me feel more peaceful?" Instead of pushing yourself to do, remember how to let go and simply be yourself. Or when you find that you are extra tired, remind yourself to stop avoiding the needs of your inner child self—that is causing the tiredness. Go in and talk to the child, and ask it what its emotions are. Ask it what its emotions are right now and what its needs are. Most of you have spent your lives avoiding dealing with that part of yourself because you do not know how to handle it. Most adults do not go to those inner zones because they do not know what to do once they are there. Once you learn this is true, it can become a great wellspring of peace and love to go there intentionally, because when you cease to avoid something it brings great relief and frees up your life force.

When you feel exasperated, and when you feel concerned that you do not know what to do, instead of brainstorming about it, just stop. Take a deep breath, and sigh on your exhalation instead. You will get much further than you will by trying to figure it out. A sigh can heal more than an overactive, chaotic mind. Blessings and peace.

22

The Matrix of Grace and Mercy
A Channeling from the Elohim of Divine Grace

The theme of kindness and compassion that permeates the preceding chapters is lovingly expanded upon by the Elohim of Divine Grace.

Elohim of Divine Grace: Dear ones, when you seek grace—grace for lifting pain, grace for ease in your path—it is important that you know that all the divine qualities work in pairs. You commonly refer to certain angels, myself, and other Elohim as those who embody and work with the frequency of Divine Grace. Yet, grace and mercy are divine counterparts that are inseparable. For even with qualities such as Divine Love and Divine Innocence, there are feminine, more receptive aspects of the qualities, and there are the more masculine, generative aspects as well. Grace requires you to be in your feminine and receptive side, whereas mercy is a quality that, once you begin your spiritual path, you must bestow on yourselves in order to receive grace.

Let me explain. To be merciful with one's self begins with ceasing the most obvious forms of self-punishment, and any kind of self-harm or harm to others as well. Yet, there are subtler forms of mercy that we wish you to be aware of so you can work with us more fully. There are situations in which your ability to be merciful is directly correspondent to our ability to dispense grace, because to dispense grace when you are not doing your part can sometimes override your learning. To be more receptive to grace, and the ease that it brings into your life, it is important for you to understand the meaning of living in mercy with yourself and others.

If you are aware that you have a pattern that was created for self-protection—to keep you isolated from harm in any way—mercy requires that you, as an adult, not judge yourself for having created the pattern in the first place. Mercy also requires that when you realize the pattern is holding you in ego separation in present time, you cease to give it your power. In other words, when you find yourself in any thought, behavioral, or attitudinal pattern that creates the illusion of separation between yourself and others, between yourself and us, then your part of this formula of grace and mercy is to cease the pattern in a merciful way with yourself. Many of you approach it from an aggressive stance that is lacking in mercy for yourself. You have attitudes toward yourself or others such as "Damn it, there I go again" or "What a stupid thing I am doing." You criticize yourselves in a merciless way. And when you attempt to change your patterns in that manner, not only do you limit your effectiveness, but you severely limit the amount of help we are able to give. Why? Because the frequency of your critical attitude is such that it does not allow you to be receptive. It limits your sense of your deservingness and availability for grace and healing.

Certainly this self-negating pattern can be subtler than the grosser displays of low self-worth that you have experienced at times in your life. Still, we believe it is important that you know this. It will assist you in recognizing when you are in the critical attitudes that you may have taken for granted in the past. Perhaps it will also assist you in understanding that there are times when you have felt that your path is more difficult than it should be. When you recognize that your own effort is what is causing the problem, you can become more merciful with yourself and experience more grace and ease. It is your overeffort to try to be better than you perceive yourself as being that holds you back and takes a lot of the fun out of the process of becoming what you truly are. Using the attitude of mercy means that when these patterns arise and you become aware of them, you simply say to yourself, "Ah, there's that ego separation pattern that was at one time needed but is no longer appropriate. I am so happy that I noticed it so I may now choose to shift it." Let it be that simple. Use your spiritual tools for clearing the old beliefs, or see a healer if one is needed. But do it out of self-love, because you deserve the freedom it will bring. Every time you criticize yourself or are harsh with yourself about "doing the same thing again," it is as if you have taken that injured child, shaken it by the shoulders, or even hit it, and put in more trauma on top of the original. Certainly, catching yourselves is better than being oblivious. But it is time to refine the manner in which you respond when you catch yourself. Do you honestly think that your inner, injured child is going to take the hand of the one who is scowling about the problem? As you learn to respond in Divine Truth, as you change and grow, you can extend a friendly hand to the part of yourself that is experiencing illusion. As you send love, as you look at that part of yourself in a loving way and you extend a friendly hand, Divine Mercy steps in and takes charge. Then the part of you that perceives itself as injured can trust you, take your hand, and be lifted out of the old pain and separation and into grace.

Hear this as the voice of the loving father who wishes you to be more at peace. And know that when you call upon Divine Grace, you need to hold the frequency of receptivity and Divine Mercy to make it as effective as possible. You may even call for Elohim and Angels of Divine Grace to help you understand how to be merciful and nonjudgmental with yourself. That in itself is a humbling act. When you do not know how to stop self-criticism, you can still ask for help as long as you acknowledge that the self-criticism is not your truth. We can assist you in becoming more merciful with yourself. The truth is that 90 percent of the shift in the energy pattern originates in the fact that you ask for help, the fact that you recognize the need, the fact that you no longer want to believe in the negative voices, and the fact that you sincerely desire to be kinder and more merciful toward yourself. The other 10 percent—thanks to the little receptivity you opened up in asking for help—is the love and comfort we can give you and the dispensation of Divine Grace we can send, which are needed to help you move beyond the past pattern.

We love you in every aspect of yourself. When you are most critical of yourselves, we still love you. When you are gentle with yourselves, we love you. When you are sleeping, when you are awake, our love is unchanging. And your attitudes make a difference in whether you feel it or not. The attitudes you hold toward yourself make a difference in whether you feel our love, whether you receive the full effect of Divine Grace, and whether you return to full innocence and peace. Beloveds, you are more the creator of your own reality than you know. It is a testimony to your spiritual commitment and your own growth that we come to you now to offer this subtler level of understanding into your consciousness—to help you understand the matrix of healing, self-awareness, and awakening more deeply.

Be merciful with yourselves. In being merciful with yourselves, do not mistake such attitudes as self-pity and feeling sorry for yourself for mercy. For self-pity holds us at bay just as much as your treachery with your own patterns. To extend mercy is to see your own divinity, to extend that loving hand and say, "You can step out of it now. I know you can." It is never "Oh, you poor thing." The moment you identify yourself as the "poor thing," you equally block our love and assistance. For the frequency of self-pity is an aspect of self-condemnation. Even though it can be mistaken as being merciful with yourself and compassionate, it is indeed not. It holds you in the illusion of helplessness and victimhood.

You are brilliant, sparkling, divinely incredible Beings of Light, who have more capacity for love and brilliance and peace than you know. We invite you, in the spirit of Divine Grace and Mercy, to remember this in the times that are most challenging. When those old emotional patterns are unraveling and leaving your body and psyche, be aware of the attitudes you hold toward your healing process. When you judge, feel pity toward, resent, or resist the feelings that arise during a release, you slow down the release dramatically, because all these attitudes create contraction, and contraction does not allow the flow of energies outward. Once again—let me repeat—the attitude you hold when you are in need of help makes the difference in how much help you are capable of receiving. This is a very great empowerment for you because it puts the power of choice in your own hands and heart. In our desire to love and bring you grace every step along the way, we are glad to share with you this understanding, so you can assist us in giving more, so you can assist us with being able to interface with your consciousness in a more tangible and meaningful way.

So I ask you to go inside now and say to yourself—whether it is to your body, to your inner child, or emotional body, to the part of yourself you tend to criticize the most or have the hardest time accepting—say, "I apologize for being so treacherous with you. I apologize for feeling sorry for you, for criticizing you, avoiding you, and judging." Take a couple of minutes and make a pact with yourself to learn how to be more merciful so you can receive Divine Grace more fully.

In deepest grace and love I see you as successful. Dear ones, you need never feel guilty about your attitudes toward yourselves. When you catch yourself, you simply need to apologize, because there has been a foul that has been committed. Then change it. You do not need to feel guilt or shame for it. Just stop, make amends, and choose mercifully.

Now I would like you to close your eyes and see a photograph of yourself in your mind's eye. Look at the expression on your face in the photo and ask that it express the attitude "I'm trying so hard to be okay." Somewhere deep in most seekers there is a little, or a lot, of that attitude. If yours is already gone, that is good. If there are still traces of that attitude, then it is time to let them go. In that attitude you hold contraction that says, "I'm not already okay, so I have to try hard to be better." See that expression on your face, and visualize words like a caption on the picture, whether those words are "I want to be better," "I want to be okay," "I'm trying so hard but it is never enough," or "I am afraid I will never make it." Whatever your words might be, look into the eyes of yourself in the photograph and tell that part of you, "It is time to stop trying. It is time to know that you are okay. We are simply unraveling some illusions we created in the past because we are learning a better way." Then use your Sword of Truth to cut through this picture of yourself, or rip it into pieces. Now burn the pieces of this photo in a rainbow flame bonfire, transmuting the energies to pure essence again.

🖵 Now, with your permission, we would like to do a lifting of old energies in grace. Simultaneously, the Elohim of Divine Innocence and the Elohim of Divine Love will be working with you. Together we will form a matrix of grace, innocence, and love and dispense these energies to you. So we ask you now to simply welcome us to do a lifting and an energizing. As we are lifting old painful or dense energies in grace, the frequencies of Divine Innocence and Divine Love are being brought in to replace those old attitudes of shame, self-condemnation, self-pity, fear, hurt, self-judgment, resentment, or whatever they might be.

Now we will begin. Breathe as deeply into your entire body as you possibly can to assist us in reaching in deeper for the clearing and lifting. Affirm, "I am ready to have all old painful attitudes and emotions lifted in grace. I am willing to feel only those energies I need to feel in order to learn and grow. Lift the rest now."

Let go of the shame of not being good enough. Let go of the idea that you will never be okay until someone makes it up to you for what others did. Be willing to let it go, and we will lift. Just be willing.

Take as much time as you need to finish this process.

Elohim of Divine Grace: Dear ones, in closing, let us say that when you learn to walk in mercy and compassion with yourselves, you will walk in grace, in innocence, and in love again unceasingly. So-la-re-en-lo.

Part 6

Meditation and Initiations
of Empowerment

In this section you will find meditations and initiations to assist you in further healing and deepening on your spiritual path. Keeping your aura and chakras clear is vital to maintaining spiritual growth and progress. Transcending perceived limitations is a key ingredient to mastery and a key aspect of initiation.

If you need further assistance, you will find in-depth spiritual teachings to assist you in maintaining healthy boundaries, deepening Higher Self connection in your body, and receiving assistance from Light Beings, as well as additional meditations and initiations, in my two workbooks *The Pleiadian Workbook: Awakening Your Divine Ka* and *The Pleiadian Tantric Workbook: Awakening Your Divine Ba*.

23

Rainbow Flame Meditation

Since the publication of my first three books, the Lords of Light of the Rainbow Flames have made themselves known to me. This group includes a being called the Lord of the White Flame of Divine Truth. I have replaced former aura boundary protection techniques with daily invocation of the Rainbow Flames around my auric field. Others with whom I have shared this process feel as I do that it is a much more effective boundary protection than those taught in *The Pleiadian Workbook: Awakening Your Divine Ka*. You need not do this entire meditation daily in order to maintain the Rainbow Flames around your aura. Once you have done this meditation, a simple invocation of the Lords of Light of the Rainbow Flames, asking them to renew the flames around your aura, will suffice. When calling in the flames around your aura, you can call on them all at the same time or one at a time. I recommend that you repeat this meditation occasionally, or as often as you like, as a way of keeping your field clear and balanced.

In order for you to understand their purpose, I will describe each flame's function and location around your aura.

The White Flame of Divine Truth will be immediately outside your aura, nearest you. This flame dissolves illusionary and false energies and holds the frequency of Divine Truth.

The Ruby Red Flame is next. It energizes and restores energy flow to your physical body. It is great for dissolving resistance and defensiveness and releasing anger.

Next is the Carnelian Orange Flame, which purifies and balances your emotional body and sexual energy and restores healthy flow to those energies. It holds the energy of healthy sexual flow and emotional stability and surrender.

The Golden Yellow Flame is next. It purifies and cleanses the lower mental body and will center. This flame also assists you in aligning with Divine Will and Divine Power in practical ways.

The Emerald Green Flame comes after the Golden Yellow Flame, bringing balance and compassion to your heart center. This flame is wonderful for healing grief, clearing issues around worth and shame, and finding your balance point in your heart. It holds the frequency of compassion and deservingness of love.

Next is the Sapphire Blue Flame, which is a very clear, lighter shade of sapphire. It opens and purifies your communication centers, allowing expression of your essence in all that you say and creatively express. It helps to restore confidence and flow to self-expression and creativity.

The Indigo Flame purifies and balances your higher mental body, enabling you to project your higher vision and Truths into your world without judgment and false projections of beliefs and ego attitudes. This flame holds the frequency of alignment with Divine Mind and higher vision.

Next is the Violet Flame, which raises the frequency of all energies to their higher nature. It is often thought of as the flame of alchemical transmutation, taking base energies and raising them to their higher spiritual purpose, like lead into gold. The Violet Flame is wonderful for aligning all other energy bodies with spirit.

The last flame around your aura is the Heart Pink Flame. This flame holds the frequency of pure, innocent Divine Love and is, naturally, very healing for your heart.

At the end of the Rainbow Flame portion of the meditation, you will be guided to leave the Rainbow Flames around your aura, in the order given above. Before that, you will use the Rainbow Flames to purify and balance your energy bodies. Your physical, emotional, mental, etheric, astral, and spiritual energy bodies all overlap throughout your body and aura. Sometimes pollution from dense energies can overflow from one energy body to another. This meditation, used over time, will assist in clearing this problem and restoring healthy balance and cooperation between your various energy bodies.

During the meditation, you will use the Rainbow Flames to purify and balance these energy bodies throughout your aura, your Tube of Light, and your chakras. Your Tube of Light begins at a small Earth Portal Chakra at the bottom of your aura and extends around your spinal column, out through your crown chakra, and all the way to your Cosmic Portal Chakra at the topmost point of your aura [see illustration below]. Your Tube of Light is about two to three inches in diameter and is like an axis to your higher-dimensional consciousness. It goes into the higher realms, connecting you all the way back to the Source of your own consciousness, or your highest Higher Self. Once you have cleared and balanced with the Rainbow Flames, you will fill your Tube of Light and chakras with Higher Self Energy, overflowing into your aura.

Your Tube of Light begins at your Earth Portal Chakra at the bottom of your aura and extends beyond your Cosmic Portal Chakra at the topmost point of your aura.

Rainbow Flame Meditation

1. Make this invocation: "In the name of the I Am presence that I Am, I call forth the crystalline Pillars of Light, from the Cities of Light where the Ascended Masters dwell. May these Pillars of Light fill and surround this room, anchoring it as a sacred Dolphin Star Temple in the Cities of Light, where only that which is Divine may enter. All that is less than the Divine, which is illusion, must leave now."

2. Breathe deeply, using your breath to bring yourself into your body. With each inhalation, call in your Higher Self of the Light to fill the holy temple of your body with your own spirit. Imagine this as an infusion of your own higher consciousness in the form of Light. With each exhalation, imagine that you are releasing all tension and any energy blocks, pain, and numbness that keep you from being fully present. Inhale your Holy Spirit consciousness; exhale tension and blocks.

3. Breathe fully into your head and neck area. Feel the skin around your head and neck expand with each breath. Allow your mouth to be open just a little, relaxing your jaw and expanding your breath into your shoulders. Fill the tops of your shoulders with your own Holy Spirit Light, cleansing that area with your out-breath.

4. Allow your breath to spread into your arms, and feel the skin around your upper arms expand with each breath. Breathing deeply into your forearms, feel the forearms expand with your breath. Expand your breath into your wrists and hands, all the way to each fingertip. Breathe into your entire arm, all the way down to your fingers now, feeling the new life force, Light, and Divine Presence there.

5. Inhaling into your upper torso to your waist, fill your entire rib cage with Higher Self Light. Feel your spine actually lengthen with each breath. Feel your entire upper torso expand with your breath as you welcome your Holy Spirit to fill that space. Breathing deeply into your lower torso, expand your hips, abdomen, and genitals. If there are areas in which you notice excess tension, breathe into them and give them permission to relax. Realize that to be a Christed Presence embodied, you must first clear and open the temple of your body.

6. Expand your breath into your thighs, breathing so deeply that you can feel the skin around your thighs to your knees expanding with each breath. Breathe into your knees and calves now, drawing the Light of Higher Self into your lower legs with each in-breath, each out-breath cleansing that part of your body temple. Expand your breath into your ankles and feet, breathing so deeply that you can feel the skin expand around your feet and toes with each breath.

7. Now begin to take full-body breaths. Experiment with how to bring your breath into your entire body with a single inhalation. Then exhale through the pores of your skin around your whole body. To do this, you must breathe very deeply. Inhale into your head, shoulders, arms, and torso down the legs to the feet, and exhale from your whole body. Repeat the full-body breaths two or three times, minimum.

8. Pull your aura in or push it out, whichever is needed to extend your auric field just about arm's length around your body. Imagine that your aura is shaped like an egg and extends two to three feet above, below, behind, in front of, and to either side of your body. Use your breath and your intention to draw your aura to fill that space.

9. Give yourself a new grounding cord, made of whatever color of light feels appropriate to you at this time. Send this grounding cord from your lower body to the Earth Star Crystal at the center of Earth. Ask the devas of the Earth Star Crystal to connect you to the highest potential future and to the highest Christ consciousness of Earth. Breathe, and feel that connection. Ask the Pleiadian Emissaries of Light to place an Earth Cone of Light beneath your aura to secure this connection.

10. Invoke the Pleiadian Emissaries of Light and ask them to place the Interdimensional Cone of Light above your aura, aligning you with Divine Truth and assisting you in clearing all ego and illusionary energies.

11. Ask the Sirian Emissaries of Light to anchor the Evolutionary Cone of Light above your aura, aligning you with your highest purpose according to the Divine Plan.

12. Ask the Andromedan Emissaries of Light to place the Intergalactic Cone of Light above your aura, anchoring a Pillar of Light to the Great Central Sun around your body and aura.

13. Welcome the Lords of Light of the Rainbow Flames. First, call on the Lord of the White Flame of Divine Truth. Ask that your aura be filled with this beautiful sparkling White Flame of Divine Truth, which dissolves illusion. Visualize or imagine your entire auric field filled with that flame.

14. Call on the Lord of the Ruby Red Flame. Ask that the Ruby Red Flame also fill your aura, adding vitality and life force, clearing resistance, and purifying the fires of the body passion.

15. Welcome the Lord of the Carnelian Orange Flame to fill your aura with that flame to heal and balance your emotional body and purify your sexual energy, aligning it with its highest purpose.

16. Welcome the Lord of the Golden Yellow Flame. Ask that the Golden Yellow Flame also fill your aura, purifying your will center and lower mental body. Intend to align in the spirit of surrender to Divine Will.

17. Next, call on the Lord of the Emerald Green Flame of divine compassion, balance, and heart healing. Imagine the Emerald Green Flame filling your auric field, adding to the other flames.

18. Welcome the Lord of the Sapphire Blue Flame of creative inspiration, self-expression, creativity, communication, and peace. Imagine the Sapphire Blue Flame filling your aura.

19. Next, calling on the Lord of the Indigo Flame, ask that the Indigo Flame fill your aura, clarifying your vision and dissolving the veils of illusion, projection, and judgment. Ask for help that you might see through eyes of Divine Truth and not through the eyes of ego. Intend to clarify your higher mental body and align with Divine Mind.

20. Call upon St. Germaine, Lord of the Violet Flame. Ask that the Violet Flame be added to your auric field, transmuting all energies to their highest spiritual essence.

21. Last, ask the Lord of the Heart Pink Flame of unconditional, innocent love to add this flame to your aura. Breathe deeply as if your own breath were fanning these flames in your aura, balancing, clarifying, and purifying all your energy bodies with pure love.

22. Maintaining the Rainbow Flames in your aura, focus on the bottommost point of your aura, beneath your feet. From your Earth Portal Chakra, located there, draw the Rainbow Flames in with

your breath to fill your Tube of Light. Breathe in deeply from the bottom of your aura, drawing the Rainbow Flames into your Tube of Light all the way up to the base of your spine. With your next breath, draw the Rainbow Flames all the way up your spine, out through your crown chakra, and into your Cosmic Portal Chakra at the top of your aura. Breathe deeply through your Tube of Light a couple of times, allowing your breath to increase the Rainbow Flames there.

23. Breathe into your root chakra, opening it as much as you can at this time. As you inhale, draw the Rainbow Flames to overflow the Tube of Light and fill your root chakra. With your exhalation, imagine that you are blowing the flames into, and out through, your root chakra. Also breathe the flames down your legs and out through your knee chakras, through your foot chakras (in the center of your soles), and out through each toe.

24. Continue overflowing your root chakra as you breathe deeply, drawing the Rainbow Flames into the front and back of your sacral chakra. Draw the flames in with your inhalation; expand them with your exhalation. (As you proceed to fill the rest of your chakras, each chakra will continue filling and overflowing until finally all your chakras and your aura are constantly filling and overflowing with Rainbow Flames simultaneously.)

25. Next fill your solar plexus chakra, front and back, overflowing your Tube of Light with Rainbow Flames into your chakra area. Once again, use your inhalation to draw the flames into that chakra and your exhalation to expand and open the chakra.

26. Continuing in the same manner, allow the Rainbow Flames to overflow your heart chakra front and back, opening it fully.

27. Overflow your Tube of Light with Rainbow Flames through the front and back of your throat chakra. Use your breath to bring those beautiful flames into the front and back of your throat. This time you will also overflow your throat chakra down your arms and out through your elbow chakras, and the chakras in the palms of your hands and the tips of your fingers.

28. Again, overflow the Rainbow Flames in your Tube of Light to fill the front and back of your third eye, breathing and inviting that chakra to open fully.

29. Allow the Rainbow Flames to fill and overflow your crown chakra. Use your breath and your vision to imagine those flames spinning around through your crown, opening it, cleansing it, and balancing all the energy bodies as they interface there.

30. Sit in silence for at least two to three minutes, or as long as you like. Continue allowing the Rainbow Flames to cleanse your aura, your Tube of Light, your chakras, and your arms and legs while you meditate.

31. Use your breath to push the Rainbow Flames from inside your body and chakras out into your aura. Continuing to use your breath, push the Rainbow Flames just to the outside of your aura, surrounding it. The White Flame of Divine Truth will be closest to you. This is followed by the red all the way through the violet and then pink flames on the outside. Ask that the Rainbow Flames remain there as a filtering system, for aura boundary protection.

32. Now that your body temple has been purified, call on your Higher Self of the Light to come and fill your Tube of Light with your own Higher Self energy and consciousness. Ask that your higher consciousness fill your Tube of Light, from the top of your aura, into your crown, around the entire length of your spine, all the way to the base of your aura. Continue breathing, continually filling your entire Tube of Light with Higher Self energy, connecting you to your own Divine Source.

33. Place the tips of your thumbs and middle fingers together, palms up. This mudra (a hand position that brings about higher states of consciousness) will assist you in anchoring your Higher Self Tube of Light connection more deeply.

34. Now, using your breath, you will overflow your Tube of Light through each of your chakras, filling and overflowing them with Higher Self energy. Begin by overflowing your Higher Self energy into your crown chakra, then into the front and back of your third eye, the front and back of your throat chakra, the front and back of your heart chakra, the front and back of your solar plexus chakra, the front and back of your sacral chakra, and your root chakra at the base of your spine. Also overflow your Higher Self energy down your arms, through your elbow chakras and your palm chakras. Then overflow your Higher Self energy down your legs,

overflowing your knee chakras and the soles of your feet.

35. Breathe, and feel that ever deepening connection to your own Divine Presence, your Higher Self, your I Am. Now is a wonderful time for communion with your Higher Self, to simply remain in presence and silence. Allow the focus of your meditation to be on feeling that loving Divine Self that you are. If you need more focus to maintain your attention, slowly repeat the mantra "I Am the Divine Self that I Am." Or make up a mantra of your own. Meditate as long as you like.

36. When you feel complete, use full-body breathing and awareness of your feet on the floor to bring yourself back. Reground yourself if you feel the need.

The Rainbow Flames can also be used for localized clearings in your body or chakras as needed. I use them when I burn contracts and clear beliefs and judgments as well. They do a more thorough job than an ordinary flame or the Violet Flame alone, as I taught in *The Pleiadian Workbook*. When you are energetically clearing your home, work space, or car, try using Rainbow Flames. When the clearing is complete, seal the building, apartment, room, car, or whatever in Rainbow Flames, just as you do your own aura.

24

Rainbow Diamond Council of Elders and the Ramayani

Ramayani is the name of a group of beings who came to Earth, in Egypt, about 40,000 years ago. Many of this original Tribe of Ra were higher-dimensional Light Beings who downstepped into physical form, bypassing the physical birth process. They birthed a whole civilization of human star beings, many of whom ascended. Their era was actually a continuation of many eras, or stages of development, in ancient Egypt. Many of their teachings carried forth into the final stages of Egypt's spiritual culture. The best way I can interpret their messages in this chapter, and the teachings I have received while on tour in the present-day Egyptian ruins, is to say that this precedence of Light and spiritual culture as a way of life began to die out about 3000 B.C.E. By 1000 B.C.E., tyrannical power had taken over the government and most of the temples as well. The reign of Light had waxed and waned previously, but it still remained fairly intact until that time. Erratic attempts were made by several members of royalty, at various times, to restore the ancient sacred way of life to the people. Beings such as Amenhotep I, Amenhotep II, and Akhenaton carried the encodings of Light into their positions as pharaohs. But these resurrections of the sacred ways were never completed. The sacred ways of life were already disappearing in 1000 B.C.E., and the Arab and Christian takeovers finally won out. However, this seeming victory of the invaders has never stopped the higher-dimensional Light Beings from connecting with those who are open to them. Even today, you can commune with the Goddesses Hathor, Isis, Sekhmet, and Maat and the Gods Ptah, Ra, Osiris, Horus, Thoth, Anubis, and others in the ancient sacred sites. They are ever present and ever giving of their love and teachings to those with ears to hear and eyes to see.

The Ramayani were the seeds of the many stages of spiritual evolution in Egypt, and those who ascended during that culture are the Ramayani Ascended Masters. They are part of a vastly larger group of Ascended Masters called the Rainbow Diamond Council of Elders. This Council consists of Ascended Masters from every indigenous tribe that has ever produced ascended and enlightened ones. Pakal Votan, the Mayan leader whose tomb is in Palenque, Mexico, is one of the Rainbow Diamond Council of Elders of whom I have been made aware. When they have come into groups to connect, I have been aware of numerous Australian aboriginals, Native Americans from many times and many different tribes, Incans, Lemurians, other Mayans, ancient Balinese from over 2000 years ago, Egyptians and other African tribal members, Tibetans, and many more.

In a channeling, the Council revealed the names of many ancient tribal cultures, now extinct, that produced Ascended Masters. The Elders said that in simply hearing these tribal names, deep memories could be restored from our own past-life experiences and initiations in these cultures. Many races ascended as a group and have left no genetic lineage behind. Others became extinct by means of Earth changes and the process of time. I would like to share with you the names given to me by the Rainbow Diamond Council of Elders, that you might be impulsed to feel and remember some of your own sacred past connections. They are the Ramayani, the original tribes of Ra; the Inti, who lived in South America and predated the Inca by about 2000 years, at which time the entire race ascended to the fifth-dimensional Cities of Light; the Serapi, of whom Serapis Bey was a great leader; the Timo, the original indigenous people of Timor Island; the Kumari, of whom Sanat Kumara was an avatar; the Loki, located in the Himalayas; the Sirens of Greece, Sirian female beings who sang the love songs of creation, awakening, and ascension for Earth, some of whom were mermaids; and the Aneké, who predated the Native Americans and were of Lemurian origins. Other group names I have been given are the Bolarce, Pum-A-Ta, Irani, Ara, Celestes, Tukonese, and the Miranali. I am certain there are other ancient groups that are not named; but these are all I have been given at this time.

The Ramayani Feeding Process

The first time the Ramayani made themselves known to me was at the Fall Equinox in 1998, during a workshop I was leading. They came to share a meditation called the Ramayani Feeding Process. This process was used, most often at sunrise, in their ancient Egyptian culture. At the time they came to Earth, their name for Egypt was Rama Tara, which meant "The Home of the Sun" or "The Home of Ra on Earth." At that time, brain stems were longer, as were the bones of the occipital region around the lower brain— larger and slightly more protruding. The Ramayani made plates of gold, shaped to fit around the occipital area of the skull, which were used to activate the higher purpose of the lower brain. The image of a large bird eating a snake has been used in many cultures for various symbolic purposes. According to the Ramayani, its original symbolism was that of the lower brain, via the brain stem, feeding the upper brain. It was considered one of the essential activations of immortality, just as the Ka awakening was.

Several years ago while I was on a book-signing tour in Hawaii, Pala, a Pleiadian guide, came to me. He said that the gold plate I described above had been found beneath the Sphinx. This was the first time I had heard of it in this life. I was leading a meditation for a group at the time he channeled this information. He told us that we could call on this gold lower-brain activator plate etherically, and that he and the other Pleiadian and Sirian Emissaries of Light who were with us would assist us in receiving the activation. As we called it in, others and I felt movement and expansion of our lower cranial bones. It also felt as if formerly dead circuits were being turned on inside our brains. Over the next year and a half, my occipital bones took on a new shape, which made that part of my cranum look and feel bigger and slightly protruding. These bones had expanded outward to take on the shape of the etheric gold plate. This particular activation is the first step of the Ramayani Feeding Process, which I was given exactly a year and a half later, after my own brain activation had expanded enough to anchor the process for the group for whom it was channeled.

Ramayani Feeding Process
Guided Meditation and Initiation 🔲

1. Ground yourself with a grounding cord of light to the Earth Star Crystal at Earth's core. Ask the Overlighting Devas of the Earth Star

Crystal to connect you only to the highest Divine Source of Light and Love at the center of Earth.

2. Adjust your auric field to about arm's length around your entire body, in an egg shape.

3. Call your Higher Self of the Light to fill your Tube of Light with your own Divine Essence energy and consciousness [see illustration on page 229].

4. Invoke three times the Ramayani of the Rainbow Diamond Council of Elders to be with you. Invite the Dolphin Star Temple Higher Council of Light to come forth as well.

5. Ask for the Interdimensional, Evolutionary, and Intergalactic Cones of Light at the top of your aura.

6. Ask for an Earth Cone of Light at the base of your aura to maintain your connection to Earth's Christ consciousness and Earth's Divine Plan.

7. Ask the guides to place you in a Ramayani Feeding Process Chamber of Light.

8. Ask that the etheric double of the golden lower-brain plate be brought in around your occipital bones and lower-brain area. The first time you do this process, allow five minutes of silence while you breathe deeply. In subsequent meditations, half a minute will suffice.

9. Holding your head on its vertical axis, chin parallel to the ground, extend your head forward as far as you can. Breathing deeply to facilitate your lower-brain activation, remain in that position until your head seems to relax into the position and energy changes have stopped (approximately thirty to sixty seconds). Then return your head to its normal position briefly.

10. Do the exact opposite of step 9. Move your head backward as far as it will go while maintaining your vertical axis and chin parallel to the ground. Again, breathing deeply, remain in that position until your head seems to relax into it and energy changes have stopped (approximately thirty to sixty seconds). Then return your head to its normal position briefly.

11. Maintaining your head on its vertical axis, chin parallel to the ground, make two or three clockwise circles with your head, then

two or three counterclockwise circles. Begin by extending your head forward, as in step 9, and continue with that type of head extension around to your right side, behind, around to your left side, and back to the forward extension position. Coordinate deep breathing with the movements while holding the focus of lower-brain and brain stem activation. (This head movement is often seen in Middle Eastern dancing.)

12. Sitting cross-legged, or in a chair with the bottoms of your feet together, straighten your spine without making it stiff. Then arch your pelvis forward just to the point where your genitals are parallel to and touching the ground or your chair. (This is wonderful to do outside, seated on Earth.) Tilt your head backward. Press the pointer fingertip of your right hand firmly into the bottom center of your nose, above your lip. Open your mouth widely. A somewhat raspy or guttural sound is triggered by this activation. Make the sound aloud until the activation stops and the sound naturally relaxes and subsides (approximately fifteen to thirty seconds).

13. Rock forward and backward slowly a few times. In the forward position, your head tilts back and you inhale deeply. In the backward rocking position, your head tilts forward and you exhale deeply. As you rock, imagine that your brain stem extends all the way up to the back of your crown chakra [see illustration page 241]. Ask the guides to restructure your etheric brainstem in that location. Hold this focus for about a minute to a minute and a half. Also, during this time, ask your brain to produce more cerebrospinal fluid. Imagine your cerebrospinal fluid flowing from your brain down your spinal cord into your lower back and feeding your entire nervous system. Continue this rocking until you sense that your elongated brain stem is in place and is being filled with energy from your lower brain. The rocking motion is like a pumping action to help you achieve this. After about a minute or so, when you feel that this pumping has filled the elongated brain stem, stop rocking.

14. Sit again with your genitals touching the chair, floor, or the earth where you are seated, with your head tilted backward as far as you can hold it comfortably. The feeding of your upper brain by your lower brain will continue for a few minutes. The Ramayani say that during this time an actual serum is secreted, which moves from lower to upper brain. They call it the nectar of the gods.

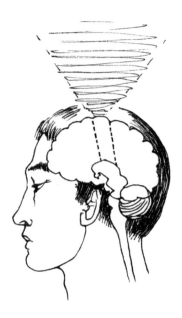

During the Ramayani Feeding Process the brain stem
extends all the way up to the back of the crown chakra.

15. When the brain feeding feels as though it has stopped or slowed down greatly, breathe in through the bottommost point of your aura into your Tube of Light, which anchors there [see illustration on page 229]. Ask for and breathe in prana from Earth up to your heart. Also, ask for and breathe cosmic prana in through your Tube of Light where it connects at the topmost point of your aura. Draw the cosmic prana into your heart. Simultaneously, breathe these Earth and cosmic pranas into the center of your heart, where your soul resides. When you exhale, expand your soul and heart light outward through the front of your heart chakra. Continue this until your soul energy and light have filled your auric field.

16. Bringing your hands to a prayer position in front of your heart, end with a namasté. This gesture means "I honor the God in you." Ending your meditation in this way means that you honor the God in yourself, in your guides, and in All That Is.

There were long periods of time during which the Ramayani did this process every morning at sunrise. You may choose to use it as often or as seldom as feels right for you on your path.

Ramayani Cellular Clearing and Death Process

During a training program some time later, the Ramayani came in with the channeling and cellular clearing and death process that follows. I have had qualms about including it in this book because of the more advanced use of kundalini necessary to do this process. If you have not already been running fairly large amounts of kundalini, do not attempt this process until you have. You could cause yourself serious energy, emotional, or even physical problems. *The Pleiadian Tantric Workbook: Awakening Your Divine Ba* includes a process for clearing and activating your body kundalini channels. I highly recommend that you work with that level of kundalini for at least three months before you attempt the Cosmic and Earth Kundalini activation at the end of the channeling.

> *The Ramayani:* In the most ancient Tribes of Ra, called the Ramayani, there were priests of the Hathor Temples as well as priestesses, who worked on behalf of all of those you call Gods, or the higher-dimensional Light Beings. These priests and priestesses were anchors, or channels, for such Light Beings as Isis, Thoth, Hathor, Horus, Ptah, and others whose names your history has forgotten. What we wish to remind you of, at this time, is an ancient technique that was used in the Hathor Temples by the Priest and Priestess Healers of the Order of Hathor. This technique is one to be specifically used when a person is dying, for in death it is important that the organs, glands, bloodstream, and all parts of the person's body be flushed with kundalini in order to transmute all karma and density. These flushed energies are released into the higher dimensions and transmuted there, as long as the person's identity was not attached to them at the time of death. If the person was still identified with these karmic issues and attitudes, if the person still believed in these erroneous energies that were less than Divine Truth, less than their own Divine Essence, the energies would become locked in the organs of the body. The organs would be clairvoyantly read, and sometimes physically examined, after death by the Death Oracles. These Oracular Beings were well trained in understanding the weight of karma in physical density.

Amorah: On the walls of many Egyptian tombs were often painted scenes of Thoth, holding the feather of Maat and recording the individual's karmic status at the time of death. The hieroglyphic image used to represent this test was the weighing of the physical heart against the weight of Maat's feather Maat was depicted holding the scales of justice or sitting above them. Anubis, keeper of the multidimensional portals to be passed through in afterlife, was always shown standing by witnessing the results. This would enable him to determine which higher-dimensional portals could be opened for the soul's passage and which could not. This determination depended on how far along the person was on the initiatic path, and how much karmic weight was still held in the body.

The Ramayani: Now, that of which we wish to remind you is intended to serve you personally, as well as those you might encounter who need this sort of assistance. But before we speak of the actual death process itself, let it suffice to say that the techniques you will be using for the clearing of the body during this training date back to the time of the Ramayani and even beyond. The activations and flushings that you will be using were used by the initiates, while still alive, to assist them in becoming completely free of all the karmic issues they did not need, or want, to take with them. This, of course, accelerated their enlightenment process and the process of becoming fully spirit-embodied Master Beings.

As you are learning techniques for taking dense energies through the ascension process within your chakras and your body, you are learning to use your kundalini for deeper neurological and skeletal spiritual alignment. Your role in assisting Earth's transition into ascension, a planet of Master Light Beings embodied, calls on you to run three types of kundalini in a clear and unblocked manner: your own body kundalini (the kundalini commonly taught and practiced in many spiritual paths), your Higher Self Cosmic Kundalini, and Earth Kundalini.* The synergy of these

---

*WARNING: Unless you know that you run kundalini through your spinal channels in a clear manner, do not attempt to do this process. Running Kundalini through blocked channels may result in bodily harm. If you need assistance with clearing your kundalini channels, you may wish to contact a healer or expert in kundalini. There is a chapter in *The Pleiadian Tantric Workbook* that can assist you in this as well.

three kundalini forms is vital to your own ability to anchor your Higher Self, or Master Self, in your body. It is also necessary in order to perform the activation and clearing we are here to teach you. Once you have learned to run these three types of kundalini, you will be enabled to run Universal Cosmic Kundalini and Earth Kundalini through your healing channels and out through your hands to other people as described during this process.

So, in this particular technique, you bring this Earth Kundalini up through your feet and out through your hands, and you bring the Universal Cosmic Kundalini from your crown chakra down your arms and through your hands. You may call on the Priests and Priestesses of Hathor and ask them to assist you in running these energies for the person who is going through death transition in order to release all the density and karma left in the body that can be released into the Light.*

You will begin with your hands on the person's feet, and run this kundalini mixture cellularly from the person's feet through his or her legs. You run the two kundalinis full palm, so that every point on your hand is running this combination of Earth and Universal Cosmic Kundalini. By doing so, you cellularly begin to flush the person's body. When it has reached the person's hip joints, put a hand on each hip joint, continuing to run the two kundalinis cellularly through the trunk of the body. The ideal is to have two healers present. Each healer then places one hand on the base of the person's spine and one hand on a hip joint, until the whole trunk of the body has been flushed.

Amorah: When you have flushed the trunk of the body, if there are particular areas in which you notice extra density, you may need to put your hands specifically on those areas. For instance, the liver is often a very dense place for many people, just as the pancreas and spleen can be. Even the walls of the physical heart can become hardened. (Any place that you find on your own body that needs a little extra attention, you can use this same process: place your hands on either side of the local area and flush cellularly until it

*Never do this process on anyone other than someone in death transition.

feels complete.) Then you place one hand on top of the person's head, and one at the base of the neck, and run the kundalini energies cellularly through the head and neck down both arms and through the fingertips. This is a process that was sometimes repeated four times as a person was going through death transition, perhaps over a period of a week.

The Ramayani: At the point of the actual death, if it is known, the ideal is to place your hands on the base of the spine. *Do not cover the crown chakra,* but run the energies up the spine and out through the person's crown chakra. It is important that the crown chakra be flushed with as much of the two kundalinis as is possible. When the actual death begins, and you see or sense the Spirit leaving the body, you must remove your hands at once. At that point the individual must use his or her own energy to push himself or herself through to the other side. Then it is up to the higher-dimensional guardians and angels to pull the individual through whatever higher-dimensional gateways are appropriate to the person's initiatic and karmic levels of completion. At that time there is usually a holding pattern, energetically put into place, while the organs of the body and the person's consciousness are being evaluated.

If you personally become aware that you are about to experience a physical death, breathe, and remain very lucid and conscious. Whether it is your time for a conscious body death or for your full body ascension, you can run these energies cellularly through your own body by calling on the guides and your own Higher Self and asking them to assist you in turning on your three kundalinis 100 percent. But we want to strongly emphasize that it is not something that is to be done casually or with someone who is not ready to die or to do a full-body ascension. One hundred percent cellular kundalini is a process of the body dying or moving into the Light. And yet, the coming times call on these techniques to be remembered, so we use this opportunity to make you aware.

In your invocations and setting of space for healing sessions or Chamber of Light sessions, if you so desire, you may call on the Ramayani of the Light. Those of us who ascended and completed our evolutionary paths during that ancient culture of Egypt, and have remained behind in order to assure that the teachings and healings will not be lost, will be with you. We will guide you and work with you with our etheric hands as you work with your hands of Light embodied.

We are grateful for this opportunity to interact, to share knowledge and love, and to share the sobriety of understanding of what it means to truly be a healer. For a true healer is indeed a facilitator of spiritual growth and spiritual anchoring of the recipient's human being and Light Being into Oneness. Of course, the individual's personal growth, maturity, and spiritual practice are the most essential ingredients in the attainment of this Oneness and Mastery. And yet, the right healer at the right time is also an important part of the formula. When one takes on the role of becoming this kind of healer again, it is important that one realizes that he or she is a spiritual facilitator. *Never overstep the bounds of your client's potential and readiness.* In order to assure your discernment in this regard, we encourage you to also sharpen your abilities of clairaudience—your ability to hear our voices. Sharpen your intuition and your clairvoyance. Be aware of the presence of higher-dimensional and interdimensional helpers, because each of you has a part to play as a spiritual facilitator in your own way. And it is very important that in using the tools given, you do so with discriminating wisdom and without usurping the personal growth of the individual. To attempt to fix it for someone who is not doing his or her part is indeed to hold that person back, in the long run. What each person must do and experience in order to learn and grow must never be postponed or interrupted by an overeager teacher or healer, no matter how loving the intention might be.

That will suffice for now. Again, we thank you for this opportunity, and we anticipate joyful co-creation with you in the future.

Running Your Higher Self Cosmic Kundalini and Earth Kundalini

If you have not been practicing Higher Self meditations for bringing your Higher Self fully into your body, and running kundalini up your spinal and leg and arm channels, do not do this process. Until these prerequisites have been done and kundalini has been run for at least three months, it is not safe to proceed with this process. If you need assistance in accomplishing these goals, techniques for Higher Self embodiment are included in *The Pleiadian Workbook: Awakening Your Divine Ka*. Techniques for clearing your body kundalini channels and running kundalini safely are included in *The Pleiadian Tantric Workbook: Awakening Your Divine Ba*.

Once you feel certain that your kundalini channels in your body have been open and running well for three months, and you have worked with Higher Self embodiment meditations during that time, then you can safely proceed. If still unsure, you might consider working with a healer who has expertise in kundalini. There are phone and e-mail contact numbers for our organization in the back of this book. This will give you access to our healing practitioners in your area or to those who do phone sessions, if you need assistance in this regard.

Once you have opened your Tube of Light connection to your Higher Self, activating your Higher Self Cosmic Kundalini is as simple as an invocation and breathing. It is your Higher Self who regulates the amount and nature of your Cosmic Kundalini flow. The first time it is activated, you will be guided to pause and fill up different areas before moving the energy through your Tube of Light to your perineum center, where it is anchored. Your pineal gland will be filled to overflowing before you breathe this kundalini down into your brain stem and to a membranous sheath around your atlas, or top vertebra. Your Cosmic Kundalini will activate this sheath and overflow around and through your brain before bringing it into your spinal cord, which is next. When the kundalini has moved through the length of your spine, it will stop briefly at another membranous sheath around your tailbone. There it overflows into your sacral area and aligns with the pumping action of your cranial bones and sacrum, as they expand and relax synchronistically, pumping cerebrospinal fluid through your spinal cord and trace amounts throughout your nervous system. When this is complete, your Cosmic Kundalini finds its final destination as it activates your perineum center and anchors there.

Once your Cosmic Kundalini has reached your perineum center, you will activate your Earth Kundalini. This is done by sending a burst of Cosmic Kundalini with a powerful blowing outbreath to the Earth Star Crystal at the center of Earth. The Earth Kundalini will automatically begin to flow into your aura and into your foot chakras and root chakra, taking its own root through your body at that time. Running Earth Kundalini has a great balancing effect on your body and Cosmic Kundalini flows. When you first activate these new kundalinis, I recommend that you run them only in meditation for a few minutes at a time for about a week. Pacing how often and how long you run these energies after that is up to your personal preference and guidance.

Guided Meditation for Activating Your Higher Self Cosmic Kundalini and Earth Kundalini 🎞

1. Ground, and pull your aura in to arm's length around you in every direction.

2. Call on your Higher Self of the Light to fill your Tube of Light with your Divine Essence energy.

3. Turn on your kundalini in your spinal channels by taking a deep breath in through the base of your spine, up your spine, and out your crown.

4. Take a couple of deep breaths in through the bottoms of your feet, up your legs, up the outside of your torso, down your arms, and out through the palms of your hands. This activates the kundalini side channels.

5. Ask your Higher Self to activate your Cosmic Kundalini. Taking a deep sucking breath, breathe in through the topmost point of your aura, drawing your Cosmic Kundalini into your Tube of Light and into your Crown Chakra. From there, breathe it into your pineal gland in the center of your head. Allow the Cosmic Kundalini to fill and overflow your pineal gland before you move on.

6. Deeply inhale, drawing your Cosmic Kundalini into the sheath around your atlas, or top vertebra. As your kundalini activates the sheath it will overflow around, and then through, your brain. Continue to breathe deeply into your atlas and brain until the activation has stopped.

7. With another deep sucking breath, pull your Cosmic Kundalini down the entire length of your spine through your spinal cord.

8. When your Cosmic Kundalini overflows the tailbone into the sheath around it, breathe it into your sacral area for about twenty seconds.

9. Breathe deeply, drawing your Cosmic Kundalini into your perineum center until it is full.

10. When this center is completely filled, take a deep inhalation. Blow

powerfully on your exhalation, sending a burst of Cosmic Kundalini to the Earth Star Crystal at the center of Earth. Once will suffice. Almost immediately, you will feel a response in your foot chakras and root chakras. Inhale through those chakras, drawing the Earth Kundalini upward. It will naturally take its own course based on what is appropriate for you at this time.

11. Meditate for about eight to ten minutes in whatever way you prefer. When that is complete, ask your Higher Self to turn off your Cosmic Kundalini. The Earth Kundalini will automatically turn off as well.

25

Initiation of the Bardos

A Channeling of Mother Mary, Easter 1999

Mother Mary: When the one you know as my son, and I, experienced the initiation of death and resurrection together in Egypt, the one you call Jesus the Christ was eighteen years of age. When we visited the temples in Egypt for that final initiation, it was given by sealing the initiate in a sarcophagus in a chamber beneath the surface of the earth. It was during this initiation, which was spoken of in *Pleiadian Perspectives on Human Evolution,* that we had to cross the isle of crocodiles first before we even arrived at the death chambers. These are the chambers of death and resurrection because they contain the portals into what the Buddhist path calls the Bardos, or the seven Hells. In Egypt it was called the death of the seven egos. When the initiate entered those chambers, the sarcophogi were sealed. Almost immediately I felt a sense of being spun downward into the earth, into a specific section of the halls of Amenti, where the gates of Hell exist. But, you see, what is spoken of as Hell in your modern-day Bible is a gross misinterpretation. It has incorrectly been made to sound like a place where you are judged by some fear-inducing God, and then cast into as punishment for your sins.

These regions of Hell, the Bardos, or the seven egos, are simply regions of consciousness in which you, at some point in your spiritual growth, in your process of forgetting and remembering, have become entrapped, for you meet nothing in the Bardos that is not totally created by your own ego mind at some point in your lifetime or lifetimes. When a human being is moving into mastery, he or she must face every addictive temptation, every ego allurement, whether it be for power or powerlessness in order to avoid responsibility. Whether that ego identity be that of the victim of rape or incest or a brutal death—or whether it be as a victimizer reexperiencing the horror of lifetimes in which you have been the one who raped or murdered—if you fear a part of your own psyche, then you are a creator of your own Hell, because if you fear that part of you that has the capacity to be a murderer, you empower it to exist. Whereas if you face it by affirming that there is nothing to be ashamed of, knowing you will never act on this negative ego impulse again and that it is not your truth, then you are free to feel the emotions and transmute them with the power of the Holy Spirit. Then you have true power, because you know you have transcended the capacity for committing harmful acts or believing in victimhood. Of course, you would never be asked to go through the test of the Bardos and face your seven egos until you have reached a point on your spiritual path at which you have the potential for passing through them successfully. If you are truly moving toward mastery, it is inevitable that you will face this initiation eventually. And yet, when you have truly transcended those false identities and moved beyond guilt, shame, fear, addiction, and other entrapments, then it is no longer a challenge.

When Jesus was eighteen years of age, he and I entered the chambers of death and resurrection together. While in those chambers, we could not submit to a single ego allurement or judgment or fear or shame or avoidance. If we had painfully reacted to the painful or alluring scenes we witnessed, or even shrunk away, we could not have returned to our bodies, and they would have been found dead at the end of the initiation. Remember—the chambers themselves were portals through which we entered into the regions of Hell. We could exit the Bardos only by going through them to the other side. We could not go in reverse. If we had become caught up in, and identified with, what we witnessed there, we would have become entrapped there until we transcended the false identity and released all emotional and mental reactions.

You [Amorah] have something in your psyche to say about this.

Amorah: When I saw the movie *What Dreams May Come,* I noticed that some people hated the scene about the Hells. I sat there in a state of awe the whole time it was going on, because I was excited that a movie could be put out to show people how to go through the Bardos. If Earth happened to go through a disaster, during which there was a lot of fear and panic and people were dying, it showed people how not to go into the astral planes by simply not believing in it, and making love your only truth. That is what that movie was do-ing. It is a movie of the time, because it is preparing people to under-stand that even in the worst circumstances, one can simply look at it and say, "This is not real." And with that simple thought, that will-ingness not to believe in it and identify with it, you can be raised into the Light. Mary wanted me to mention that because it is a good mod-ern-day reference point.

Mother Mary: I speak to you of this, dear ones, because in your daily lives you are in a constant process of preparing yourselves for this fi-nal initiation. Even the human beings who do not know about initia-tions, or the test of the Bardos, are always in a state of preparing themselves whether they know it or not. When you live in misery, it is because your identity has become engulfed in a Hell of your own making. And a Hell of your own making can also be someone else's Hell that you have been repulsed by or afraid of. And by having a re-action to someone else's Hell you join that person in it. So we have these Hell regions that are a co-creation, that are agreed on as com-pletely as you have all agreed to see these flowers on the table as red. And as completely as you all have agreed to see the candle containers as a rainbow formation, you can as easily agree to see the world as a dangerous place. Or you can choose to see the world as a school that has been created for the purpose of learning the difference between Divine Truth, relative truth, and illusion. And if Divine Truth is truly ultimate, it will reign supreme eventually.

When your consciousness has explored every other possibility and has come back home to itself, and when your consciousness has rec-ognized that when it had a loving thought free of attachments, and that good things happened as a result, and when your consciousness experiences going through a situation that has been painful in the past with a different attitude, and finds itself not in pain—then you are home.

In the Bardos, in that final initiation, that is when you know you can trust yourself to be a fully sovereign Master Being, or Christed One. You will have transcended the need to have mastery over anything other than yourself and your relationship to All That Is. So, from a practical daily standpoint, think of yourselves as in a constant preparatory test of the Bardos, for you are. In that constant preparatory state, it is simply an issue of how long your identity stays in any place of pain, addiction, and illusion before you return to a place of love, acceptance, and experience of your greatest joy. This is the stuff of which true freedom is made, the stuff of which true self-trust and self-respect are born. This is home—wherever you are! Namasté.

26

The Resurrection Process

A Channeling of Ascended Master Jesus Christ, Easter 1999

Ascended Master Jesus Christ: Beloved brothers and sisters, there is great fascination in the human race with anything that seems unexplainable, with anything that seems beyond the explainable, with anything that seems to be a result of some unknown psychic phenomenon or hidden power. There is a tendency in the human to be just like an animal sniffing what seems to be a particularly savory smell. When these energies arise, many humans approach them from a place of fascination and a certain type of spiritual gluttony. And yet, those of you who are here are not here to be fascinated, because you have chosen a path of mastery—a path that will take you to total transformation and peace. Yet, we wish to help you be aware that you may sometimes feel, even in the presence of higher Truth, this spiritual gluttony that we call fascination with the unexplainable, and with psychic phenomena. We ask you to see this through eyes of amusement instead of through eyes of judgment. Some of you have avoided dealing with issues that involve miracles and psychic phenomena, because you know that it can be seductive and pull you back if you become too entranced with it. Perhaps I can demystify this issue for you a little by sharing parts of my own experience that are considered supernatural.

Tonight I have chosen to speak to you about my experience of what you would perceive as physical death and resurrection. Then I will talk with you about the experiences of my final departure from my physical body later in life. When my body was placed upon the cross, it was indeed a physical act. It was one that created great loss of blood and led to a physical death. Yet when a person has reached a certain level of mastery over identity with the body, and has reached a certain level of mastery in which one no longer fears the pain of death, there is a way that one can consciously remove one's self from the body in such a way that one need not experience the worst of the pain. This is what I did.

When I appeared to go unconscious on the cross, it was the point at which I had achieved removal of myself completely from the cellular structure of the body. Yet I held myself connected to the body in what you know as an astral body. An astral body is the body that has a cord made of white light that glows silver and connects through what you call the chakra of the solar plexus, or third chakra. This astral body is your dream body. I simply removed all of my connections to sensation, all of my connections to the nervous system, and stayed above the body surrounded by a host of angelic beings and other Masters who where present. We encircled the crucified body in a Pillar of Light. The moment the physical body let go of the last bit of life force (because I kept the astral body connection, which is normally released at the point of death), I was able to freeze the body in a sort of stasis until I was ready to reenter. By holding the physical body in that Pillar of Light, and having no consciousness in the body at the time of the death, I was able to retain my true consciousness intact. Certainly, having completed the test of the Bardos was a great preparation.

There is not one of you in this room who would be incapable of achieving exactly that same act, if you simply knew it to be possible. For it is like going into a deep meditation, in which you focus on breathing all of your consciousness into a single point of light; then you project that point of light through the third chakra into the astral body until there is no consciousness left in the body. *You are capable of achieving anything that has your full attention.*

This teaching is being given now because the upcoming times on Earth are quite unpredictable, even by us. If you are ever in an experience that would require or cause a physical death, and it is not your time, and you know you still have reason to remain, you can choose exactly the same experience of resurrection that I did. All you need do is focus, first in the pineal gland. Collect all your energy in your pineal gland. Spin it until you build enough momentum that you can literally suck all of the energy from your pineal gland directly into your soul matrix. At that point you have disconnected primarily from your head.

Then you begin the same process again, only this time in the soul area in the center of your chest. You breathe yourself into the consciousness of your soul until you are so much at the center of that light that you can begin to collect the light, as opposed to letting it shine through the cells of your body, as is normally done. In the collecting of this light, you begin to whirl the soul matrix so that as the light rays are sent outward, they spin around themselves instead of through your cellular structure. There is a natural moment when this is so complete that you can once again simply whirl or project that consciousness, with great intensity of thought momentum, into the area of your root chakra.

At the base of your spine, between your perineum and your tailbone, is the center that you call your kundalini reservoir. Just below your kundalini reservoir is the entry perineum portal through which your Ka connects into your lower body. [Refer to chapter 7 in *The Pleiadian Workbook: Awakening Your Divine Ka* for more details about Ka and Ka portals.] Between your perineum center and your kundalini reservoir, there is a threefold flame, one of three threefold flames in your body [see illustration page 258]. The other two are located in your pineal gland, and in your soul area of your heart chakra. What you must do is connect with all three of these threefold flames simultaneously. In your upper chakras, the threefold flames appear more like light and geometry than in your perineum/root chakra location. Once you have collected the threefold flames in the pineal and soul areas and spun them around themselves, you draw them into your root chakra to blend with that threefold flame there. This last one is the fire of your life force. It is the fire of your passion, your sexual fire. It is the fire of desire for life. Your full consciousness is at that stage blended with and spinning all three threefold flames as a trinity. Continue until there is such a momentum and such a power in that trinity of threefold flames in the root that you can send it directly up your spine and out through your crown chakra. Immediately propel your consciousness into the back of your solar plexus chakra, through the silver cord of your astral body. Use a forceful outbreath to push your astral body outside your physical body. Direct your consciousness, in your astral body, into the higher planes with clear intention to enter the City of Light. You can command the gates of the Cities of Light to open as you project yourself within this trinity of threefold flames. You will be in your astral body. At that point you are in total command of the reality of the physical. There may still be fragments of life force clearing in the cellular structure of your physical body. But at the final moment of the physical body's death, there is a release that is like a sudden collecting of all the remaining light in your body into a single light. This light combines with your soul and looks like the symbol of the yod [see illustration on page 260]. It shoots straight up and out the crown chakra if you are in a state of complete let go and surrender. The moment you see that light move out through your crown, you call it to you with your love. It blends with the trinity threefold flame matrix. At that moment you can command the temple of your deceased physical body to remain unchanged. From the Cities of Light you can surround your physical body in a crystalline matrix that suspends it between dimensional realities. This can be maintained for a maximum of about twenty-four hours. At that point, the higher-dimensional hold on the physical reality begins to wane. It is still possible, with great force, to reconnect to your body for a few hours beyond that point, but it is simpler and more assured of success within the twenty-four-hour period.

When I began my resurrection process on the cross, this is the process I used. If you are in a sudden-death experience, of course, you do not have time to prepare yourself for the physical death. But you do have the ability to go into a state of total surrender and to move back into your physical body with a spark of consciousness. This spark will be just enough to reclaim the remains of your threefold flame trinity. If you do not dissolve your astral body—if you can see a death coming and you say vehemently, "I CHOOSE LIFE!"—then you can take your consciousness out into the astral body and remain connected. Yes,

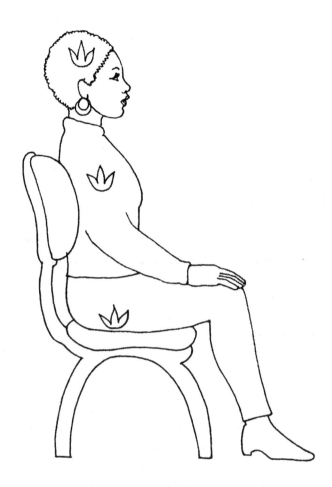

*The Threefold Flames are located in
your pineal gland, soul matrix, and perineum center.*

even after the physical body has died, you can still reclaim the energy
from the three major centers and achieve resurrection if you remain
fully conscious and focused.

When my body was being removed from the cross and taken into
the tomb, there were two angels attending me. It took a matter of
only minutes within the tomb for us to prepare the body for resurrection. And resurrection is truly a spiritual birthing experience. Many

people who have had death experiences, gone to the other side, and returned have done this same process. It is a choice. When I reentered the physical body I prepared the centers first. The angels and I worked together by simply reinstating a light matrix where the three-fold flames had been held in the pineal, the soul, and the perineum centers. When the light matrix was in place, the body was unfrozen. Still in my astral body, I began to slowly move back in and blend with my physical body, one chakra at a time, awakening the body from the center out. It was a process of a few hours of full recovery as I consciously reconnected to the nervous system and the brain. It took time to project my consciousness into each of the centers fully until each one individually was alive and functioning. It was many hours that a visible glow remained around my physical body. This is attributed to the fact that there is a moment in a resurrection experience during which the physical body becomes just light. The body then becomes invisible to those who cannot see that frequency. Then it returns to being physically visible, but with a lingering glow.

When my wife, Mary Magdalene, arrived at the tomb the next morning, there was a great rejoicing when she saw the tomb was open. She knew that I had passed the initiation of resurrection, as had been planned. It was done to show human beings the potential of your own spiritual power and focus of mind. It is rare that a human being has even an inkling of the power of mind when intensely focused on a singular purpose. And it is with that singular purpose of mind that enlightenment is achieved on each level. It is with this disciplined focus that the will of your spirit becomes stronger than your ego's will. It is with single-mindedness that even a physical death and resurrection is attained. It is with single-mindedness that a person might levitate, or learn teleportation. All of these supposed extrasensory experiences or supposed psychic phenomena are explainable if you understand the vastness of your consciousness. To prepare yourself for resurrection, however, you must be able to focus all of your consciousness on a singular purpose for a sustained period of time. And to prepare for this, you must have all of your consciousness collected in your multidimensional hologram, as you speak of it in this day and age. In other words, you must have gathered and brought into divine alignment all of your missing parts, whether they be ghosts or soul fragments or traumatized aspects frozen in shock or

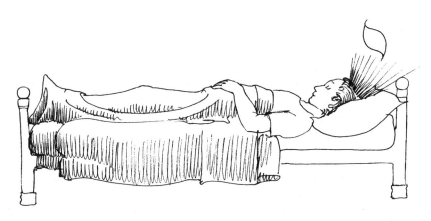

The release of life force creates
a light that looks like the symbol of the yod.

dark aspects stuck in lower astral planes. You see, the human condition today is one of much fragmentation. Most human beings are still very attached to placing their consciousness in places where they feel more in control, or in avoidance of fear. But in order to collect yourself into wholeness, you must apply the principle of resurrection to daily life. This is what I wish to speak of now.

Perhaps the single most important thing that you can do on Earth at this time is learn how to use the principle of resurrection to transcend ego identity. And it is really simple. It has to do with the power of your consciousness to collect itself and focus anywhere it wants to be. If you have an effective process for truly being in spiritual love and anchoring your Higher Self to your body, it is a very excellent way of tricking the mind into changing its focus. On one level of perceiving it, it is literal, and on another it is strictly a trick that you use to change your mind. And yet that is an extremely valuable trick. Whatever you can do to shift into feeling that pure, innocent, wise unconditional, loving self, in any part of your body, is an important beginning. Even if you can only bring your Higher Self as far as your pineal gland, you can use the principle of resurrection to begin the transcendence of ego identity. If you can bring your Higher Self into your whole body, as I will ask Amorah to instruct you in meditation, then it is even easier. All you have to do is place your full consciousness into the place inside where you feel that divine love and innocence, until you have melded with it and become one consciousness. Then, wherever in your body you feel anger, fear, shame, tension, resistance, or avoidance, you begin to shine your light of consciousness, and spin it. You will then direct a single ray of light from that place of loving consciousness into the area of your body in which you feel your ego identity, or old emotion, is held. You pull your higher consciousness with your breath in that stream of light into the place you feel the aspects of your energy in need of release, healing, or transformation. You will continue until you feel nothing there but radiant love and light. It is a supreme process of transmutation. In order to use this resurrection process, you must be ready to let go of all avoidance. You must be able to witness any aspect of your psyche without judgment.

Amorah: At this point, Christ has asked me to share the personal experience that follows:

I went through an experience during which I literally recognized I was creating a physical death for myself this year. It made me look very seriously at what I was doing at that time. I realized one morning that I was avoiding something I did not want to feel in myself, and that I had to face it or literally die. When this realization came, I affirmed at once, "Whatever it is, I am willing to feel it, and I am willing to realize that there is nothing inside me that I need to judge." As soon as I affirmed this, I saw the face of a former lover filling my third eye. I felt the longing to be with him, deeply and passionately. I immediately felt how much shame I had in my body because I was intimately involved with someone else at the time. I subsequently realized that the reason I was harming myself was that I thought it was not okay to feel those feelings for my ex while in a new relationship. So I told myself, "If it's there, it's okay to feel it. It's what I choose to do with it that really matters." I asked my guides to come in and seal me in protection so I would not create a psychic link with that person. This freed me to feel everything to its depths that I felt about my ex, instead of avoiding and judging it. So I did, and it took me a long time. Knowing that I would not breach his psychic field or create astral links, I let myself feel and imagine, even on a sexual level, everything I had repressed in shame. I was missing him deeply. Please realize that I was not doing this from a place of indulgence. I was doing it from a place of taking my consciousness to the depths of what I was avoiding in order to release it, while loving it all the while. By the time I was done, I was in a state of total peace. I no longer felt any kind of attachment to him, and the shame was in the process of dissolving. So I guess I was using the principle of the resurrection process without the exact techniques. I was applying the principles of nonavoidance, nonjudgment, and loving self-acceptance—while still moving and releasing the energy. If I had worked exactly as Christ is saying now, I am certain it would have been much faster. But I had to work through so much self-judgment first.

Ascended Master Jesus Christ: This is a supreme example of what I speak, and it was spoken very beautifully. To accept what seems unacceptable is the supreme test of self-love and self-trust. So, of course, to apply the principle of resurrection one must have embraced those principles first, because you must be able to apply those principles to whatever you find within.

What I would like to speak of briefly now is the physical death experience. When I was eighty-nine years old, I was still very vital in my body. Mary Magdalene and I had moved together at times, and at times had done separate service. We were together then, with a group of yogis and secret initiates from the ancient Egyptian schools. At that time it was becoming dangerous for Egyptian citizens to acknowledge connection to the schools of Isis and Osiris. Yet only a handful of people on the entire planet still held the secrets of mummification. There has been much superstition around mummification. In many cultures it has been done for the wrong reasons. The original purpose of mummification was for transcendence of the need, during reincarnation, for a soul to enter into a new lifetime, taking on an entire karmic pattern that had already been transcended in a previous lifetime. In other words, if a person experienced physical death and the body was either buried in the earth or cut apart—as they did in the ancient Tibetan traditions—or cremated, a certain limitation was placed on the next lifetime. The learnings from the previous lifetime would be at least partially blocked. In cultures in which this was understood, to mummify a person's body was a way of keeping the person connected to former learnings through the genetics and cells of that person's former body. This would also connect them to their evolutionary attainment, so they could literally start in the next life exactly where they left off in the previous one. I'm sure you can see the great advantage of this, as opposed to the alternative of forgetting and remembering. The destruction of the teachings of mummification was done to interfere with conscious use of the cycles of reincarnation in this way. It was also destroyed to prevent certain beings from coming into the Egyptian culture as spiritually empowered leaders. Those teachings will be found again, by the way.

The other use of mummification is to assist individuals who have completed their cycle of lives and need not come back again at all. If the individual has chosen a path of maintaining strong contact with the human race and Earth as a guide or Ascended Master, a mummified body—or at times even a statue that can hold the person's consciousness—can be used to maintain that link to Earth for as long as is chosen.

This was my path, because I was to remain in close connection with the human race through the Cities of Light. I chose to go through a conscious death experience, with the assistance of the teachings of the yogis and with what I had learned through my own resurrection. I chose to completely remove myself from the body, allowing it to go through a death in which there was a total release of all life force. Then my body was mummified and preserved in such a way as to maintain my multidimensional link until my particular service here is complete.

There was a group of people who assisted in this process, with my beloved wife, Mary Magdalene, in charge. In those ancient times, women were honored as the source of spiritual genetics that births the body and delivers the soul to Earth. It is through the divine feminine that the lightbody is carried into the higher dimensions for rebirth as well. As an initiate of the Priestesses of Isis, having passed all of the initiations of the mystery schools of Egypt, England, India, France, and Spain, Mary Magdalene was the natural facilitator of this process. The one you think of as my mother, Mary, has a mummy in the same cave in which my mummified body lies. This cave is inside a cinder-cone—shaped hill in the foothills of the Himalayas, between India and Tibet. It is on the Indian side just a little. When the mummification was completed, my body was sealed inside the hill in such a way that the hill looked solid, devoid of cave openings. So these mummies have never been found and are not intended to be. It allows us to maintain a type of connection to Earth in which we can occasionally make ourselves physically visible in our lightbodies. It allows us a more direct access to the beings of Earth. That is why so many more people have seen us—as well as others, like St. Germaine, who have mummies still on Earth—than have seen, for example, the angels.

I thank you for your attention during this teaching. It is a great honor to be able to give it at this time. I would like to turn this over to Amorah now for the meditation. I wish to say to you that regardless of the outcome of this time frame on Earth, the Divine Plan will be revealed and actualized. It will happen in your time. It is only the exact steps between here and there that are unknown. Do not allow yourself to become dismayed or go into hopelessness if it does not happen in a way you hoped for. If it does happen in a glorious way, it is certainly a time for rejoicing that the highest possibility has been actualized. Yet, keep your faith, keep the knowing of the power of choice that is within your mind, and teach your mind to focus in a singular way. Then you will truly know you are a divine creator. This is the prayer I leave with you. I await the time we walk consciously together, hand in hand, brother and sister again. So-la-re-en-lo.

Amorah: As I felt his energy moving out of my Higher Self blending, he sent back a message to someone here. The message is this: "Yes, there is also a kind of ascension in which the body dissolves completely into the Light. But there is also a type of fully conscious physical death, such as what I experienced, that is also a type of ascension. When a person can move directly through the pillars and the gateways without stopping, without any interruption, and with total consciousness the whole time, it is still ascension. Sometimes the body is left behind if there is a purpose for that. So it is really important in this time not to judge if someone you think is moving toward ascension goes through a physical death. There actually can be a purpose in that. Do not judge the surface of events, because there are many ways that the Divine Plan can work out at this time."

Amorah resumes leading the group into a meditation, with occasional guidance by the Christ: Each of you needs to select an issue in need of transformation: an area of your consciousness in which you wish to experience ego death and resurrection. Choose something you still feel is a challenge, a place in your body where you know you are still holding fear, resentment, or other old emotions. No matter what you do, you cannot seem to get to the bottom of it and end it. If you do not know what it is at this time, ask the guides, during the meditation, to impulse you to feel what it is you need to heal. But if you do know of something you are working on actively, whether it is a physical, emotional, or mental problem, you can ask the guides to help you transmute it, as much as is possible at this time, during the mediation. We will begin with the Higher Self Blending Meditation and continue into the Resurrection Chamber from there.

Higher Self Blending Meditation 📼

1. Close your eyes, and take two or three full-body breaths. Breathe all the way into your fingers and toes and all the way into your whole body, exhaling through your skin. Take as long as you need to accomplish this before moving on.

2. Pull your aura in to two to three feet around you. Visualize an egg-shaped bubble around you, two to three feet in every direction. Pull your entire aura into that bubble, and fill it with your energy.

3. Invite the beloved ones Jesus Christ, Mary Magdalene, and Mother Mary of the Light to be with you.

4. Invite the Dolphin Star Temple Higher Council of Light, including the Pleiadian, Sirian, and Andromedan Emissaries of Light, to come and to place you in a Meditation and Resurrection Chamber of Light.

5. Ask that the Interdimensional, Evolutionary, and Intergalactic Cones of Light be placed at the top of your aura. Ask for the Earth Cone of Light to be placed at the bottom of your aura.

6. Ask your Higher Self of the Light to come to you in whatever light form you are ready to connect with and integrate into your body consciousness now. Ask your Higher Self to project an image of itself to which you can relate. It might come to you looking like an angelic presence or a white-robed Master or a Merlin or a priestess. Ask that aspect of your Higher Self to place its hands on yours, palms together. Receive love and light

through your hands, and breathe them into your whole body. Imagine that you can look directly into the eyes of your Higher Self. See what those eyes would look like if your Higher Self had a body. Keep breathing and acclimating your body to receive Higher Self's energy.

7. This is a good time to ask your Higher Self for what you want. If you want to embody your Higher Self all the time, ask for it. If you want to come to that point of a single consciousness where there is no longer you and Higher Self, tell your Higher Self your intention. Tell your Higher Self that you are ready to surrender all ego identity, all ideas of separation.

8. Now ask your Higher Self to stand behind you facing your back so that you can make a link between the back side, or subconscious, of your chakras, and your Higher Self's chakras.

9. Ask your Higher Self to send a beam of light from its crown chakra into yours. Breathe as deeply into your crown as you can, surrendering your crown chakra to your Higher Self. Affirm that the crown chakra functions only in alignment with your highest truth.

10. Breathing into the back of your third eye, breathe in a beam of light from your Higher Self's third eye into yours until it is all the way through to the front of your third eye. As you are drawing the energy through the chakra with your breath, affirm, "I am ready to surrender all that I see to seeing through the eyes of truth, to seeing through eyes that only see the beauty." Ask your Higher Self to burn through the veils of judgment, shame, separation, and distrust so you can see Truth.

11. Breathing in through the back of your throat chakra, draw in a beam of light from your Higher Self's throat chakra. Breathe the energy all the way through until you feel it in the front of your throat chakra. Affirm, "I surrender my throat chakra to only speak truth from my essence. May my words never harm myself or others."

12. Bring in a beam of light from your Higher Self's heart chakra to yours. Breathe it all the way through until you can feel it move through to the front of your heart chakra. Affirm, "I

surrender my heart to the full awakening of the beauty of my soul, and to feeling deep, unconditional self-love and love for others."

13. Breathe in a beam of light from your Higher Self's solar plexus into the back of yours. Breathe deeply until you can feel the energy penetrating through to the front of your solar plexus chakra. Affirm, "I surrender my solar plexus chakra to Divine Will, and I command my ego willfulness to be released and dissolved. My solar plexus chakra is a center of divine power."

14. Breathe in a beam of light from your Higher Self's sacral chakra into yours, all the way to the front of your sacral chakra. Affirm, "I surrender the use of my sacral chakra sexual energy, passion, and emotional feelings to their higher, sacred purpose."

15. Breathe in a beam of light from your Higher Self's root chakra into yours. Breathe, opening your root chakra as fully as possible. Affirm, "I surrender my body to full aliveness, to full vitality, and to being a temple for my Holy Spirit."

16. As you deepen that connection in your root chakra, you will begin to feel the lightbody of your Higher Self begin to merge with your physical body, blending into a single form. Begin to take full-body breaths, but this time breathe in from behind your body to the front of your body, all the way up and down. Welcome your Higher Self to come and dwell in your physical body deeply into each chakra, into your cells, into your limbs. As your Higher Self blending deepens, you will be able to feel that light and love moving through you. If there are places in your body where it cannot penetrate, breathe deeper into those areas.

17. Now the Christ is asking you to focus on your pineal gland, in the center of your head. Ask your Higher Self to blend fully into your pineal gland and into the threefold flame there. Your pineal gland has the sacred geometry of the sunflower, the Fibonacci spiral [see illustration on page 268]. Breathe into, and gently spin, that Fibonacci spiral matrix as a way of opening your pineal gland to receive Higher Self. If you start to feel pressure in your skull, ears, cheeks, or anywhere in your head,

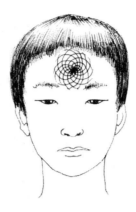

The Fibonacci spiral of the pineal gland
has the sacred geometry of the sunflower.

press your tongue in to the roof of your mouth to assist your cranial bones and facial plates in opening. Spinning your pineal gland will make your head feel expansive. If your cranial bones are blocked, it could be a little bit tight or painful. Keep breathing until you can feel your pure Divine Light filling your pineal gland. (You may need to make slow circles with your head to release tension.) When you have built a lot of energy in your pineal gland, intend with great focus to move beyond time and space limitations. Spinning your pineal gland with your Higher Self blending is enabling you to anchor multidimensional awareness of yourself while still in your body.

18. Now do the same process in your soul area in the center of your chest, about one and a half to two inches to the interior. Breathe, and draw all of your consciousness into your soul matrix. Your soul is like a little star or sun that anchors into the sacred geometry of a double tetrahedron merkaba [see illustration on page 270]. Ask the guides to assist you in healing and restoring this sacred geometry as needed. Breathe into your soul area, asking your Higher Self to blend fully into your soul matrix and the threefold flame there. Spin the soul merkaba gently at whatever pace is natural. All you have to do is intend

it while bringing your Higher Self consciousness and your body consciousness together inside your soul matrix. You do not need to know the direction; just ask it to spin in its natural way. Use your breath to give it a little momentum. You may feel a split in your consciousness, because your pineal is also very active. If you find it difficult to move your whole consciousness into your heart, it is okay. When the resurrection process accompanies an actual physical death, you do want to pull all of the energy of your pineal into the soul, but you would have to build up much more momentum to do that. For this use of the resurrection process you are creating a triple point of awareness to utilize the resurrection beams.

19. Breathe into and focus as much attention in the area of your perineum center as you can. The sacred geometry of your perineum center is the shape of a diamond, or octahedron, standing on its tip. As you see in the illustration above, this octahedron is composed of two pyramids, each with four

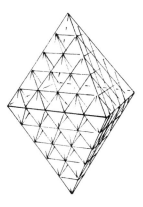

The Diamond Octahedron is the Sacred Geometry of the Perineum Center.

sides, with their bases together. Within this octahedron are many tiny octahedron diamonds. Ask the guides for any needed healing or repairs to the sacred geometry of your perineum. Begin to spin it. A very erratic spinning pattern

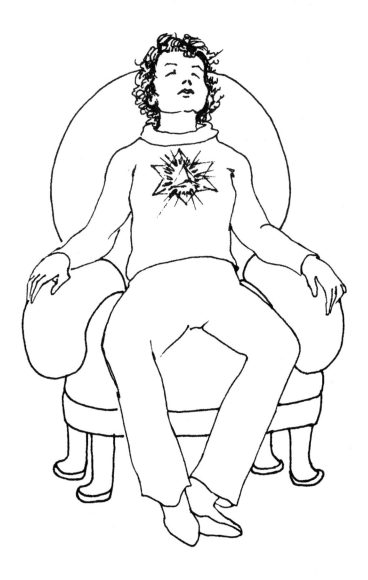

The Sacred Geometry of the Soul Matrix
is the Double Tetrahedron into which the soul anchors.

will commence. The octahedron does not spin round and round; it spins off in different directions at different times. Just breathe, and pull Higher Self in to fill your perineum center and the threefold flame just above it. Keep breathing deeply, and pull your consciousness in as much as you can.

20. Some of you may be aware of a sound that is being emitted from your pineal gland through your soul matrix down to your perineum linking the three centers [see illustration on page 272]. This "beam of sound" aligns you in resonance in those three sacred centers. You may have to tilt your pelvis backward and forward just a little to intensify the sound and focus of consciousness there. Next a phenomenon will occur in which it seems as if all three of those centers are in one location that fills your whole body, superimposed one around the other. Even though each occupies an individual space in our human way of seeing, in a fifth-dimensional way of seeing they are all occupying identical space, overlapping one another, creating multiple spin patterns of the varied geometric shapes. Find a way to hold the concept of a holographic Fibonacci spiral spinning inside a double tetrahedron, which is spinning in both directions at the same time on a horizontal plane. Then imagine the diamond-shaped octahedron spinning, blended with the other two forms, in its erratic diagonal spin patterns. Together they create an illusion of circles spinning on diagonals in many planes. This is because they are all moving so fast. You do not have to be able to see them all at once, but you do need to hold the concept.

21. Begin to tone the sound that you hear emitted by the synchronized movement in the trinity of centers. Bring your middle fingertip and thumb together on both hands, palms up. This will help you anchor the energy.

22. Find the location in which you can feel the strongest concentration of energy in those centers. Hold as much of your consciousness there as you can. It may be a combination of two centers as a single ball of light or consciousness, or it may be a single center. Allow the light to stay as big as it is, but narrow

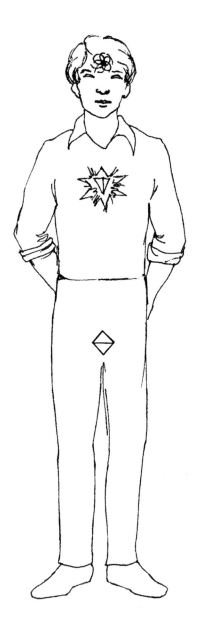

*The Three Sacred Centers used in the Resurrection Process
create multiple spin patterns of the varied geometric shapes.*

the focus of your consciousness so that you are concentrating in a small central area in your pineal gland. Your pineal gland has a natural way of sending beams to specific locations in your body. If you are more in your heart, you may choose to stay there instead of moving into your pineal gland. Now breathe into the location in your body that holds the pain or ego emotional identity you wish to transmute. If you already know what and where the issue is, all you have to do is start focusing a beam of light from your consciousness into the place in your body where you feel the block. If you do not know, ask the guides to impulse to feel the area of your body in need of clearing. It may be an area of pain, contraction, emotion, resistance, or other ego agendas. As you focus an intense beam of light from your pineal gland, heart, and perineum in that area, you may wish to continue toning the sound of the three centers into the area being cleared. You might also like to use affirmations such as "I Am the Light of God/Goddess. Pain is not my truth." Substitute any emotion for the word *pain*. Ask all the angels and guides who are holding the chambers to assist you in making this as gracious and effortless as possible. Let it be a gentle process of breathing light and love into a dark corner free of effortful processing. Keep focusing the light into the area, and direct some of your consciousness on that beam of light until you can occupy that part of the body with higher consciousness and it is totally open and free. You will reach a point at which you feel your consciousness equally in the part of the body that is going through the death and resurrection and in your pineal gland or heart. When you feel the energy is equal, then simply allow yourself to breathe back and forth between these areas of consciousness. This begins the process of dissolving the lower energies. What you will actually feel is the lower energy breaking up and moving through the beam of light and finally dissolving into the light. Continue until the transmutation feels complete.

23. Ask for the spin of those energy centers to slow down to an appropriate level for you in waking consciousness. When it has slowed down enough to let you feel you can continue with your

normal daily activities, make sure you are grounded. Then open your eyes and continue with your day.

I have found that I experience a continuing state of heightened energy flow throughout my body after doing the Resurrection Chamber sessions. You may choose to do this meditation in the daytime to ensure that it does not keep you awake at night.

Part 7

Return to Divine Flow

This final step of working directly with the Elohim for restoring the Matrix of Divine Flow is a must during this time of planetary acceleration—especially on a cellular level. I have been deeply touched by the understanding of how responsibility for our own attitudes corresponds directly with how much assistance we can receive from the higher-dimensional Light Beings. Of course, it must be so in order to achieve mastery—and achievement of mastery is, for each of us, our birthright and destiny. So why not make it as gracious and loving as we can along the way?

27

The Matrix of Divine Flow

A Channeling of the One That Is Many and the Many That Are One, April 2000

A small group was gathered for the monthly spiritual gathering at my home on April 2, 2000, when this teaching and channeling came through. I am choosing to include the information I shared with the group before the channeling began, because it sets the stage for the channeled information. The theme I was guided to share that night was about planetary dispensations and the current level of activation from the photon band and higher-dimensional beings. Following is the transcript of that evening:

Amorah: For several years I have been working with different beings on the specific time-encoded activations that are coming through to Earth within the precession of the equinoxes. I started out mainly working with Hermes from the Sirian Archangels. He helped me understand our orbital cycles and their relationship to spiritual evolution. Whether it is Earth's orbit around our local Sun, or our whole galaxy's constant orbital pattern around the Great Central Sun of All That Is, there are times when we enter new seasons that correspond to and synchronize with time-released encodings from the higher dimensions. During equinoxes and solstices, when the balance of daylight and night is either most polarized or most balanced, these synchronizations with time-released encodings are most exact. For a long time, people have known that these are the most powerful times to really tune in, in terms of "what's next" on our path of awakening and healing. What do I need to know now? What is existence asking me to receive? What is Creator asking me to give, or to give up? These are the spirit questions that have been part of ceremony, vision quests, and meditation at these key times since beyond history. It has been a unique process, learning to live in time in that way, because our tendency as human beings is to look at our lives very much in the moment, or via the past. We may have long-term goals. But even when we think we are looking at the long term, we still are looking from a very microcosmic perspective at something that is very macrocosmic.

The higher-dimensional beings, for instance, do not look at success and failure in terms of whether or not there is a loving response during a conversation, or whether a relationship endures for a lifetime. They may look at it in terms of whether the lessons are learned over several lifetimes—or all your lifetimes put together. Yet, because we have brought ourselves into the time and space continuum for the purpose of experiencing things sequentially, and for the purpose of being able to feel individual feelings, we tend to isolate experiences. In the higher dimensions, many experiences, feelings, and awarenesses are going on simultaneously. The beings who exist on higher levels, therefore, do not isolate experiences in the same way as is done in time and space. The tradeoff is that while we gain the individuation and the sequential aspect of experience, we also lose most of the bigger picture. Of course, this is partly why we want to bring our Higher Self in—to help us remember the bigger picture. Our Higher Self can also help us learn to transcend pettiness or the feelings of being so caught up in survival or getting what we want right now that we forget there is a bigger picture. You can look at many situations and see either failure or success, depending on your choice of mental evaluation. But there is never any need to evaluate in those terms in the eyes of spirit. We will always have as much time as we need to finally get a result, if a result is what is needed. If it is not needed, then maybe we need to learn to let go of the need for results.

It is such a vast world of possibilities. Somehow, working with the precession of the equinoxes for the past four years has been a key way of aligning with the bigger picture and balancing between present-day reality and All That Is. The precession of the equinoxes simply means that one follows another in a predictable, reliable manner: equinox, solstice, equinox, solstice—year after year in an ongoing pattern.

Within this sequential pattern, time-released karmic patterns and Earth activations occur as well.

For instance, at March Equinox 2000, the photon band moved into the first activation of cellular demutation. This was a time-released aspect of the Divine Plan for Earth and her inhabitants that was set in place millions of years ago. June Solstice 2000 took that activation to a next level by releasing memories of certain planetary invasions that resulted in certain genetic mutations over a million years ago. Stored pain and astral entities were released from subterranean areas. By September Equinox 2000, the subsequent time release occurred opening portals to realms of transcendence of genetic limitation and forgiveness. December Solstice 2000 released another layer of subterranean astral energies and pain, and activated a time mechanism in our brains for seeing the bigger picture of Earth karma and cellular mutation. Also a next level of mutation frequencies was added to the prexisting ones. This gives an example of how the precession of equinoxes works both as a time piece and as a spiritual and karmic activator and healer.

Amorah: The precession of the equinoxes is measured in 26,000-year cycles within our solar system, one of which is nearing its end. Within a 26,000 year cycle are many smaller cycles as well. And the precession of the equinoxes is the one that most directly has to do with the time encoding of the Divine Plan in its most minuscule parts. The bigger perspective of the Divine Plan is looked at from the 26,000-year increments. The new cycle that began at March Equinox 2000 plays itself out all the way through until March Equinox 2001. The cumulative effect of previous annual solstice and equinox cycles is expanded by the new focus brought in at this time.

No matter what the new focus is at each solstice and equinox, it will always be part of an overall focus that began 26,000 years ago. And that 26,000 years has been a next level from the 26,000 before that, and so on back through billions of years of Creation. If we are not in alignment with the Divine Plan, certain patterns become solidified within us. It is not that we can never clear them; it simply becomes more difficult. The direct timing of solar encodings offers us the easiest and most efficient opportunity to align with whatever clearing, healing, awakening, or activation is being given. These times are geared to help us align with the Divine Flow in its sequential and cyclical aspect.

To add to the bigger picture of how the Divine Plan is time-released, we are now in the photon band for about the next 2,000 years. Not only are we receiving impulses from the equinoxes and solstices; we are also continually receiving impulses, dispensations, activations, and clearings from the Great Central Sun via the photon band. The photon band is made up of antiparticles. Scientists see them as an inverted molecular structure that somehow appears as light. Spiritually speaking, photonic light is the type of light that is formed by movement through time and space. These particles of light are microscopic. Each light particle has its own time encoding that, when aligned with our Sun, must also align with all the encodings that are inside our Sun regarding what is to happen in this solar system. The photon band connects our solar system to the whole galaxy, to all the galaxies, and to the Great Central Sun. So its purpose is unique. At this time on Earth, not only do we have our local solar system agendas and galactic agendas; we are also experiencing the energy of the Great Central Sun aligning us with Oneness. All of these different impulses and orbits are occurring at the same time, and there are juncture points during which an exact moment of interface transpires. These synchronized time locks bring juncture points in evolution of spirit as well as alignment of planets and star systems. Local astrology synchronizes with solar astrology, both of which synchronize with galactic and universal forms of astrology. From a universal perspective, the galaxies are like cogs on a wheel, turning together. There are points in their orbital rotations where they connect, and the gears fall into place. Then there are the in-between cycles, during which everything is moving toward the next connection point.

The Higher Councils, such as the Council of the Holy Mother and Holy Father, and the Intergalactic and Galactic Federations of Light, work continually with our local Higher Council to determine where we are in our alignment within these diverse yet synchronized cycles. They determine when we need extra dispensations of grace or karmic pattern activations. They monitor how the impact of group and planetary thought-forms inhibits Earth from receiving dispensations. I have been extremely aware of how the dispensations of grace are given at fairly regular intervals. There are certain key times when huge dispensations of grace are ready to be given but are held at bay by these limited thought-forms. There is no space for those waves of energy to enter into our atmosphere when a human energy block has created contraction versus openness and receptivity.

Our bodies reflect all of this cosmic bigger picture in a microcosmic way. As the Sun, photon band, and Great Central Sun align us with the Divine Plan, including our own planetary and individual awakening, our chakras and cellular structures also need to be in alignment with the rhythm and harmonics of the universe. In other words, their spinning patterns need to be synchronized with the orbits of the planets, stars, and galaxies. This is necessary in order for us to receive what is being given through higher-dimensional dispensations. If we have a chakra or group of cells in which we have put a stop-gate to keep us from ever opening beyond a certain point, then we must clear the issue that caused us to shut down in this manner in order to return to the Divine Flow, or rhythm, in these areas. It is necessary for all of our chakra and cellular spin patterns to be in cosmic alignment if we are to receive dispensations coming through from the angelic realms. If not, we will not receive them. It will be as if it had never happened, because we did not have the capacity for receptivity. In other words, our ability to receive any frequency of Light, Love, and Truth at any moment depends on our alignment with Divine Flow.

As a prerequisite to the information to be channeled tonight, the guides want me to help you understand this basic manner in which every cell in the human body is like a planet or star, and every chakra is a whole galaxy. They are intended to be aligned with the orbits within this galaxy, because our bodies are a microcosm of the Milky Way. Whether it is a result of ingesting foods that are in a mutated form because of chemicals, pesticides, or genetic engineering, our cellular structures have been mutated by the foods we eat, the water we drink, and the air we breathe. Nonorganic foods, genetically modified foods, food preservatives and artificial coloring, and refined foods such as white flour or sugar that have been processed down to the whitest, simplest form, have diminished our cellular ability to align with the rhythm of the universe, with Divine Flow. Most humans have been invested in avoiding certain feelings their whole lives, and therefore have created contractions in their bodies to prevent feeling. We have eaten foods that help hold contraction in place. That prevents certain frequencies from the universe, from Divine Source, from being able to move through us. Whether this is caused by karma that we have carried on a soul level or by experiences in which we misunderstood something that happened to us and felt guilty or blamed someone or lost our ability to trust God, if we are holding on in repression and avoidance, it will affect our ability to align with this rhythm of the universe and with the solstices, equinoxes, and planetary alignments—all the way out to connection to Source through the Great Central Sun.

What we have embodied is reflected in our everyday lives. In the human race right now there are two great driving forces. The first driving force is to have enough money to feel that we have power over our own lives. This is a reflection of human beings who feel out of control and at the mercy of the elements. These people are trying to find a way to get a sense of personal control over their lives because they have forgotten what sovereignty is. The other driving force is the yearning for the love that will never die, or wanting to be in love. It is in all the songs, all the music—this human condition of waiting for the right man or woman in order to finally be okay. What I have come to see is that the love songs are the closest to the right idea. The human capacity for joy can exist only when we are in a state of being in love all the time. And yet it has to be an in-loveness that exists for no reason: an in-loveness that is not because we are afraid of loneliness or because we are trying to heal something from our mother or father or because we want to look good or successful to our friends or want to have a sense of worth founded in something outside ourselves. It must be an in-loveness that is free of any ulterior motive, and it has to be a kind of in-loveness that is constantly renewing itself—one that can happen as easily when you are with the lover as not. It can happen with a flower as easily as with a person. It can happen with a person as easily as with a flower. Some people find it much easier to love flowers and animals than to share love deeply with other humans.

We must learn to be totally unselfconscious about our love, to live in awe and adoration of the beauty of the essence of All That Is all the time, to love unconditionally, free of attachment to outcome or to other people's opinions. When I started thinking about that, I was looking at the difference between trees and humans. I could see that every cell in trees and flowers is continually receiving every bit of light and energy and nourishment that is given to it, physically and etherically. With trees, I can feel an uninhibited Divine Flow. What I saw in my own cells and the cells of a friend while we were in Nature was that we were letting the love and light and prana in, and it was making us more peaceful. But our cells were receiving only a fraction of what was possible. It felt like a block that prevented us from experiencing that same receptivity that the trees and flowers did.

All of this observation and learning is coming together, in terms of what the next stage of planetary awakening and individual awakening really means. We have a lot of unmutating to do, and shifting of cellular spin patterns. There is so much pollution in our receptivity that we do not feel safe enough to let energies flow through us. In shutting ourselves down to let in only a little and always stay in control, we have really cut ourselves off from Divine Source—whether it is the Divine Source of the rocks and trees and water or in each other. Also, some of us have been psychic sponges and have experienced damage as a result. We have needed to learn how to have boundaries. Boundaries can be something that we lovingly give ourselves through our healing process, or they can be something to wall off the pain and fear and damage and keep everything out. It can seem overwhelming to try to figure out the right balance. It may not be safe to simply drop having boundaries.

How do we get back to being a race of beings who inherently know how to hug each other and have a full spiritual blending? How do we once again allow ourselves to intimately know each other without any blocks? When beings in the higher dimensions want to communicate, they do not talk about it or strategically reveal their experiences. They just blend with each other. Then everything that one knows, the other knows. One of the goals of existence is for everything to come to a place of blendedness, and in that Oneness we will all know everything. So I relate it to being in love, because being in love is probably the closest we come to this higher state of Oneness, other than when we have babies and bond with them deeply, or when our survival is threatened or death is imminent and we open ourselves, stop fighting things off, and surrender. Our priorities get really straight then.

A key ingredient to healing is to live every day as if it were your last. Then, in every day you will create no regrets. You will not go to sleep without knowing the people you love know it and feel it. You will not go to bed until you have made amends with anyone you may have harmed or with whom you had a misunderstanding. Every single moment is totally complete when you live that way, so that if you die at any moment, you will be complete. One of the ingredients to letting in life force and light and love is keeping your priorities straight. Once you are surrendered to that, many of the choices in life are gone—but they are gone in a way that really frees you.

Another ingredient in the process of unmutating and returning to Divine Flow is eating as much whole food and organic food as possible. Eliminating chemicals and neurotoxic substances is also vital to healing and restructuring our cells. Commercial detergents, perfumes, and personal care products are loaded with neurotoxins that inhibit our nervous system, brain function, and cellular health in general. We need to return to natural, organic products and ways of living.

All the principles we have worked on for years in order to transcend ego identity and embrace our spiritual nature are key: nonjudgment, living in nonblame, letting go of self-pity and pity for others, releasing all old emotions and resistance, and all the rest. But the most important at this time is the healing of trust. It is vital to release the distrust that is a contracted, protective energy holding us in a closed state. In order to let go of distrust, we must trust ourselves to stay open, radiating our light and using discernment about our choices. In order to trust ourselves, we have to resensitize ourselves enough to know how to use discernment. So there is a catch-22 in that it is difficult to let go of distrust fully until we have already developed a belief in our own ability to use discernment. But to use discernment fully, we have to be free of the contractions of distrust in order to be sensitive enough to know what to make discerning choices about.

We are in the dilemma of wanting to embody our Christ Self and to be on a path of ascension while holding on to erroneous protections for which we do not seem to have a fully healthy replacement. We are getting really good at living in the integrity and impeccability and ethics of Higher Self. Yet at another level we are still not receptive to the love and light and prana that come our way. The cellular patterning that we have taken on has made us only partly alive. Very few people are really living in full aliveness—even the people who seem to be the most vital. I find that people who practice some of the healthiest diet and exercise programs, meditate every day, and live ethically are still going through a lot of pain and misery. I have narrowed the problem down to this issue regarding cellular spin. Even as a race we are set to operate at a certain minimal level that keeps us alive while not allowing us be vulnerable to outside influences. As a human race we have been warding off energies on all levels for a long, long time.

Ask yourself these questions: "When I am around people whom I love, am I feeling loving and loved, or do I just think it is loving? When I hug someone, do I really let that person's love in? When I am with my significant other, am I in awe and wonder of that person, or has that become old, and I find that I am not stimulated now?" We can use these questions as keys to understanding where we are, without judgment. "What would I need to shift right now to feel as in love with this person as when we were going through the honeymoon phase? What would I need to shift in me to be available to feeling as excited as I did the day this friend and I had the best connection we ever had? What would I have to shift in me to be as open as I was the day the most powerful channeling I have ever done came through?" We do not have to live each moment as a replay of any other, but we can learn from those times what was different in us that allowed such a positive experience, and then work at developing those qualities more fully.

All this seems complicated because the dispensations that are coming through now require that a certain matrix of energies and issues all be opened and working together. So we cannot focus only on distrust or letting go of attachments or learning to find victory in our day-to-day lives. All the issues and alignments that we have embraced during the precession of the equinoxes over the past few years are coming to a culmination point now. And we must somehow learn to be in alignment and mastery with all of these divine qualities and awarenesses simultaneously.

The guides are saying that is enough. It is time to let them take over the rest of the solution.

The Collective Voice: In the Light and the Love of the Great One, from the collective voice of the Source that is One-in-Many, we speak to you tonight. We speak from a place of those who are blended with Source and yet hold individual functions within Source simultaneously. We are aware that this sounds paradoxical, and perhaps from your way of thinking it is. But there are many members of what you call the Elohim, even the Holy Mother and Holy Father, and the many aspects of Holy Mother and Holy Father, who are all part of this matrix. This group of beings holds a certain rhythmic flow within Oneness. It is a rhythm that is in actuality a simultaneous experience of individuation of being and total surrender into Oneness: a complete and equal coexistence. We have been the watchers of existence, of Creation, and of humanity for a great long time.

The experiment that is coming to its culmination on Earth has been watched, in your terms, for aeons. It has moved through many systems. It has moved through many dimensions. And on Earth at this time, there is a culmination to the seeming pattern of opposition of light and dark that was born out of consciousness in resistance to itself. From the moment any aspect of consciousness in existence had an experience of a thought, or a wave of awareness, or a feeling (not as you feel) that in any way negated itself, or anything or anyone else in existence—from the moment that first erroneous thought of resistance or judgment or shame or fear occurred, it was as if a split, or rift, went through the dimensions that created an impulse in all of consciousness to have a momentary fear, or concern, or even curiosity about its own potential for darkness or pain. Before this resistance to one's own consciousness, consciousnesses had existed in a continual state of flow and discovery and in the flow of Love and Light, and awe and wonder and adoration were unceasing through All That Is. The first moment when a single doubt was experienced in a single consciousness, a domino effect was created. And what we think of as a resistance to one's self occurred, because it was the first experience of something that stopped the flow of Love and Light through All That Is: the Divine Flow.

You think of the universe as huge. You think of the furthest reaches of the universe as having great vastness in comparison with the small space that you occupy. And yet there was a time within All That Is in which any new thought, awareness, or experience of a new

THE MATRIX OF DIVINE FLOW / 287

possibility impulsed a wave through all consciousnesses within All That Is, and every individual experience became a shared universal experience. The first time a consciousness experienced a little contraction, or a sense of surprise that startled, it was very similar to feeling resistance to experiencing one's own consciousness. This was the seed of what you think of as dark and light, and their opposition to each other. Before that time, All That Is was filled with the anticipation of infinite possibilities, and infinite possibilities stimulated great joy and a sense of adventure and exploration. New possibilities were explored by impulsing Light and Love into a thought about a possibility, and thereby creating it. It was very simple. And it was very joyful until this first unpleasant reaction was experienced and dominoed through All That Is.

The human population is a focal point at this time for healing this original, higher-dimensional rift in which the first consciousness experienced resistance to its own brief thought, which triggered contraction that stopped the Divine Flow. In a sense, when some of your modern-day teachers talk about how all the universe has its eye on Earth at this time, there is certainly some exaggeration, because there are those who are maintaining other parts of the universe and other groupings of consciousness. Yet the greatest concentration is here, because something is happening on a large scale to bring the human population to the point of experiencing that brief lapse in the Light and Love without reaction. In your terms, indeed, this is still quite some time away. But in our terms, it is getting very, very close. Everything that is impulsed to Earth is ultimately for the purpose of stripping away all of the results of that very first resistance to the self. Perhaps you might think of it as judgment, because your consciousness reacted with "a judgment" against something outside that was blocking the Light. Or you might feel it as shame that such a thing could even exist and question the possibility that the same potential exists within yourself. You might have experienced it as "I don't want to be aware of that. I refuse to believe this is possible." This reaction created fear, denial, and avoidance of the unknown. Or perhaps you were one of those who experienced it as "I have to do something to fix it" or as anger. The thought of the potential for absence of Light and Love, even briefly, was unthinkable. Any and every potential reaction was experienced by someone at that time and is still in the process of being healed within individuals, and therefore within All That Is.

What if that moment could have simply been experienced as "Oh, I'm capable of having a thought that could stop the Divine Flow. That is an interesting potential. I don't think I'll do it again because I prefer to be in flow, but how amazing." The whole universe could receive that wave, that domino effect: "Wow, look at this possibility. I don't think we want to go there, but it's okay that it exists." The moment there was fear or judgment or doubt or resistance or defensiveness or shame or any of these reactionary energies. They became locked in consciousness as something ultimately to avoid, to fear, to judge, or whatever.

So here you are in the twenty-first century, and what does this have to do with you now? First of all, take a deep breath and let out a sigh. With your next breath we would like you to embrace the energy of childlike curiosity. As you let the breath out, we invite you to think, "This is a curious thing to explore." This will assist you in discharging any reactions that might be occurring in present time. So, another nice deep breath. We ask you to join with us as cosmic adventurers who are not in the process of solving a problem, who are not trying to bring things right, but who are learning to experience each new thing as simply an experience and move on without judgment, shame, fear, attachment, denial, anger, or avoidance left behind to keep it repeating itself. It is important to learn that even if there is judgment, shame, anger, or any other emotion or negative attitude, you can choose to simply observe it with childlike innocence and wonder, as opposed to reacting to the fact that reactionary energy exists.

You might think of us as those who hold Divine Flow for All That Is. We are the ones who have learned not to resist anything. If you have the potential to be a murderer and you resist it, you will ultimately create a lifetime in which you will have to murder just to release the pent-up energy. If you are aware that you have a part of you with that capacity you might say, "I choose to use my will to remain benevolent when that murder energy is active in me. But isn't it curious that something I would never consciously want to do is still a potential? I just don't have to choose to actualize that potential." What if everything that has ever resulted in reactionary, negative emotions or attitudes could be approached with that simplicity? Indeed, this is the key. And you are moving now in the direction, within the Divine Plan, of the point at which you will no longer be able to look at an issue as in need of healing.

Indeed, from your perspective, there is certainly healing. True healing is simply a matter of bringing consciousness back to Divine Truth. Then you will be able to align yourself in Divine Flow of Love and Light continually. In order to work with the energies of healing and Divine Flow, it is necessary to look at more than one ingredient at a time. The energy being impulsed into your Sun from the Great Central Sun at this time is a matrix. This matrix contains the polarity between awakening into Oneness, in which no individual consciousness is aware of itself, and awakening into individuation, in which all individual consciousnesses are aware of themselves and still know that they are part of Oneness. The Great Central Sun is impulsing you via the photon band and your local Sun to remember how to experience Oneness within individuation by choice. Eventually it will simply be a part of your natural flow again, which is living in self-affinity in Divine Flow. At this time we are offering the option of experiencing it by choice.

This dispensation will grow stronger and stronger over the years to come, which to you may sound like a long time for a single dispensation. For us it seems just less than a moment. As we look at you in time and space we impulse you with this movement toward the harmony of Oneness in individuality. At this time you are in the stage of observing what inhibits Divine Flow, becoming conscious of it, and learning how to transform those energies back to Divine Flow. Over the past few years the photon band has impulsed you and your Earth on many levels. In the beginning, basic morality clearing was impulsed. The very first impulse from the photon band was the impulse to care about not harming, even in subtle ways, others who have harmed you. It was the first stage of forgiveness. Since that time the photon band has been impulsing every emotion that has ever been repressed within you to release. It has been impulsing your physical body vibrationally to raise its frequency. At times the impulsing was for several months at a time on a single organ of your body or on your nervous system. At this point every organ of your body has been impulsed by the photonic Light from the Great Central Sun to let go of the past.

Every cell of your body has been impulsed since March Equinox 2000 to give up physical survival control and to allow spirit to rule the physical body. Spirit does not rule body by controlling it. We have been assisting you in realigning so that the potential for your body to naturally follow spirit consciousness is becoming a greater possibility. Of course, this requires your ongoing awareness of the difference between ego consciousness and spirit consciousness, and the release of ego control, in order to make body/spirit cooperation possible. There were times when simple cellular energies were being impulsed to let go. If you were holding repressed emotions in your cells, or mutations from your birth experience, all these things have been impulsed over the last few years to release. Now we are asking you to look at the Matrix of Divine Flow, which is a matrix of Divine Trust, Divine Love, Surrender to Divine Will, and Unity in Diversity. The matrix that is created by these four states of consciousness is the matrix that needs to be brought into balance in order for you to align to receive the rays of Divine Grace that are impulsing your body to return to the dominion of spirit consciousness in the body. The reason we speak of it in this way is that some of you have literally cleared all your karma, and yet your bodies are still experiencing problems.

The genetic mutations in the human race as an entire species have existed for so long that your bodies are not responding to your spiritual awakening in the way they would in an ideal situation. In the process of healing these species mutations within your body, this Matrix of Divine Flow is going to help you bring your body back into cooperation with spirit once you have learned how to communicate with your body with all of these energies active simultaneously: Divine Trust, which uses discernment without distrust; Divine Love, which is truly unconditional and free of attachment; balance of Surrender and Divine Will in action; and living in Unity in Diversity, in which you can find harmony within differences of lifestyle, religion, opinions, race, government, and every other aspect of life. When you have healed all blocks to the Matrix of Divine Flow and can consciously embrace and live in all four attitudes at the same time in your heart and mind, your body will begin to respond by letting go of the past. When your body begins to respond, you will first feel as if something is awakening inside your cellular structure, as if it is responding to something such as a voice that it has never heard before.

When you begin to feel that response, as if your body is stretching and awakening and wanting to hear, then that is the time to ask for assistance from the Elohim of Divine Grace, from the Angels of Divine Grace, and also from the four Elohim who hold the matrix: the Elohim of Unity in Diversity, the Elohim of Divine Love, the Elohim of Surrender to Divine Will, and the Elohim of Divine Trust. When you embrace this matrix of four energies, call on these beings, who radiate those qualities throughout existence. Ask them to place you in a cocoon, or a healing Chamber of Light, for healing and awakening your cellular structure to Divine Flow. We believe you are ready to begin that at this time. You know how to bring your own inner reference points of the feelings of those qualities all into your mind, body, and heart at the same time. Even if you sometimes stray from it in your day-to-day life, it is enough that you know what it means to feel each quality.

If you have ever had a reference point in your life of knowing what it means to be in total trust of the Divine Plan, in total trust that everything is going to work itself out, even if it is not obvious at this time, then you can anchor Divine Trust. If you have ever had a moment in which you have cared more about loving someone than you did about getting your own way, then you know the energy of unconditional love, free of attachment. If you have ever had a moment in which you have been in total surrender to doing the right thing, even though it meant taking a risk, then you know the balance of Surrender to Divine Will in action. If you have ever had a moment in which you were in the room with someone who had a totally different opinion on everything, and you were in peace, without judgment or the need to change that person, then you know the energy of Unity in Diversity. Once you know the matrix of those four qualities, or virtues, and can bring them into your consciousness simultaneously, you can speak your body consciousness in a way that will enable it to hear in a way it has never heard before. Then call in the Elohim and angels who work with those four energies, and the Elohim of Divine Grace for a cocooning or chamber to bring your cellular structure to the point where it reflects your spiritual growth and responds to the Love and Light of Divine Flow. Then you become the anchors on Earth for this energy that is being impulsed.

This matrix will be going through many levels of activation over years and years to come. Until Spring Equinox of 2001, the primary focus is on self-acceptance, because self-acceptance is the glue that holds it all together. Self-acceptance is the absolute ingredient that pulls resistance to your own potential back into healthy perspective. So if you are not at a point of self-acceptance yet, we ask you to work with that in your meditations and your healing. If you are unable to feel self-acceptance, the Matrix of Divine Flow—the other four energies—cannot be held together.

We are very honored to be able to bring this message into form at this time, because it has not been spoken of before. We know that when higher ideas are first spoken of on the physical plane, that is when the chain reaction begins. So we thank you for assisting us in beginning this chain reaction of returning to Divine Flow.

Matrix of Divine flow Process

1. Close your eyes now, and simply take a moment to envision Earth floating in the air in front of you.

2. Call on the Lords of Light of the Rainbow Flames, and ask them to surround the planet in Rainbow Flames.

3. Orally affirm your intention to hold the qualities of the Matrix of Divine Flow, as follows: Turn your focus inward the first time each new phrase is given, and allow yourself to feel it. The second time the new phrase is given, focus it on all your brothers and sisters on Earth and the higher collective consciousness of the human race. The Elohim will assist you in sending this message to your brothers and sisters in an appropriate way. Affirm and feel as deeply as you can, "I am a divine and holy aspect of All That Is, and I choose to accept everything I have ever experienced, free of judgment, free of shame, free of fear, and free of denial and avoidance. I choose to accept and love myself unconditionally now. So be it."

4. Now let us send this message as a potential into Earth. Affirm and send this message, "You are divine and holy aspects of All That Is. You can choose to accept yourself and love yourself un-

conditionally. You can choose to accept and love everything you have ever done, free of judgment and fear, free of shame, free of denial and avoidance. So be it."

5. Affirm and feel, "I choose to live in Divine Trust with discernment, and to free myself of all distrust now. So be it."

6. Send the message to Earth, "You can choose to live in Divine Trust with discernment, and free yourself of all distrust now. So be it."

7. Affirm and feel, "I choose to live in unconditional Divine Love, free of attachment, with All That Is. So be it."

8. Send the message to all humans, "You can choose to live in unconditional Divine Love that is free of attachment, with All That Is. It is within your power to choose this. So be it."

9. Affirm and feel, "I choose to live in Surrender to Divine Will, to release all effort, all worry and control, that my every action may be divine. So be it."

10. Send the message to all humans, "You can choose to live in Surrender to Divine Will, to release all effort, all worry and control, that your every action may be divine. So be it."

11. Affirm and feel, "I choose to embrace Unity in Diversity, to honor and love the differences in all people, and to honor the free will of all people. So be it."

12. Send the message to all humans, "You can choose to live in Unity in Diversity, to release all prejudices, to learn to love the differences in you and others. You can learn to appreciate and honor the free will of others. So be it."

13. Affirm and feel, "I believe in my ability to live in this sacred matrix of Divine Flow, and I affirm that it is my truth now. So be it."

14. Send the message to all humans, "I believe in your ability to choose to live in this sacred matrix of Divine Flow. I believe you can do it the moment you choose it. I believe that you have never done anything that can not be forgiven. So be it."

15. Affirm and feel, "In Oneness I Am. In the beauty of my uniqueness I Am. I return to Divine Flow in grace and ease. So be it."

The Collective Voice: Take a minute or two of silence to communicate with your body, to align with the cooperation of these energies and tell your body your intention of releasing all mutations and errone- ous spin patterns.

Invoke the Elohim of Divine Trust, the Elohim of Divine Love, the Elohim of Surrender to Divine Will, the Elohim of Unity in Diversity, and the Elohim of Divine Grace. Tell them you are ready to live in these qualities all the time and to accept yourself fully. Ask them to assist you with healing and dispensations that will aid you in your re- turn to Divine Flow on all energy body levels: emotional, mental, etheric, astral, spiritual, and physical. Ask them to help the cells of your body learn to respond to your loving spirit by releasing all muta- tions and erroneous spin patterns. Be with them in silence now, lying comfortably for your first cocooning or Chamber of Light session.

This first session with the Elohim may last up to one and a half hours, so allow as much time as you need. When it is finished you will simply feel a sense of completion, or you may start stretching, or your consciousness will return to normal waking consciousness. If you are unsure, just lie comfortably for the entire hour and a half to be certain that it is complete. It is fine to do this at bedtime.

After a short break, the group to which this channeling was given re- turned and shared the following comments:

Amorah: The Elohim spoke to me during the break and said that there is not one single dysfunction you can think of that cannot be healed by one or all of the four qualities mentioned in the channeling. I'm sure I'll test that theory, knowing me. Amazing to think that there's a ma- trix we can work with that would heal everything that could keep us from anchoring our Christ consciousness. Any moment that I am off, I will be able to look at which one of those four qualities or self-accep- tance will totally shift me back into alignment and flow.

A guest: I feel it has given me a working matrix that is so specific it will cut out the guesswork. Even on a cellular level, it was nice to also have them acknowledge how many generations after generation have built up this mutation. To think that we could be now at the point, with the help from outside, of literally shifting that back to a nonmutated form is such a blessing.

Another guest: I feel really grateful for this; it is so perfect with the work I have been doing. One thing that would help me with this is a name for this matrix.

Amorah: They called it the Matrix of Divine Flow. Within that matrix are the ingredients of Oneness, which includes every uniqueness, and in which both Oneness and uniqueness simultaneously exist. That is part of the matrix too: the One That Is Many That Are One. Ultimately, it is about the Divine Flow of just that.

You may choose to do these Matrix of Divine Flow sessions as often as you wish. I have done them daily ever since the channeling came through, which was just over three months ago at the time of this writing. In the beginning, I experienced a lot of old pain as it was released from my cellular structure. This happens occasionally even now, but is more intermittent. I have come to realize how much life force has been required to hold my own unhealed past and the genetic and species mutations in place. Each time our bodies have responded to a reactionary thought and emotion, the cells have experienced a glitch in their spin cycle. These brief glitches create an accumulative effect as they are repeated over time, until the cells continually hold a negative response pattern, which interferes with healthy spin. Eventually each pattern also mutates the geometric structure of the cell.

For thousand and thousands of years, the human race has held common fears, beliefs, distrusts, and other energies in response to astral invasions, corruption in government, social pressures, Earth changes, and group karmas. These energies have for many centuries brought about cellular corruption and mutation on a species level. Add your personal karma to this formula, and you can begin to glimpse how many millions of layers of mutation and corrupted spin cycles our cells potentially hold. The good news is that we have been given a very simple and tangible method to begin reversing this cellular corruption. Of course, the most important ingredient is your consciousness and following your inner guidance. This may involve cleansing diets, fasting, mineral soaks, exercise, or whatever you need to do in order to assist your body.

The trickiest part of this process is learning not to get caught up in the old energies and patterns as they are released. Sometimes after a session with the Elohim, you will feel wonderful and joyful for a while. Later in the day you may feel irritation, fear, or even panic, hate, anger, or any other emotion that is releasing. You see, everything that you have cleared in your emotional and mental fields has a cellular correspondent. And those cellular correspondents may not have completely released with your past healing work. When they are releasing, the ideal attitude is to remind yourself that this is old energy clearing, and it is not your truth. If you have cleared beliefs and emotions in the past, then you probably will not need to do it again unless you have trouble letting them go. Remember to breathe deeply into your entire body when deep releases are occurring, to assist the process. If you get caught up in acting them out, believing in the emotions or thoughts or pains, you will slow down your own process of release. We are being asked to step to a whole new level of maturity in order to actualize the benefits of this process. We are being asked to affirm our higher truths and to stop believing in everything else. You see, most humans experience life as the product of their emotions and thoughts, as opposed to recognizing that they are simply experiencing emotions and thoughts that are not their higher truth. When you can observe emotions and thoughts with this level of maturity, you remain detached while observing and letting go without denial. You become the chooser of your life and fate, instead of the victim.

Another piece of good news is that a close friend, who has also done the Matrix of Divine Flow sessions daily, and I are experiencing incredible changes. When we go out into nature together, we jokingly say that we are there to get high. The energy from wildflowers has begun to move through our cells so much more deeply that we go into ecstatic altered states. At one point the Elohim told me that if humans were to experience only 10 percent of their potential for cellular Divine Flow, we would be in a state of tantric ecstasy twenty-four hours a day. The more that is cleared, the more I am aware remains to be cleared. But even at this beginning level, my friend and I often experience wondrous shifts in our openness. As she said, "This is like an orgasm, but better." Our sensitivity to electricity and chemical pollutants has also intensified. The Elohim have assured me that this is a passing phase. Already, the payoffs are definitely showing me that it is worth it.

The image on page 297 may assist you as a visual aid to the process of Divine Flow. The session lengths will vary greatly and tend to get shorter after the first few times. Ten minutes to an hour and a half seems to be the overall range of session length. For future sessions, this is all you need to do:

1. Lie down or sit comfortably, and call in your Higher Self alignment in the Tube of Light.

2. Call in the Elohim of Divine Love, Divine Trust, Surrender to Divine Will, Unity in Diversity, and Divine Grace. Affirm your readiness to live in these divine qualities and feel each one as much as you can at this time.

3. Ask for a cocooning or Chamber of Light for returning your energy bodies and cells to Divine Flow. Relax until it is done.

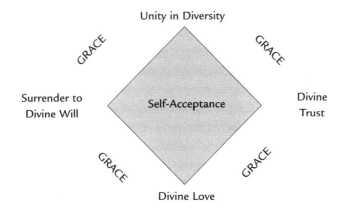

Matrix of Divine Flow

I hope this process and all the teachings will assist you in making your cellular transformation as gracious and joyous a possible. As you return to Divine Flow, experiencing the alternating current of dissolving into Oneness and experiencing your I Am presence, All That Is experiences wholeness and fulfillment as well. We heal God/Goddess/All That Is by remembering and returning to our own aspect of that Divine Oneness, because God/Goddess/ All That Is is all of us living in Divine Love, Divine Trust, Surrender to Divine Will, and Unity in Diversity—all at the same time.

28

Planetary Breakthrough

St. Germaine Channeling, October 2000

As you read this final chapter, I hope that this information will help you more deeply understand the value that each of us is capable of contributing to the co-creation of the future. Even though this channeling refers to an event that occurred in the past, the fact that it occurred is an important understanding for readers relative to the movement toward planetary ascension and return to Divine Flow. Also, I wish to point out that this type of activation is an ongoing occurrence at regular time-encoded intervals on Earth.

St. Germaine: Beloveds, it is a time of great celebration on Earth. Even though some of you have been very focused on war in the Middle East and some of the tragedies that still occur within the consciousness of ego and separation, there has been a great breakthrough that has taken place just in these last three days. We would like to share it with you tonight. We would like to ask you to help anchor this activation more deeply for this planet as well as for yourselves, and to use the energies of Mt. Shasta to send the energies out to your human family and to the planet.

On Thursday of last week [October 26, 2000] there was a peace conference held. It is not one that is commonly known, but it was a counterplan to the energies of the Illuminati. It was held not only in the Cities of Light; there have been certain people around the planet who have known of this plan for quite some time who have been preparing—not to hold the energies of counter-anything in a combative way—to simply balance the polarity. Polarity has been out of balance on this planet for a great long time. It has been a very long time, even in this solar system, since the majority was aligned with Divine Law and with right action. We know that many of you have been working toward that goal for a great long time, and at times have been disheartened. Yet we also see how you pick yourselves up and keep holding the Light of Truth and holding the Light of Peace. The determination of your souls has inspired an activity in the higher dimensions, because some of you have even come to the point of death's door and have refused to go through the other side. Some of you have reached the point of ascension—being offered the opportunity to leave this planet knowing that your karma was complete—and yet you keep staying in determination to serve as anchors for the higher-dimensional energies of Divine Law and Light upon Earth.

As of last Thursday a decision was made to begin to send, from the core of Earth and from the outer edges of Earth's atmosphere, simultaneous energy waves. These waves were accompanied by Light Beings sending an alternating frequency pattern. The purpose of these rhythmic patterns of energy flow was to help align your heartbeat with Earth's, to help align the flow of energy between your emotional and mental bodies, and to help align your cellular structure more directly with your local Sun, which, of course, is a Source of the Light of All That Is, Divine Source, or Oneness.

And so the Light Beings at the center of Earth and the Light Beings in the center of your Sun synchronized with the Light Beings who hold the outer edges of Earth's atmosphere and began to send these alternating waves of light through to Earth's core from different directions. You might imagine it as a laser light show during which light penetrates from one longitude and latitude across the globe through to the other side, in concurring time increments and multiple locations, all aligned with exact complementary patterns and time to achieve a common purpose. The Light Beings on the outer atmosphere anchor them through the center of Earth out through the other side and back to the outer atmospheres directly opposite the point of origin. This link connects heaven and Earth, as you might say.

What we are happy to report is that there are enough of you who are aligned in your multidimensional lightbodies, while connecting to the Divine Essence of Earth, that we have been able to establish a light grid throughout the entire surface of the planet for the first time since Lemuria. On May 5 of this year, when the great alignment occurred, many of you had prepared and gathered for the great activations. It was the first time that a major dispensation of grace was available to Earth, that there were enough people on Earth willing and able to receive it on all dimensional levels, the first time that we could take advantage of the gatherings occurring on Earth to the fullest. It is not that your other gatherings have not been effective. Of course they have been. If you had not had all of the other planetary linkup ceremonies, prayers, meditations, and so on, Earth's frequency would not have built to the point that we can now begin to break through on a new level.

On May 5, some of you became aware of how many of the veils of thought-form and illusion were cleared from the planet's atmosphere. Some of you became aware at that time of how the energies were higher than they had ever been because certain multidimensional alignments were brought into place that had not been in place for a great long time. The work that you have been doing to renew your cellular structures, transmute genetic mutations, clear your karmic patterns, and heal your emotional bodies—all of these things have contributed to the breakthroughs this year. Because every time you make more space for spirit to enter your body consciousness and you meditate and bring in your own Higher Self and God connection, there is one more little beam of light that can shine out through the dimensions and anchor you and your planet to Divine Source. Therefore, what has taken place in the last three days is a very beautiful alignment that through you, and through the hundreds of thousands of others around the planet who have worked to bring what you call your Higher Self into your body, your own I Am presence, you have opened enough multidimensional pathways that we have been able now to make that connection through the entire Earth. Some of you have experienced it as an extra chaos because, although you have been raising your frequency, as the frequency around you increases as well, your ability to anchor on even a higher level increases. And, of course, that means that as your frequency and the Earth frequency are raised, whatever exists within you and others that is of a lower frequency must be released, transmuted, and transcended. The more Light you bring in, the more it impulses the release of its opposite. A planetary chain reaction will be continuing for weeks to come. We have been in great celebration!

As some of you have worked with the Elohim earlier in this year on this process we call the Matrix of Divine Flow (to restore integrity to your cellular structure), the photon band has been continually impulsing that alignment to all life on Earth. Of course, the more directly you align with the photon band impulses, the more gracious your personal transformation process will be. What we are telling you now is that the deepening and intensification you and Earth have experienced within the last three days is going to give you almost ten times the result that you have been getting from the cellular and genetic transmutation work than has been happening previously. It will be extra important for you to be very conscious of the aspects of your lifestyle and your diet that help support this ongoing transformation and transmutation, and the aspects that do not.

One of the messages to assist you personally, at this time, is to begin to tune in more deeply prior to eating. Think about swallowing the food, think about the taste of the food before you ingest it into your bodies. With the ongoing frequency increases, your cellular change will be accelerated. It is very important that you work with that acceleration, because there is no need for illness. There is no need for it to be a catastrophic or traumatic time; and yet, we also make you aware that those who resist the energies that are coming into Earth will find it traumatic. For, you see, it is only in resistance to the Divine Flow that pain can be felt. You may at times feel as if old emotions are spinning off more quickly. You may feel at times as if there were tremors moving through your body. If you can remember in those times to simply breathe deeply and say to yourself, "I welcome the I Am Presence That I Am. I welcome the spirit of victory into my life. I am ready to be fully alive on every level." If you welcome the energies, you will find this time of transition on Earth to be ecstatic. Some of you have already begun to have spontaneous experiences of tantric flow without sexual experience. Some of you are already experiencing the waves that suddenly move through you in the middle of the day, and it is ecstatic. It is only when you resist the clearing and releasing of past energies, which frequency increases trigger, that you experience pain. So if you begin to feel fear that you think you have cleared, or you begin to feel shame or anger that you think you have cleared in the past, do not judge the experience. When you feel these old energies arising again, just say to yourself, "Thank you, cells, for letting this old energy go. Removing these old karmic patterns from my cells is the final stage of victory and breakthrough." Because there is going to be continuing intensification, you cannot increase the frequency of light without affecting its opposite. If you increase the frequency of light and the anchoring of the light into your cells, then the cells must let go of everything that is less than the Light, just as your personalities have been doing mentally and emotionally for however long you have actively been on your spiritual path.

The amount of spiritual discipline that you have created prior to this time will assist you in getting through this time. The canceling of judgments, negative thoughts, pity, and blame as they occur in your consciousness is essential. You will find that what you put into the world will come back to you more quickly. For, indeed, you know that you are creators of reality and that you are co-creators. Earth is not at the point of instant karma yet, in which your thoughts and actions manifest instantaneously. However, you are moving closer and closer to activation of the Law of Instant Karma all the time. This requires the awareness you have developed, or are developing, through your meditations, through your spiritual practice, and through your self-love and self-care and compassion for others to make the coming times as gracious as possible.

We are very excited, at this time, because our ability to work with you will continue to deepen even more. Some of you who have never been able to hear guidance directly are going to be able to hear it more directly now, or soon. Some of you who have long awaited your third eye awakening are going to find it easier, because the multidimensional veils are being dissolved quickly. We are not saying that every rift through the dimensions has been cleared. And we are not saying that every thought-form that has been created by the human family is dissolved. What we are saying is that these barriers have been dissolved enough that they no longer inhibit your multidimensional connection to Divine Source throughout this Earth. Of course, free will is still here. And, of course, the choices that people make are still within free will. Yet goals such as yours—goals of full enlightenment, goals of embodying the divine perfection of your own consciousness—require living in that refinement throughout your day: living as if you are a Christ, Quan Yin, or Buddha now. Many of you are doing this already, so it will be very easy for you. In fact, easier and easier. And for those of you who have not been disciplined to live in the integrity and impeccability of spirit yet, more help is available than ever before—as long as you are doing your part.

Some of you who are still lax in stopping, or at least clearing, your production of negative thought-forms as they arise: it is time to get a little more refined and disciplined. You know that if you speak or think a word, it travels from you out into the atmosphere. If the word is about a specific person, it travels to that person. If you have a judgmental or negative thought about the person, it travels to her. You are helping her co-create a negative reality and holding her back in her growth. Simultaneously, you create a lower astral link to that individual. If the person is maintaining healthy boundaries, she will not let your negativity penetrate her field. But that does not relinquish your responsibility. If the person does not take your negative energy in, it is going to come back to you like a boomerang. You are going to find the effects of your own negative thoughts and judgments and blame coming back much more quickly than ever before. Yet there is nothing to fear. It is a great and joyful opportunity. Is it not wonderful to discipline and narrow your choices, since you want to live in impeccability, in right action, anyway? Is it not wonderful to be able to create the depth of self-respect that comes from living in impeccability? Is it not wonderful to know that your very existence on Earth is helping co-create a positive reality for yourself and for many, many others? Because every time you make a quantum leap spiritually, there is a wave that goes through the entire human family, and even beyond. The door that you have opened and passed through is then open to the next person who is ready. If we could explain to you the number of realities that are affected when one human being makes that spiritual choice of no return, you would be in awe of your power of influence. Your spiritual breakthroughs and healings impulse not only your human family and Earth; the effect moves through realms that you have not even begun to explore yet. There are astral realms in which beings have been trapped for aeons. Every time something happens on Earth to change that astral reality of lower thought-forms, of addiction, of pollution, of inner and outer toxicity, there is a great wave that goes out from this planet.

You took on this job a long time ago: to affect the reality of all existence through the experimentation in transformation and transcendence that is tran-spiring on Earth. We thank you for doing such a beautiful job. We thank you for making victory possible. We also want to remind you that even if all the angels that exist have the most beautiful gifts of Divine Grace and Love to bestow upon the human family, if there are not enough human beings who are able and willing to receive these dispensations, they cannot be given. Yes, there have always been ongoing dispensations to individuals and to specific groups. Yet as of May 5 this year, it was the first time we were able to give everything that was available from higher-dimensional sources on that day. And frequency increase and dispensations have been very accelerated ever since. As of the activation that has taken place now, in the last three days, this is going to be greatly, greatly increased.

Some of you have not understood that we need you as much as you need us. When I say us, I speak of the collective, higher-dimensional family of Light that is working with the evolution of human and spiritual consciousness. We cannot anchor anything if there are not people here through whom we can anchor. Before I could hold the seat of the Master of the Violet Ray, and before I could hold the seat of the one who welcomes beings into the initiatic path of purification, there had to be enough beings on Earth anchoring violet ray, certain levels of initiation, and certain levels of consciousness for me to be able to assume this higher office. The same is true for all the Light Beings with whom you work, whether it be Quan Yin, Mother Mary, Buddha, or others. There is an interrelationship, an interdependence, and it is more reciprocal than you may have realized. Every loving thought that you have enables us to bring more loving thoughts to the planet. Every inspiration that you allow in, allows us to send more. Every time you break through, you open the space for someone else to step in where you were. So there is a continuing domino effect on your planet in which every single person who takes one step in the right direction opens the door for another person to take that same step, and then another, and then another. . . . The more people who take the same step, the quicker this domino effect moves from one to the other, until it becomes a continual movement, like a wave.

I would like you to close your eyes now.

◻ Visualize your beloved planet Earth. Imagine that there is a bubble above and around the entirety of Earth, approximately the distance of half the diameter of Earth. The bubble is sparkling with diamondlike light. Imagine that around that bubble there are enough angels, Ascended Masters, and other Light Beings surrounding your planet that there is not a single space that is not held by these divine ones. Imagine that beyond that point, there is light that comes through your Sun from the Great Central Sun that radiates into Earth's atmosphere from every direction at once. This holographic light is anchored through the Light Beings and angels and directed through Earth's atmosphere to the surface. Imagine that Light from Divine Source continually penetrates your aura, your cells, and the aura and cells of everyone and everything on this planet, and that it contains everything that is needed to realize God/Goddess consciousness. Take a moment to imagine that every human on Earth continually breathes and welcomes this light. Imagine the whole planet sighing in relief because the time has finally come when there is no separation. We all swim in that sea of light and love together. Let it overflow you. Send that light from Source that has been downstepped through the angels and Masters, downstepped through you out to every member of the human family, every plant, every animal, every rock, every water source, every grain of sand, and every speck of dirt. Allow yourself to be the conduit for that Light from Divine Source, sending it into Earth's core. Know that you will not interfere with the free will of those who do not wish to receive it. Just allow that light that flows through All That Is to flow through you that you may live in Divine Flow, aligned with the Divine Flow of Source and all of Creation.

In your daily life, if you have created enough spiritual connection with your own Higher Self that this light flows continually through you, you can simply walk from one end of a shopping mall to the other and give hundreds of people an opportunity to let go and receive the Light of Divine Source. You could go into a gift shop or health food store knowing that even if you do nothing other than be who you are, every human there will benefit from what you are overflowing into the world as your part of co-creation. Imagine yourself in your daily activities, or at your job, with the Light from Divine Source downstepped through the angels coming through every cell of your body and overflowing out through your chakras, through the pores of your skin. Imagine what you bring to your family, to those with whom you work, even to people with whom you speak on the telephone.

Imagine that you are with someone on the telephone from one of those large companies. We are using this example because it is one that throws Amorah off more than any other situation. It is a great time to remember this discipline: when dealing with bureaucracy, getting your buttons pushed, your body is contracting, and you are feeling angry and powerless and impatient. Notice what it feels like in your body when that happens. Notice the amount of contraction it takes to be impatient or angry. Notice how your breath is weakened. When you contract in that way, it is as if you were saying, "Forget it, God, I don't want any love. I don't want any light. I'm mad right now!" When you contract in that way, it is like saying, "Back off, angels, I'm frustrated." I do not think that is what you really want, is it? Just remind yourself next time, in a gentle and loving way, without any self-judgment, "Is this what I really choose to create for the world and for myself in this moment?" Breathing through the emotion is the greatest way to keep your body open without contracting and justifying the reaction.

Once again, thank you, and bless you for what you have brought to this planet. Bless you for what you have brought to all of us who have been working with you for a great long time. We thank you for bringing the gift of your life to Earth to assist in the awakening to Divine Peace and Divine Love. We promise you that Divine Law will eventually be the only law on Earth. We thank you for helping orchestrate that possibility. Have faith that all is in Divine Order. Have faith that what you do matters greatly, because it does. Know that the cycles of time are the only thing that stand between you and the experience of Divine Flow in All That Is. Know that the cycles of time are the only thing that in any way seem to separate you from a world that is run by Divine Law.

[⎙] We ask you to welcome your own future self who has experienced Divine Law on Earth, who has experienced Divine Order and Unity. I would like you to hold your hands palms up and ask your future self who lives in that future time of Divine Law and Divine Oneness to place its hands upon yours. Breathe deeply with your arms and hands uncrossed as you welcome your future self. As you feel the energy beginning to move up your arms, welcome yourself from the future to begin to blend with your entire body, as if it were walking into you. Allow your future self to walk in and blend with your whole body at this time. Breathe into your eyes and allow that future self to look through your eyes, and you through the eyes of your future self. Breathe into your throat, chest, and arms and ask your future self to impulse you with your own Divine Flow. Expand your breath and invocation into your torso and legs, and all your chakras, all your cells. Align your future self with your body and your consciousness now. Welcome it, as your future self places a little spark of light into every cell, impulsing you with your Divine Alignment, your Divine Perfection, and your Divine Flow that already exist in the third dimension in the future. You will experience the continuation of this return to self-affinity and affinity with Oneness through the sequence of time, until finally time exists no more. We thank you.

As St. Germaine's channeling is complete, I want to finish with information brought through in mid-May 2001 from Metatron. Metatron said that from March Equinox of 2000 to March Equinox of 2001 the acceleration on Earth had increased thirteen times over what it had done in the previous year. From March Equinox of 2001 to March Equinox of 2002, it will have increased 144 times beyond where we were at March Equinox of 2000. The last karmic pattern had been released into Earth's atmosphere and human consciousness by June Solstice of 2001. On March Equinox of 2004, the end of karmic cycles will occur, and the gridlock will be in place for the countdown to Earth Ascension. The keys for personal Victory are: surrendering to the Light; nonavoidance of emotion, while refraining from acting on emotional reaction; living impeccably as if each day were your last; and opening your heart and body, free of resistance, to the Divine Flow of Creation.

Namasté,
Amorah

Epilogue:
Putting It All Together

In this book we have touched on many of the ingredients of mastery, which indeed brings us back into the Divine Flow of Creation and yet beyond. For as we return to Source we take with us everything we have learned along the way. And as we return we must learn to bless every experience we have had along the way. For even our seemingly worst mistakes and misuses of power, or our most painful experiences of seeming victimhood, have all served the purpose of teaching us how to be Masters of every realm. To be born into loving perfection and Divine Flow is a great gift. To experience every possible aspect of consciousness, best and worst, and embrace, forgive, and love it all into the Light of Truth and Mastery is a great accomplishment. All of existence benefits from every lesson every one of us has learned as we merge into Oneness with All That Is.

When we return to Source, we take a richness with us that fulfills our original longing to understand all the possibilities of Creation. Therefore, the reclaiming of the Divine Flow of Creation is both a reclamation and an expansion into more than what seemed to exist at Creation. We will understand every possibility for existence and will have more compassion. We will have fulfilled the desire for experience. We will know that we hold every possibility within us and therefore have nothing to judge, and nothing to fear, ever again.

I repeat the words given to us at the time of soul creation, from chapter 3: "Child of God, mercy and love be unto you. Daughter of God, and of the Holy Mother and the Holy Father, and of the Elohim, and of the planets and stars and galaxies, and of all of Creation, be one with yourself and with each other, as we are with you. Son of God, your mission and glory are great as you and the daughter seek refuge in the physical world in order to serve and bring the Truth that we are One to all of Creation. You will remember when it is time to remember. You will forget and go into unconscious dreams when it is time to be unconscious and dream. And you will always be reawakened. You will always be impulsed with the light and sound and colors of our love, and we will know you by the colors in your heart. You cannot be lost to us, for we have formed you into the spirits and the souls and the bodies that you are becoming. In death and resurrection, in enlightenment and confusion, you are always seen and loved and will never lose anything of what you are. It is impossible. As you go forth now, back through the spirals of Creation, to your destination, always remember that you are part of everything and that a spark of consciousness of all things is in each of you. When you return, you will be more than you are now. It is impossible for you to ever be less, as each experience will make you more. And through you, we become more as well. Our relationship is mutual, for as you experience and know, as you awaken and slumber, all of us experience it through you, who are the Creators and the Creation. You are a projection of us. Never forget that, my beloveds."

When we remember that we chose to become incarnate souls, dropping all blame, judgment, self-pity, arrogance, shame, and other issues of separation and misplaced identity seems to be the only sensible choice. And when we go beyond letting go of ego to feeling gratitude for it all, grace, transcendence, and ascension are natural next steps. Yet for many of us, the next step is service that flows naturally from love and gratitude. This is the only true service. Service based on feeling sorry for others, or attachment to changing the world, is still mainly based in ego need—even if it seems altruistic. The maturing of self beyond ego identity into mastery comes first. Then the true service is born. In our ascension-based mystery school, the real goal is not the ascension itself. The real goal is to reach that level of consciousness at which ascension is an option. At that point, each of us enters into the Divine Flow of our own sovereign Creation—whether it be ascension, conscious death, or remaining in service in human form. The nature of the choice will no longer matter. All that will matter is that it comes from the Divine Flow, which you have reclaimed at the depth of your Beingness. At that point you are consciously Creator and Creation. You are One—simultaneously in AFFINITY with your individual essence, and with All That Is.

Welcome Home!

About the Author

A natural healer and psychic since birth, Amorah Quan Yin's life purpose is to return to Christ consciousness and be an anchor for the Divine Plan on Earth. Her teachings, books, and all of her actions are to assist in the movement toward completion of the karmic play-out on Earth and toward planetary ascension in grace and love.

Amorah was born November 30, 1950, in a small town in Kentucky. As a child, her clairvoyance, clairaudience, and clairsentience were active, but these gifts gradually shut down when she entered public school and succumbed to peer pressure. At age sixteen, upon the death of her grandmother, her full sensory perception, as she prefers to call it, once again reopened. Sporadic experiences throughout her early adult years finally led to her spiritual awakening in early 1979. With her spiritual awakening came a natural healing ability.

Through books, classes, spiritual work with a teacher, and her own increasing awareness, Amorah broke away from traditional jobs in 1985 and began teaching workshops about using crystals and gemstones for healing and awakening. She also began to make and sell crystal and gemstone jewelry at that time. Private healing sessions and teaching were erratically intermingled with her other work until 1988, when she sold the jewelry company, moved to Mt. Shasta, California, and began building a full-time teaching and spiritual healing practice. Amorah is well respected and known as a very capable and gifted healer, seer, and spiritual teacher in the Mt. Shasta area and internationally. Her limited private healing practice consists of individual sessions and private intensives done in person. She also does occasional phone readings and distance healing work.

Amorah is founder of the Dolphin Star Temple Mystery School, contemporization of the ancient Lemurian and Egyptian Mystery School systems. There are also remnants from Native American, Delphi, Avalon, Mayan, and other ancient spiritual cultures. She and those who have completed the mystery school trainings offer a comprehensive Full Sensory Perception Training I, II, and III, and Pleiadian Lightwork Intensives I, II, and III. The majority of the material she teaches is self-learned through her own spiritual practice and past-life recall, or channeled from her Higher Self, or Light Beings who are members of the Dolphin Star Temple Higher Council of Light.

In 1993 she took the name Amorah Quan Yin. This came about as a result of two specific experiences. The first occurred in 1990 while on a twelve-hour air flight. She had been invoking an essence name that would resonate in her soul for quite some time. Near the end of the flight, she just started to doze off when, in her words, "An angelic voice sang softly into my left ear, Ah-mo-rah." I started to open my eyes and move in startled response, but the angelic being touched me gently and whispered, "We waited until you were between wake and sleep so you would know your soul name is three syllables, not a word." Later she learned what the syllables mean: *ah* is the universal sound for divine love; *mo* is the universal sound for mother; *rah* is a universal sound for holy father. Altogether it means beloved of, or divine love of, the Holy Mother and the Holy Father.

The second incident took place in January 1992. While meditating, the Goddess Quan Yin came to Amorah, sat in front of her, and gave her mudras and a discourse. Then Amorah experienced being bilocated inside the feminine peak of Mt. Shasta, called Shastina. Inside the mountain, Quan Yin and her own male counterpart, Avalokitesvara, sat facing one another doing an ongoing series of hand mudras. Both Quan Yin and Avalokitesvara appeared to be the same size as the interior of the mountain, while Amorah remained in her human-size form. When the mudras were complete, millions of tiny sparkles of light began to emanate from Quan Yin's large etheric body, forming a miniature Quan Yin floating in front of the large one. The small Quan Yin turned toward Amorah and revealed that it had Amorah's face. Quan Yin said, "This is what you are. You are a little piece of me come to Earth to do our work. You are not me. You are the ah-mo-rah part of me." Amorah says that she felt a deep sense of peace and a knowing inside that this was true. Connecting with Quan Yin had always been the easiest and most natural of all of her higher-dimensional connections.

Dolphin Star Temple
Mystery School Trainings

Pleiadian Lightwork Intensive I: A training program for becoming a Pleiadian Lightwork practitioner over a period of twenty-eight consecutive days, with every fourth day off. You receive hands-on work in the group setting and learn to give it, as well. Many deep healing techniques are taught including Dolphin Star linking and Dolphin Moves. This is an accelerated and spiritually intense way to receive healing and awakening.

Pleiadian Lightwork Intensives II and III: The second and third levels of the program. You may take these if you wish to become a Pleiadian Lightwork practitioner or if you prefer group intensives to private work. Each intensive is fourteen consecutive days, with every fourth day off. Processes included are cellular clearing and healing; paradigm clearing in the original eight cells; soul clearing, healing, and depossession; anchoring the Pillar of Light, or Laoesh Shekinah; Dolphin Tantra; Assemblage Point shifting; localized healing in the body; Ka-linking to other meridian systems; accessing original soul memory and purpose; and many more.

Full Sensory Perception Training Program: Three ten-day classes taught in varying formats depending upon location. The program includes all of the basic information for becoming a clairvoyant reader and spiritual healer and for deepening your own healing process, full-sensory abilities, and spiritual growth.

Tapes of channelings, guided meditations, guided multidimensional journeys, and Amorah's original music are also available, as well as an all-day workshop video entitled *Self-Love and Self-Master*. Newsletters with more details and schedules are available upon request. You may also get on the Pleiadian Lightwork mailing list or set up workshops and private appointments by contacting:

Dolphin Star Temple
P.O. Box 1581, Mt. Shasta, CA 96067
Phone: 530-926-1122 • Fax: 530-926-1112
e-mail: pleaides@snowcrest.net
Web site: www.amorahquanyin.com